في ذكرى

مارك لينز

KATAJUN AMIRPUR

New Thinking in Islam

The Jihad for Democracy, Freedom and Women's Rights

Translated from the German by Eric Ormsby

In memory of Nasr Hamid Abu Zaid

GINGKO
LIBRARY

First published in Great Britain in 2015 by
Gingko Library
70 Cadogan Place
London SW1X 9AH

First published in German in 2013 as
Den Islam neu denken by Katajun Amirpur

ISBN 978 1 909942 73 8
eISBN 978 1 909942 74 5

Typeset in Optima by MacGuru Ltd

A CIP catalogue record for this book is available from the British Library.

Printed and bound in Spain by Liberdúplex.

www.gingkolibrary.com

**The translation of this work was funded by Geisteswissenschaften International
– Translation Funding for Humanities and Social Sciences from Germany, a
joint initiative of the Fritz Thyssen Foundation, the German Federal Foreign
Office, the collecting society VG WORT and the Börsenverein des Deutschen
Buchhandels (German Publishers & Booksellers Association).**

Contents

Translator's Note: In her citations from the Qur'an, Katajun Amirpur uses the standard German translation by Rudi Paret. In the translation I have drawn on the English translations by M. A. S. Abdel Haleem, N. J. Dawood and Alan Jones, depending on which best suited the author's context; I have sometimes modified these slightly with reference to the Arabic original. Details of these translations are given in the bibliography. I have also changed the author's transliteration of Arabic terms to correspond to current usage in the UK.

Foreword

My mother liked to be called "Umm Nasr" – the mother of Nasr. I
myself addressed her this way. Later I wondered why a woman was
called after her eldest son; I wondered about the image of woman
that is expressed in this form of address. My mother taught me that
the traditional image of woman and the sharp polarity between
man and woman were things to be overcome. My readings of the
Qur'an were influenced by such experiences. Instinctively I read the
Qur'anic verses differently which have been interpreted by exegetes
to the disadvantage of women.[1]

In this brief essay the Egyptian literary scholar Nasr Hamid Abu Zaid
(1943–2009) expressed what is perhaps the most significant point on
the agenda of reform Islam: namely, that one can read the Qur'an differently, if one only has a mind to do so, and that it is the perspective of
the exegete that predetermines the outcome. The Qur'an is thus open
to interpretation.

In addition, Muslims ought to "listen to the Word and follow
what is good in it", as verse 39:18 states. Hence, the Qur'an itself
exhorts humans to read it in the best possible way. To Muslim feminists, who read it as a text espousing justice in matters of gender, this
appears wholly legitimate. Asma Barlas designates her approach by
the concept of "Foundationalism", that is, "epistemological theoretical

---

1 Nasr Abu Zaid, *Ein Leben mit dem Islam* (Freiburg im Breisgau: Herder Verlag,
1999), 78.

Fundamentalism". Accordingly, there exist what may be called "root-convictions" that serve as the fundamental justification for other and different convictions. The designation "Fundamentalism" rests on the postulate that regards justice in matters of gender as rooted in the Qur'an.

The issue has not remained at this stage. Abu Zaid has pointed out methodological difficulties with this stance, and Asma Barlas has responded to his critique. And so we find ourselves here in the midst of a theological dispute that is all the more interesting for being still undecided. In the meantime, there are also feminists such as Raja Rhouni who represents a "post-foundationalism" position and is thereby linked with Abu Zaid. From this viewpoint, the result of an interpretation, such as that accepted by Barlas and Amina Wadud, tells us more about the outlook of the interpreter than about the text itself. To be sure, Abu Zaid did not regard the readings of Wadud and Barlas as unjustified but he himself wanted to press further and grasp the essence of the Qur'an. Hence, his focus – like that of the other three men portrayed here – rested less on a new reading of the Qur'an, and instead, on an inquiry into how the Qur'anic revelation occurred; as well as on the question as to what the Qur'an really is: speech, text, discourse, dialogue or even something else entirely? A modern Islamic theology has to address these questions since the answers may have major consequences for Islam in today's world.

By 2001 – in other words, at a quite early point in time – Nasr Hamid Abu Zaid was already concerned with the notion of a modern Islamic theology in Germany. At that time, Wolfram Weiße, director of the Academy of World Religions at the University of Hamburg, together with the Körber Foundation, invited him to reflect on this. For his part, the Egyptian scholar was of the opinion that Germany might be the very place in which to establish this field of Islamic theology; Germany might provide a space for thought that guaranteed both freedom and conditions that Muslim thinkers could not find anywhere else.

Thus, for Abu Zaid, the nature of God's word stood as one of the themes to be dealt with. The question about the createdness or the non-createdness of the Qur'an was also involved. To this diverse answers had been given in the history of Islamic theology and these in turn had led to particular ways of interpreting the Qur'an. Of course, it is axiomatic according to Islamic belief that God speaks in the Qur'an, but the history of Islamic theology acknowledges various, and contradictory, conceptions of *how* that is to be understood. Many scholars take it literally. The Ash'arite School, whose founder al-Ash'ari died in 935, took the position that God possesses such attributes as knowledge and speech, and so, both knows and speaks. So too in the Qur'an. For Ash'arites, God's word is one of His essential attributes. From this they concluded that His word must be uncreated, just as He Himself is.

Even their intellectual opponents, the Mu'tazilites, did not deny that God speaks in the Qur'an. Nevertheless, in their view the difference between human and divine speech resided in the fact that God, thanks to His omnipotence, requires no medium for producing speech. Speech in our sense does not apply to God since speech is a human faculty. Since they reckoned God's speech to be one of His attributes of action, they rejected the notion that the Qur'an could be eternal, that is, uncreated, as God Himself is.

This is all relevant for a modern theology. For with acceptance of Ash'arite dogma, concerning the Qur'an's uncreatedness, by the Sunni mainstream in the second half of the ninth century, the notion was rejected that the Qur'an might be determined in form and content by the personality of the Prophet; rejected as well was the notion that God spoke in the context of a historical situation. In this way strict limits were set on the possibility of Qur'anic interpretation, much stricter than they would have been had the Mu'tazilites carried the day in this theological conflict. A created Qur'an allows far more scope for interpretation, with respect to women's rights, for example.

Like Abu Zaid, who can be considered a neo-Mu'tazilite, so too Fazlur Rahman was receptive to the idea of the Qur'an's createdness; the two other theologians presented in this volume, 'Abdolkarim Soroush and Mohammad M. Shabestari, are Shi'ites and as such, heirs to the Mu'tazilites, and so they too share this opinion. Nevertheless, this signifies no rejection of the axiomatic divinity of the Qur'an; for all four thinkers, it remains beyond question that the contents of the

Qur'an ultimately go back to God. But they do ask, however, who undertook the formulation of the Qur'an's language – God, the angels or Muhammad himself – and they inquire as to how the revelation unfolded. Abu Zaid endeavoured to establish this theological question by recourse to modern linguistic concepts. Fazlur Rahman has raised the question, while Soroush and Shabestari have also developed their own approaches.

The essays presented here have something in common that distinguishes them from other contemporary approaches in reform Islam: here the Qur'an itself is central. As the textual point of reference of Islamic culture, it is the sole thing upon which all Muslims agree; this cannot be said, for example, about the hadith. For this reason all the thinkers represented here share the conviction that any reform must take the Qur'an as its starting-point. Unless legitimated by the Qur'an, reform has no hope of success. That does not mean, of course, that a novel reading of the Qur'an or some brilliant new idea about its nature can produce reform. More than that is needed.

That they place the Qur'an at the very centre of their efforts served, therefore, as a criterion for precisely why these thinkers were selected. A second criterion was the originality of their thought as well as its impact which they developed in different ways, and, as will be seen, within distinctive frames of reference. The thinkers presented here have something else in common. What they themselves have experienced, and how they view the Qur'an, cannot be separated one from the other. Both are conjoined. Thus, the goal of this book is not solely to present ideas but also the men and women who formulated them.

For reasons of space many exciting thinkers had to be left out. These include Asghar Ali Engineer and Riffat Hassan as well as Muhammad Iqbal, Sayyid Ahmad Khan, Chandra Muzaffar, Abdulaziz Sachedina, Abdelmadjid Charfi, Mohamed Talbi, Nurkholish Madjid, and Ali Bulaç. They deserve to be honoured here if only by mention of their names. Many others will be briefly discussed – and others somewhat more extensively – in the first chapter, as a way of clarifying the various approaches and of broadening the spectrum of reform Islam presented here.

A word about terminology: like the designations "liberal Islam", "progressive Islam", or "Islamic enlightenment", the terms "Muslim reform thinker" or "reform Islam" are also contested. At a conference of specialists in Berlin in 2005, many of those present expressed discomfort over these designations. Ebrahim Moosa suggested "critical traditionalism" as an alternative; Abu Zaid argued for "Muslim reform discourses" and 'Abdullahi An-Na'im in his turn defended the term "progressive thinking" (though for his book he used *Toward an Islamic Reformation*). A group of Islamic intellectuals who have been meeting since the events of 9/11 call themselves "Progressive Muslims" or "The Progressive Muslim Union", in order to counter fundamentalist tendencies in their community of faith. In Switzerland a "Forum for a Progressive Islam" has been founded.

Much might be said about the sense, or lack thereof, of these designations, about the lines of inclusion and exclusion which these imply, about their origin from within other contexts, other milieu, over the problem of progress in itself as well as that of reform. The idea of improvement implicit in the notion of reform has led many Muslims to reject the word "reform" as applied to Islam. Islam is complete, no improvement is needed, they argue. Some representatives of Islamic organizations even detect in the term, and the idea of, "reform Islam" an attempt by non-Muslims to meddle in internal Islamic affairs. In a position paper written by the Central Council of Muslims in Germany we read: "Islam is threatened by the danger, through political and governmental pressure, of being split into two, confessions: Islam and Reform Islam."[2]

This is not the place for a lengthy discussion of terminology; we are concerned less about designations than about contents and, above all, about the shared necessity for all progressives, advocates of enlightenment, and reformers, to articulate current problems unambiguously. The Wahhabis have not only paved over the graves of the Prophet's

---

2 Zentralrat der Muslime e.V., Grundsatzpapier des Zentralrates der Muslime in Deutschland (ZMD) zur Kopftuchdebatte, 23.10.2003, http://textfabrik.islam.de/2652_print.php

family in Saudi Arabia with their bulldozers but would just as easily do
so over Islamic thought, as Omid Safi rightly states in his introduction to
a book published by leading thinkers among the progressive Muslims.
Certain predominant Muslim positions on tolerance, law, equality, and
freedom of opinion cannot be reconciled with the principles of a free,
democratic state, and this is a fact that cannot be ignored. For this
reason terms are not the issue here. The authors presented, like many
others both in the Islamic world and elsewhere, set out to address this
problem.

In the meantime the terms "reform thinker" and "reform Islam" have
become established; the terms have been introduced into our schools
and on the internet, thanks to the Bundeszentrale für Politische Bildung
which has put Ralf Elger's *Kleine Islam-Lexikon* online (http://www.bpd.
de/nachschlagen/lexika/islam-lexikon/21634/reformislam). Because of
this, these terms will also be used in this book when dealing with
history and the founding fathers.

The title of this volume differs from its German original, a more
literal translation of the Persian nouandishan-e eslami. Those who
devote themselves to nouandishi-ye islami are called "nouandishan-e
eslami", i.e., those thinking Islam anew, literally, "Islamic newthinkers".
At least two of the thinkers included here use this new, and so perhaps
less charged, designation themselves.

As another term that needs clarification is jihad, a word that pro-
vokes negative reactions – unjustifiably so – among non-Muslims. In
its original meaning jihad denotes "striving in the way of God" (*jihad
fi sabil Allah*). In the Qur'an there is some ambiguity as to whether it
betokens a universal battle against believers of other faiths or whether
this struggle has merely a defensive objective. In the early years of
Islam the term was understood purely in the sense of a military confrontation for the purpose of spreading the rule of Islam.

This military interpretation, however, underwent a change over the
course of centuries. Later Islamic law understood jihad to mean not
simply an obligation to wage war, but rather, an individual striving to
lead a life pleasing to God. What constituted struggle on the path of
God differed from one person to the next. The mystic understood his

grappling towards knowledge of God as jihad, just as the preacher so understood his missionary activity. Among modernizers the word is understood in quite worldly terms. For example, in Tunisia the struggle against illiteracy is declared a jihad; at the end of the Iran-Iraq War, when reconstruction began in Iran, it was called *jihad-e sazandegi*, "the struggle to rebuild".

Reform thinkers also refer what they do today as jihad. So, for example, Omid Safi, a leading voice among progressive Muslims, writes about their interpretation of law as, "This progressive *ijtihad* is our *jihad*."[3] Simlilarly, Amina Wadud entitled her book: *Inside the Gender Jihad*, while Riffat Hassan described her effort for women's rights in Pakistan as *Jihad fi Sabil Allah: A Muslim Woman's Faith Journey from Struggle to Struggle to Struggle.* Such is the title of one of her essays from the year 1991. Perhaps it's no accident that women in particular call their endeavor for the rights of their fellows a jihad. The notion imparts a Qur'anic legitimation to their struggle.

In any event no book about reform Islam can do without women's voices; it must pose the question about women. Abu Zaid once called it the litmus test for Islam in the modern world and in Asghar Ali Engineer's opinion:

Muslim intellectuals, activists and academics today have to recognize that they bear a heavy moral responsibility. They must play an active role in defending the rights of Muslims collectively. For that reason, the real test is always how these intellectuals pose the question of women. As long as they do not regard it as an important matter – perhaps the most important of all – they cannot be called engaged intellectuals.[4]

---

3 Omid Safi, ed., "Introduction: The Times They Are A-Changing – A Muslim Quest for Justice, Gender Equality, and Pluralism", in *Progressive Muslims: On Justice, Gender, and Pluralism* (Oxford: Oneworld, 2003), 1–29.
4 Asghar Ali Engineer, "The Compatibility of Islam, Secularism and Modernity" in Farish Noor, ed., *New Voices of Islam* (Leiden: ISIM 2002), 34.

Accordingly, this volume sets out to discuss new efforts being made in Muslim theology, and so, new ways of reading and new ways of proceeding will be described. Here, perhaps, the objection that this will result in an eclectic interpretation, or in a hermeneutic that does violence to the Qur'an, must be confronted. Of course it might be claimed that the thinkers presented here are constructing a distinctive version of Islam – an Islam that has been conditioned, and made suitable, to the demands of a non-Muslim social majority, or a Westernized minority. But in answer to this, democracy and human rights, and their compatibility with the Qur'an, are not merely the need of a small minority but, rather, they represent the aspiration of the majority of Muslims. I am convinced of this. Secondly, a new reading of Islam proceeds from a good intention, and intention, or *niya* in Arabic, carries weight in Islam. In the end, religions are determined not so much by what the texts offer human beings but rather by what human beings make of them. Nobody can say, of course, whether the way of interpreting the Qur'an suggested in the following pages is the right one. Classical Qur'anic commentaries conclude with the formula: *Wa-Allahu a'lam*, "God is He who knows". They take the following format: in the middle of the page the sura, or chapter of the Qur'an, is given and around it the exegesis, or commentary, is written in a circular fashion; in further circles yet other commentaries appear. In Persian, this structure, similar to the year-rings in trees, is termed *hashiye*. Sometimes the views of dozens of commentators were deemed worthy of inclusion – views that could differ widely from one another and which were, often enough, wholly contradictory from one another but which, nevertheless, appeared as elucidations of one, as well as of the same Qur'anic verse. At the end, frequently placed in a corner, appeared the phrase: *Wa-Allahu a'lam*. By this was meant that in the final analysis, God alone knows. Who would try to contradict Him?

On the Way to the Modern

The Tradition of Reform Islam

In the nineteenth century Jamal al-Din al-Afghani (1838/39–1897), Muhammad 'Abduh (1849–1905) and Rashid Rida (1865–1935), who are today considered the founders of Islamic reform, were already urging an inner reform of Islam. Underlying their efforts was a sense of subordination to the West. For all three, the backwardness of the Islamic world had been caused, and exclusively so, by a fixed, inflexible understanding of Islam and the blind imitation of its forefathers. For this reason they demanded a modern interpretation of the Qur'an and of Islamic law that would be appropriate for the altered circumstances. This effort, in its essence, continues today and the same goes for the fundamental question that might be answered with its help: how can a Muslim be at once modern and genuine?

Since then, reform Islam has developed the most diverse modes of approach. Thus, Islamic modernism emerged from it, as did Islamism, i.e., fundamentalism. The cogitations of 'Abduh, Afghani and Rida led to a blueprint for an Islamic society, but they led also to the ideology of Islamism as a closed worldview. They took the position that "pure" and "unfalsified" Islam possessed all the answers to the questions of modernity. The reconciliation of Islam and modernity should therefore proceed with a return to the Qur'an and the traditions of the Prophet together with an inner renewal of the faithful. Fundamentalists and modernists could both subscribe to this, even if they drew different conclusions. Muhammad 'Abduh in particular stands as the intellectual father of both forms of Islamic new thinking.

Muhammad 'Abduh grew up in a peasant family from Lower Egypt and studied at al-Azhar University in Cairo. In 1871 he got to know Jamal al-Din al-Afghani. Jamal al-Din, an Iranian, called himself al-Afghani, that is, "the Afghan", in order to avoid having his reform-ist ideas branded as Shi'ite and thereby rejected by Sunnis from the outset. Afghani received his education first in Teheran and later in the Shi'ite centres of learning in Iraq. After several stops along the way he wound up in Istanbul in 1870. There he quickly gained access to reform-minded circles. In 1871 he went to Cairo. When he got the opportunity to address the Ottoman Viceroy Tawfiq Pasha, al-Afghani suggested to him that he let the people share in governance. Egypt should build up its own governmental institutions in order to rid itself of British rule. A constitution would set limits to the despotism of rulers. Because of these ideas al-Afghani was expelled in 1879; he then went to India and from there, in 1882, to Europe.

To be sure, al-Afghani counts as one of the leading renewers of Islam and, yet, although he wrote little, he distinguished himself as an Islamic agitator. During his lifetime he was treated with hostility by the orthodox because he strove for a revival of the rationalistic current in Islam. After his death he was styled as the hero of Islamic modern-ism, of pan-Islamism and anti-colonial resistance. Two central themes course through Afghani's thought: firstly, Islamic unity; and secondly, the demand for a reformed and modernized Islam – one that would adopt Western technology and science and by which it would then be able to overcome political and economic dependency on the West.

Al-Afghani's ideas were further developed by Muhammad 'Abduh, his most famous student. Together with Rashid Rida, 'Abduh ushered in an age of nationalistic and religious reform in Egypt. 'Abduh took from Afghani the view that Muslims had moved away from the true Islam of their forefathers and that this was the reason for its backward-ness relative to the West. 'Abduh had been introduced to European literature, philosophy and theology by his teacher and, prompted by al-Afghani, he recognized the technical and scientific progress of the

West. However, he rejected the suitability of Western mores for the Islamic world. He believed that higher education and religion, rightly practiced, would guide Egypt into the modern world.

In 1876 'Abduh completed his studies and in 1878 became a professor of history at the Cairo's Dar al-'Ulum, "College of Sciences". He wrote as a guest columnist for the newspaper *al-Ahram* and called for educational reforms. Because of his criticism of the British he had to leave the country in 1879 but was able to return a year later. He became editor of an official newspaper which under his guidance developed into a mouthpiece for reformist ideas. It called for the renewal of Islam and emancipation of Muslims from European rule.

In 1882, after he had taken a stand with the Egyptian nationalists during the 'Urabi uprising against the government, he had to leave Egypt again. In Paris, 'Abduh met up with his old teacher al-Afghani. They collaborated in putting out the reforming magazine *al-Urwa al-Wuthqa*, *"The Strongest Bond"*. Through this medium, al-Afghani and 'Abduh propagated their reform Islam which employed *ijtihad* to give new answers to current questions. In the face of the danger which confronted the Islamic world through European colonialism, Muslims would have to unite. They would become able to fight back through the practice of Islam, if rightly understood. Here too only one theme dominates: finding the true religion and, strengthened by it, having the ability to resist the colonial powers.

After sojourns in Tunis and Beirut, 'Abduh returned to Cairo in 1889 where he found a position as a judge. In 1899, he was named Grand Mufti of Egypt, a position which he held until his death. 'Abduh crafted legal opinions that had a practical relevance to the lives of Muslims in modern Egypt. For example, he addressed the question as to whether a Muslim might eat meat that had been imported from a non-Muslim country. Furthermore, in his role as Grand Mufti he authored a series of theological writings and began work on a comprehensive commentary of the Qur'an. When this was published in the journal *al-Manar*, *"The Lighthouse"*, it provoked a storm of indignation while at the same time making 'Abduh's ideas widely known. Muhammad 'Abduh died on July 11, 1905, in Egypt.

Both thinkers, 'Abduh and al-Afghani, were advocates for a rational interpretation of Islam. That is why 'Abduh wanted to reform Islamic education; he urged a stronger inclusion of modern sciences. Fundamental to his interpretation of Islam was his conviction that Islam was equal to all the requirements of modernity, because he saw it as, first and foremost, a rational religion. Rightly interpreted, Islam was not merely compatible with reason and progress but it also promoted these. 'Abduh believed that the general weakness of the Muslims of his day had its roots in two problems: firstly, ignorance about their own religion or holding a false belief, and, secondly, the despotism of Muslim rulers. According to 'Abduh, these central problems could be solved only by returning to true religion, and above all, through an improvement of the educational system and a new interpretation of religious texts. 'Abduh refused to accept the interpretations and the consensus of earlier generations of legal scholars as the only true interpretation of questions of faith; he was opposed to blind imitation (*taqlid*) of earlier generations.

In his most important work, the *Epistle on Unity* (*Risalat al-Tawhid*), 'Abduh focused on the dogmas of the faith. In this enthusiastic piece, he describes Islam as a universal faith based on reason, and as a faith active in the world. Because it is a rational religion, according to 'Abduh, the believer can remain a pious Muslim even in the modern world. To this end Islamic law is to be newly interpreted in the light of current problems by use of *ijtihad*. The basis of his new interpretation is the distinction between the mutable and the immutable aspects of the religion, between social teachings and fundamental doctrines. The dogmas of Islam are unalterable: belief in God, divine revelation, the Prophet Muhammad, moral responsibility, and reason. Islamic law, by contrast, is mutable; it is nothing more than the application of principles contained in the Qur'an. These principles are always applied only to specific, ever changing conditions. When conditions change so too do the laws. This is the fundamental starting-point of reform Islam and it remains fundamental even today. Needless to say, there is disagreement about what exactly is to be considered immutable and what is not. That is why this starting point is variously criticized as inadequate or is modified.

Secularism and Islamism

'Abduh's best-known students, Rashid Rida and 'Ali 'Abd al-Raziq (1888–1966), developed his ideas further but in quite different ways. In his book *Islam and the Principles of Governance* (*al-Islam wa-Usul al-Hukm*), 'Abd al-Raziq, in 1925, writes that it is utterly unnecessary to be concerned with the restoration of the caliphate, abolished in 1924 by the newly established Turkish Republic (despite the fact that this was supposed to occur through a congress scheduled to take place in Cairo in 1925). In 'Abd al-Raziq's view, history shows us that the caliphate was not only dispensable but even deleterious. For his contemporaries, however, much more scandalous than his rejection of the caliphate was his attempt to prove, on the basis of the Prophet's biography, that there was a separation between political rule and religious message in Islam from the very beginning. According to 'Abd al-Raziq, the Prophet did not exercise governance (*hukm*) but only a religious mission (*risala*). Moreover, his revelation dealt exclusively with the heavenly realm.

This notion of 'Abd al-Raziq's was criticized by Rashid Rida, the other important student of 'Abduh. Rashid Rida, who came from a pious family in a village in the then-Ottoman province of Beirut, had received a modern education during his student years. Through his conversations with Christian intellectuals and missionaries in Beirut, he came into contact with Western ideas. He was familiar with the journal *al-Urwa al-Wuthqa*, "The Indissoluble Link", edited by al-Afghani and 'Abduh, and it influenced him strongly. In 1897 Rida emigrated to Egypt and became one of 'Abduh's students.

From 1898 until his death Rida published the highly influential journal *al-Manar* which served as a mouthpiece for the reform movement. It analyzed the situation of the Muslim world as well as the question as to why the West was superior to the East both militarily and scientifically. From 1900 on, Rida published Muhammad 'Abduh's modernizing Qur'anic commentary, based upon his notes on 'Abduh's lectures at al-Azhar University. Following his death, Rida continued Abduh's Qur'anic commentary on his own.

After the Ottoman caliph was divested of power, Rida argued in one of his writings that the ideal caliph of all Muslims would be the leading *mujtahid*, that is, the legal scholar most skilled in *ijtihad*. This is interesting inasmuch as the notion shows considerable similarity with the Shi'ite concept of *velayat-e faqih* (the leadership of the highest-ranking legal scholar) that Ayatollah Ruhollah Khomeini (1902–1989), the founder of the Islamic Republic of Iran, developed in the 1970s and which later became the basis of the Iranian system of government. In addition, Rida argued that failure to uphold the sharia might result in the ruler being declared an unbeliever. This was a new idea that would later be seized upon by other Islamists.

His confrontations with secularists such as 'Ali 'Abd al-Raziq led Rida to pull back to more conservative positions. As a result he had a major influence on the Egyptian elementary school teacher Hasan al-Banna (1906–1946), founder of the Muslim Brotherhood. In contrast to his earlier estimation, Rida now considered the Wahhabis the real enemies of a pure Islam. Rida's ideas won acceptance after the rival movements of pan-Islamism, pan-Arabism and Arab or Islamic social-ism foundered. After the Six Day War, The nationalistic pan-Arabists were forced to search for explanations after Nasser's downfall. This created impetus for the Islamists. As the PLO fell on the defensive, the Muslim Brotherhood gained in popularity and this ultimately led to the founding of Hamas. After the Six Day War the same fate befell Arab socialism, a variant of the so-called "Third Way" between communism (socialism) and capitalism. Following the defeat of 1967, Arab socialism lost ground for the same reasons as pan-Arabism. It failed as ideology because it could do nothing to prevent the defeat of the Arab military in the Six Day War.

Islamic fundamentalists summarized the reason for this in the dec-laration: "The Jews had remembered religion and won; we had dis-tanced ourselves from religion – and lost." Consequently, Muslims should return to religion in order to find a way back to former great-ness. The further development of this phenomenon, Islamism, is con-nected in a specific way to the Muslim Brotherhood, which Hasan al-Banna founded in 1928. In reaction to Western colonialism and Western domination, al-Banna promoted religious renewal as well as social reforms as means by which he intended to return to the norms of early Islam. Al-Banna described what was to be done in detail in order to change society:

These are the most important goals of a reform based on the true spirit of Islam. In the realm of politics, justice and administration:

1. The termination of party politics and a redirection of the political forces of the nation towards a single front.
2. Reform of the law so that it stands in harmony with Islamic legislation in all its ramifications.

Secondly, in the realms of society and education:

1. To accustom people to respect for public morals; to put instructions in this regard under legal protection along with intensification of the penalties for moral lapses.
2. The question of woman must be solved in such a way that her demands and her protection be preserved equally in accordance with the teachings of Islam.
3. Suppression of public and private prostitution; to regard every sort of sexual offence (zina) as a crime for which the perpetrator receives the punishment of flogging.
4. Suppression of all forms of gambling.
5. To fight against alcohol and all intoxicants, prohibition of which spares the nation its deleterious consequences.
6. Education of women in the norms of feminine decency in order to suppress flirtatious and coquettish behavior.[1]

Many of al-Banna's ideas were later condensed by Sayyid Qutb (1906–1966) into a sort of Islamic liberation theology. Qutb was born in 1906 into a middle-class family. He attended a state school and, by the age of ten, knew the Qur'an by heart because, as he writes in his

---

1 Andreas Meier, *Der politische Auftrag des Islam: Programme und Kritik zwischen Fundamentalismus und Reformen: Originalstimmen aus der islamischen Welt* (Wuppertal: Peter Hammer, 1994), 180–1.

memoir of his childhood, he wanted, as a student in a state elementary school, to demonstrate the superiority of his own modern educational institution over that of the traditional Qur'an school.

Qutb described his childhood in an autobiographical novel called *A Childhood in the Country*. The novel is interesting just because he tells of a normal childhood. Qutb was no poor, downtrodden underdog; he did not turn into a radical out of revenge for his own social disadvantages. Here and there in this autobiography we find the themes for which he later took up political struggle: the exploitation of the peasants, and the despotic behavior of soldiers, for example. The story of this Islamist's youth is not only richly informative about a thinker who has affected world events up to the present, but it is also enjoyable to read because of its literary quality.

Qutb attended the Dar al-'Ulum school in Cairo which had been founded as an alternative to al-Azhar University. In the 1960s, after graduation, he worked for the Ministry of Education. He developed numerous proposals for reform and improvement of the educational system which were, however, ignored. Furthermore, he wrote for various newspapers, made a name for himself as a literary figure and critic, and attained a certain renown as a writer.

In 1948 Qutb was sent on a Ministry of Education mission to the United States to study the educational system. His superiors reckoned that he would return as an enthusiastic advocate of the "American way of life", but this is not at all what happened. Instead, he experienced culture-shock or, at the very least, a chastening disappointment in modern American life. His sojourn in the US led to a radical change of view. After his return, at the beginning of the 1950s, Qutb felt only revulsion for the West. The sexual promiscuity, racism, racial segregation – which affected him as an Egyptian – and the materialism radicalized him. He joined the Muslim Brotherhood and rapidly became its most important ideologue.

When his relations with the Egyptian regime deteriorated as a result of clashing viewpoints, as well as the Brotherhood's attempt on Nasser's life, Sayyid Qutb was arrested in 1954 and sentenced to 25 years at hard labour. His prison years, however, were his most productive period. He composed his comprehensive commentary of the Qur'an, *In the Shade of the Qur'an (Fi Zilal al-Qur'an)*. Moreover, he wrote his seminal work, *Milestones (Ma'alim fi-1 -Tariq)*, easily the most influential text of radical Islamism. Indeed, because of its sustained influence it is often described as the "Mao-Bible" of Islamic revolution. The first drafts of *Milestones* became available in 1962 to a wider circle; the book was published in 1964. Shortly thereafter it was banned by the censor, then permitted, and after its fifth edition banned yet again.

Qutb was released from prison in 1964 through the intervention of the Iraqi president whilst on a state visit to Egypt. When the Nasser regime decided to eliminate several irksome critics, however, Qutb was sentenced to death and on August 29 1966 he was executed.

For Qutb, Islam was an ideology, a view of life that has retained its validity even in the present day, for Islam is not merely a set of beliefs but a complete system for how conduct one's life. It conforms to prevailing conditions and the needs of society. By being turned into an ideology religion, for Qutb, becomes a motivating force. Islam is here understood as a system that is fully equipped to compete with the two other systems that ruled the world: capitalism and communism.

> Islam had to arise to construct a social, commercial and political
> system... Islam is a movement of active departure for the liberation
> of human beings on earth through means that are conformable
> with every aspect of human reality and that is conformable anew,
> according to the phase in which the movement occurs.[2]

In this way, Islam turns into an ideology of the Third Way. For Qutb it was the universal declaration of freedom for mankind "in which no one is obliged to give obedience to anyone but God." Qutb formulated a radicalized Islamic ideology directed against tyrannical regimes that had created an order akin to the age of the *Jahiliya* or "Time of Ignorance". This is how the Qur'an understands the time or heathenism before the triumph of Islam, when the Arabs still revered their tribal divinities.

---

2 Meier, *Der politische Auftrag des Islam*, 201–2.

Qutb wanted to supplant this heathen society with one oriented to Islamic law. For him a society is not Islamic simply because there are devout individuals living within it. Spiritual piety does not suffice as a criterion for a truly Islamic society. Accordingly, all the societies of his time, both his own and others, that call themselves Islamic, are heretical. God's law is not valid solely in mosques but in the state and society as well. It does not apply only in the next world but here and now; this is Qutb's doctrine in a nutshell. This new programme should be carried forward by a revolutionary elite.

Islam recognizes only two forms of society: Islamic society and heathen society. Islamic society is that society in which Islam is practiced in all its aspects: in the articles of faith, ritual, Sharia, the political system, morality and ethical conduct. Heathen society is the society in which Islam is not practiced , which is directed neither by its articles of faith and conceptual bases, its values and criteria, its political order and its laws, let alone its moral and ethical standards. Islamic society is not that which includes Muslims who call themselves Muslims but in which the Sharia is not the law of the society – whether or not they pray, fast and make pilgrimage to God's House. Furthermore, Islamic society is not that which concocts an Islam for itself out of itself – in place of what God has commanded and His prophet has determined in detail. This is what they call, for example, "progressive Islam".[3]

In *Milestones* much space is devoted to criticism of democracy, liberalism and capitalism. One proof for the injustice of democracy, in Qutb's view, is the fact that the triumphal march of liberalism and capitalism in the Western world has led to social injustice. For him, by contrast, only the rule of divine law is able to establish justice. Therefore, God's dominion, which is equivalent to validation of the sharia, is central to his thinking.

Qutb's notion of Islam as ideology was taken up by the Iranian 'Ali

---

3 Meier, *Der politische Auftrag des Islam*, 203.

Shariati (1933–1977), whose revolutionary ideas influenced an entire generation of students and so, became decisive in bringing about the Iranian Revolution of 1978/79. Shariati figures as the ideologue of revolution who reached many more of the young with his pronouncements about the revolutionary potential of religion than did Ayatollah Ruhollah Khomeini (1902–1989), the actual leader of the revolution. Furthermore, Qutb's influence is also clearly discernible in the thought of Khomeini as well. Qutb's *Milestones* must surely have been known to him. In his major work, *The Islamic State, 'al-Hukuma al-Islamiyya'*, based on a lecture given in 1970, Khomeini set's out his basic thoughts on the directives of Islam, on the Islamic state, on the necessity of establishing such a state, its leadership, objectives and formulations. In broad sections his exposition can be read as an anti-imperialist polemic. For Khomeini, the only genuine Iranian identity is an Islamic one and so only a return to Islam can rescue the land from destruction. Khomeini portrays the West, the Jews and the Shah, their henchman, responsible for Iran's problems: the Shah buys airplanes while the people go hungry and he allows Jews, who destroy Islam and aspire to world domination, into the country.

For pages at a stretch Khomeini also attacks the clerics who stay at a distance from politics. They represent a false Islam in his view; true Islam, by contrast, is political. The clerics have not earned the respect which they are accorded since they do not oppose oppression and injustice, as they have actually been commanded to do. Most clerics have assumed a colonialistic outlook and believe what the plunderers, oppressors and colonialists want them to believe, namely, that Islam and politics should be separate.

With the victory of the revolution and the establishment of the Islamic Republic, Iran took Khomeini at his word with the motto, "Islam is the solution." He believed that Islam comprised an all-encompassing system of laws and regulations meant to produce complete and exemplary human beings. Nevertheless, since human beings live in ignorance – as Qutb had also stated – they must be guided on the right path by the clergy, and if necessary, even through coercion and force. Otherwise they run the risk of falling prey to the negative influence of atheists and the enemies of religion.

2

Islamic Reformers Today

Post-Islamism

Contemporary Iranian reformers oppose just such compulsion and declare, as does the Mullah Mohsen Kadivar (b. 1959), that a human being cannot be bundled off to paradise in chains. Reformers like him dismiss Khomeini's understanding of Islam and in its place strive to reconcile Islam and democracy.

Kadivar's main thesis, which identifies him as a post-Islamist intellectual, can be summarized as follows: people expect that religion will put principles and values within their grasp while practical matters belong more properly to the realm of so-called human experience – a formulation that may be code for secular norms.

In his writings, Kadivar is concerned with the question of religious freedom. In a lecture which he gave in 2001 at the International Congress of Human Rights and the Dialogue of Civilizations in Tehran, he criticized the regime in the following way:

Although the generally accepted interpretation of Islam in many cases does not reflect the ideas of freedom of religion and belief, another interpretation of Islam does exist, based on the original sources of Islam, which is in agreement with freedom of religion and belief, as has been proclaimed in the Universal Declaration of Human Rights.[1]

---

1 Mohsen Kadivar, "Freedom of Religion and Belief in Islam" in Mehran Kamrava,

Kadivar calls the incompatible interpretation of Islam "traditional Islam", whereas the compatible form is "reform Islam", or more literally, "newly thought Islam", *"eslam-e nouandish"*. He writes:

> We come to the conclusion therefore: traditional Islam and democracy are...not compatible while newly thought Islam and democracy are.[2]

It was the loss of prestige that Islam suffered through the existing Islamism within the Iranian theocracy that induced many Iranian reformist thinkers to resist it. The cleric Mohammad M. Shabestari (b. 1936), for example, even set his turban aside in protest and explained, "No turban fits me in this Islamic Republic." Shabestari says pointedly:

> The right question is not whether Islam and democracy are compatible or not. The question is: are people ready today to allow this compatibility to emerge?[3]

And further:

> Christianity has undergone change, so too has Judaism. Why should Muslims not reform their religion?[4]

Shabestari introduced the science of hermeneutics into Iran and established hermeneutical principles for Iranian discourse on religion. According to him, every reader possesses a prior understanding and an interest in knowledge that is decisive for the understanding of the text.

---

ed., *The New Voices of Islam: Rethinking Politics and Modernity* (Berkeley: University of California Press, 2006), 142.

2 Mohsen Kadivar, "Vom historischen Islam zum spirituellen Islam" in Katajun Amirpur, ed., *Unterwegs zu einem anderen Islam: Texte iranischer Denker.* Translated from the Persian by Katajun Amirpur, (Freiburg: Herder Verlag, 2009), 79.

3 Andrea Dernbach, "Elastischer Islam," *Tagesspiegel*, 2/10/2007.

4 Ibid.

Whoever wants to interpret the Qur'an in the light of democracy can do so. He does no more violence to the text than one who winkles out a theocracy as God's ideal concept or the necessity to apply the rigid measures of retribution in Islamic penal law.

The Iranian cleric Hasan Yusufi Eshkevari (b. 1950) also emphasizes context in his interpretation of the Qur'an. He does this, for example, with the verse "Fight against them until no more dissidence exists and religion belongs to God [alone]" from the Qur'an (verse 2:193). The verse sounds combative and can be understood to mean that Muslims have the duty to fight unbelievers and bring everyone to Islam. Eshkevari argues, however, that this verse pertains exclusively to a particular historical event, namely, to ending the Treaty of Hudhaybiyya. In the year 630 CE the Prophet Muhammad broke a ceasefire that he had concluded two years earlier, and marched on Mecca. For Eshkevari, this concrete political situation alone is at issue in this verse. The heathen Meccans should be fought because they had previously sinned against the community of the Prophet. They had driven out his followers and sought to kill him. For this reason, therefore, the verse does not mean that all men should be fought, including in our own time, until they honour the one God.

Eshkevari is employing a method that Qur'anic science has been familiar with for centuries. A branch of Qur'anic science is concerned expressly with the so-called "causes of revelation" (asbab al-nuzul). Even scholars of the time proceeded on the basis of a dialectical relationship between the text and its addressee. The very fact that this science has existed for so long shows how absurd the argument of many Islamists actually is, to wit, that every pronouncement in the Qur'an must be taken literally and remains valid for all time.

> The Qur'an is a writing hidden between the two covers of a book. It does not speak. It needs a translator, and truly there are those who bring it to speak.[5]

---

5 'Ali ibn abi Talib, Nahj al-balagha, edited and interpreted by 'Ali Naqi Feiz ol-Eslam (Tehran, 1972), 386.

With these words, 'Ali, the first imam of the Shi'a, expressed himself in the seventh century on the interpretability of the Qur'an. The Qur'an has been interpreted for centuries. That is attested by the profusion of exegetical literature and the multiplicity of possible interpretations. There are mystical, philosophical and rationalistic Qur'an commentaries, the pronouncements of which differ markedly from one another. Islamic culture has perceived this multiplicity more as invigorating and natural than as menacing. Thomas Bauer in an outstanding recent study, *The Culture of Ambiguity (Die Kultur der Ambiguität)*, has shown that, historically, the Islamic world was distinguished by the fact that it could allow many truths to emerge alongside one another. There was, for example, the wine shop alongside the prohibition on wine, painting and the ban on images. Islamic culture, according to Bauer, was characterized by an extremely high tolerance of ambiguity. Plurality was prized and lived in – a fact that today is denied both by Islamic fundamentalists and by critics of Islam.

The laying down of a universally valid interpretation is thus a modern phenomenon. Only in recent times have many groups and individuals claimed a monopoly on a single interpretation of the Qur'an. It follows inevitably from the form and manner of their emergence that this is usually quite restrictive.

Islamic Feminism

Freedom of interpretation offers extensive opportunities together with the undeniably great danger of misuse. As a result, today there are men and women who arrive, for example, at interpretations that are gender-equitable with respect to the position of women. They point out that it has always been men who have interpreted the Qur'an. It isn't the fault of the source of the law, the Qur'an, that women have few rights in some Islamic societies but of the male monopoly on interpretation of the Qur'an. For this reason many women nowadays combat this monopoly by men and attempt to drub them with their own weapons.

Ziba Mir-Hosseini (b. 1952) is one example; when her husband refused to divorce her, she involuntarily discovered the theme that in following years would not only engage her personally, but also as a scholar. For almost five years she fought for a divorce in an Iranian court. According to the prevailing Iranian law, based on Islamic law, it is virtually impossible for a woman to gain a divorce without the consent of her husband. Even so, after many years, Mir-Hosseini was finally successful. She obtained her divorce by convincing the judge that it was her Islamic right, to be divorced. A further result of her "field research", in several essays on Iranian divorce law, is the film *Divorce Iranian Style*, a moving documentary about the situation of Iranian women.

In her arguments with the Iranian judiciary, and in her contacts with other women who were fighting for the same goal, Mir-Hosseini made a fundamental observation: many of these women had, like herself, used the law to their own advantage to gain their objective. Before the court these women invoked Islamic law in order to pursue their claim against those who were denying them divorce in the name of Islam. Ziba Mir-Hosseini made yet another interesting discovery. When she interviewed a series of leading representatives of reform, along with numerous conservative clerics in Iran, for her book *Islam and Gender*, she realized that their views on the question of women didn't necessarily stand in correlation with their other political opinions. Mir-Hosseini discovered, for example, that an advocate for separation of church and state and a great battler for democracy such as 'Abdolkarim Soroush held a conservative position on the question of women, similar to that held by Ayatollah Javadi Amoli, one of the greatest advocates of Iranian theocracy. Machismo is, therefore, not restricted to conservative believers.

Nevertheless, Soroush did have something worthwhile to offer Islamic feminism in Iran: Iranian campaigners for women's rights employed his basic argument – namely, his thesis about the changeable nature of religious knowledge – for their own ends. In particular, his approach was adopted by the circle of Iranian feminists associated with the journal *Zanan*. Ziba Mir-Hosseini writes that Soroush made it possible for them to reconcile their faith with their feminism: "His approach to sacred texts enabled the women of *Zanan* to argue for gender-equality."[6]

The potential for change in Islamic religion was also glimpsed by those who struggling under a secular aegis for change concerning the situation of women. Nawal El Saadawi (b. 1931) hardly counts as an Islamic feminist yet she too has stated:

> There is no such thing as a religion that is unchanging. It changes as political conditions change as well as by new interpretations of verses. That holds true for all religions, for Judaism, for Christianity and for Islam. Take the movement in Europe and the US that is called liberation theology. It interprets the Bible afresh, and says, for example, that Jesus was a black woman. So too in the Islamic world there are currents that interpret Islam in a liberal and enlightened way.[7]

Moreover, Saadawi herself has worked in the spirit of Islamic feminism. She has written about the great female figures of early Islamic history and told of their independence and their courage: A'isha, the Prophet's third wife, fought her enemies with the sword, while Khadija, his first wife, was a prosperous and influential merchant who was confident enough to contract marriage with Muhammad. Saadawi also describes how the Prophet, whose example all Muslims are bound to follow, dealt with women. Muhammad gave his wives the right to oppose him. They were expected to reprove him and make him aware of his errors and shortcomings. Furthermore, she describes how and why it came to pass that these rights were withheld from women in later times: "As far as the attitude towards women is concerned, Muhammad's successors did not walk in his footsteps,"[8] Saadawi firmly states.

---

6 Ziba Mir-Hosseini, *Islam and Gender: the Religious Debate in Contemporary Iran* (Princeton: Princeton University Press, 1999), 238.

7 Nawal El-Saadawi, Interview with the author, April 1999.

8 Nawal Saadawi, *Fundamentalismus gegen Frauen* (Munich: Diederichs, 2002), 54.

In her writings Saadawi shows again and again that many of the regulations in force today are not derived from the Qur'an.

> The problem in our region does not lie in religion and is based even less so in culture; it does not stem from Islam. All religions are capable of adjusting and they tend to change together with the political system. The Christianity of the Middle Ages is not identical with Christianity today. The feudal church is different in many respects from the capitalist church. Wahhabi Islam in Saudi Arabia is utterly different from Islam in Tunisia, Iraq, Syria or Egypt. The situation of women in Saudi Arabia is quite different from that of Muslim women in other political systems where Islam is the state religion. Religion can be interpreted in such a way as to help women and the poor, but it can also be interpreted in an opposite way as a means of fomenting oppression.[9]

The oppression of women, in Saadawi's view, has nothing to do with Islam, and so, women today lean on Islam in their struggle for more freedom and human rights. She cannot comprehend that in the West this is viewed as a contradiction and because of this she considers the West to be ignorant. Nevertheless, she also takes the notion of cultural relativism harshly to task:

> A post-modern feminist writes, "I believe in multiculturalism and diversity. I respect cultural differences and as a result, I cannot pass judgment on female circumcision." I do not agree with this. If I come to America and see that women are stoned to death in the name of honour or of anything else, I won't then say, "Okay, that's their culture." For that would be contrary to humanity. We are all human beings and so I too can judge. I can't simply say, "That's multiculturalism."[10]

This is not Saadawi's only criticism of a West that views reformers in the Islamic world as allies who cherish the same values, such as

---

9 Nawal El-Saadawi, Interview with the author, April 1999.
10 Ibid.

democracy and human rights. What is overlooked is that, for Muslim intellectuals, these values appear purely as universal and rational and so are acceptable for this reason, not because they see themselves as allied with the West. Intellectuals like Saadawi do not care to be perceived as allies since for the most part they view the West much too critically or even negatively.

> The West, the USA, have financed fundamentalist movements so that young Muslim men might fight against the Soviet Union in Afghanistan. They created Bin Laden, al-Qa'ida and the Taliban to combat Communism. Now, following the collapse of Communism, they no longer need them and now they want to sweep them away. All of this is nothing but a political game.[11]

Fatima Mernissi, to an even greater extent than Saadawi, has dealt with the Prophet Muhammad, to whom both reformers and Islamists revert in order to justify their positions. Mernissi, born in 1940 in Fez, Morocco, grew up in a harem. After studying political science and sociology at the Sorbonne in Paris, she took her PhD in 1973 at Brandeis University on the topic of sexuality, ideology and Islam.

Mernissi owes the start of her career to the national independence movement. In 1947, the then King, Muhammad V, set out a new initiative: he removed the veil from his daughter Princess Aisha and gave her a voice in urgently needed changes in Morocco. As a result it became the fashion in well-placed families to provide good education for their daughters. Fatima Mernissi was one of the first who could avail herself of this opportunity.

In 1974 she became the first – and for years the only – female professor in Morocco. Up until 1981 she taught at Rabat University; today she is active mainly as an author. Her publications deal with gender roles, female power in Islamic history, the effects of modernity in Moroccan society and the lot of Moroccan women. *Beyond the Veil*, her first book, published in 1975, has become a classic. Nevertheless, she

---

11 Nawal El-Saadawi, Interview with the author, April 1999.

became an Islamic feminist through the publication of her book *The Veil and the Male Elite: A Feminist Interpretation of Islam*. The work is a quasi-historical study of the role of the Prophet's wives; it was published in French in 1987. By the use of pithy examples she shows the context in which the chapters of the Qur'an that deal with the relation between men and women should be viewed and how they have been in part severely falsified in their interpretation.

Above all, however, Mernissi has pointed out a profusion of prophetic traditions that speak out against violence in marriage and in favour of the equality of men and women. For this Moroccan author there is only one reason why these traditions are not considered canonical: men have blocked them. Mernissi has met with vehement hostility because she has exposed many traditions that are inimical to women as inaccurate and poorly understood, and in so doing, she has not flinched from a critique of the canonical collections of traditions.

Men on the side of Women

But men too support Islamic feminists in their struggle against male dominance in interpretation. In his book *Speaking in God's Name: Islamic Law, Authority and Women* the Egyptian-born, American author Khaled Abou El Fadl (b. 1963) criticizes Muslims who try to fortify their legitimacy at the expense of women; the neurotic rejection of any equitable treatment between the sexes is glorified as a symbol for the defence of Islam in order not to be compelled to acknowledge one's own cultural defeat. In his book Abou El Fadl especially singles out Wahhabi jurisprudence that employs the most outlandish kinds of argument to meddle in the minutest trivia of daily life. He mounts a polemic against the misogynistic, Saudi Arabian legal opinions that declare, for example, that men should not sit down on a chair until the scent of a woman who was seated there previously has dissipated. He calls such pronouncements untenable and not derived from Islam. With his book he established his renown as an engaged feminist. However, the question of women represents only one aspect of his writing; he is particularly concerned with tracking down selective perceptions, strategies of repression and the possibilities for manipulation in Islamic law.

The South African scholar Farid Esack (b. 1957) puts forth a different argument but one with the same objective: to accomplish something on behalf of women. Esack explains that in comparison with pre-Islamic conditions in the Arabian Peninsula, the Qur'an improved the situation of women, for example, in matters of inheritance. And yet, what the Qur'an lays down with regard to women is not to be taken as an end-point. The archaic customs of a tribal society which do not accord women and slaves the same rights as free men, could not be rapidly altered for the very reason that the society of that time could not play along. It is the task of today's Muslims to continuously further the reform that the Qur'an initiated. Only then might one act in the spirit of the Qur'an, that is, in the spirit of justice and pluralism.

Esack's writings have been provocative when they address the Qur'anic passages that prescribe discrimination against Jews, believers of other faiths, or non-Arabs. In so doing he distances himself from the attempts at reform of many of his colleagues, male and female. Esack holds that it accomplishes nothing to construct an ethically acceptable Qur'an by means of a historical interpretation. Instead, it is necessary to see the claims to power inscribed in the text for what they are and to tackle them critically. Hence he writes:

> I have always argued that the Qur'an is an historical document.
> Its language is a human language; its context is human. It was
> sent down to a prophet who lived at a specific time and in a
> specific society. Starting from there it is necessary to discover what
> was relevant to this specific time, and what was not. Instead of
> attending to the particular prescriptions in the Qur'an it is requisite
> to direct one's attention to the principles underlying them. In
> this way one could discover a model in the Qur'an that points
> in the direction of emancipation, liberation and equality. If one
> applies and transmits this model there is no longer any need to be

concerned about the specific directives. For me that is God's will in our time.[12]

Ebrahim Moosa (b. 1957), who also comes from South Africa but currently teaches in the US, similarly criticizes specific interpretations of the Qur'an that he terms "text fundamentalism". Not only Islamists, but some modernists too, are guilty of such text fundamentalism. In direct reference to Islamic feminists he maintains that they engage in hermeneutical acrobatics as well as in a "hermeneutics of wishful thinking" (Moosa 2003, 125). In his view it makes no sense at all to scour a text like the Qur'an in the light of such modern values as equal rights. Such a claim cannot be made of a seventh-century text. He writes that, after having used this mode of interpretation himself for a while, he now considers it inadequate and unsatisfying. It makes more sense to grant history and the performative role of revelation a larger significance in any interpretative schema. The other interpretative endeavours looked exclusively for authority in a foundational text. In so doing the early jurists had already detached themselves from the text.

Text fundamentalism maintains the fiction that the text provides
the norms and we simply "discover" them. But the truth is that we
"create" the norms in a colloquy with the revealed text.[13]

Muhammad Shahrour provides another example of a modernist interpretation of the Qur'an that promotes an improvement in women's rights. Born in 1938 in Damascus, he taught civil engineering at the University of Damascus until the year 2000, following engineering studies in Moscow and attainment of his PhD at the University of Dublin. From

---

12 Farid Esack, "Den Islam neu denken," Der Wille Gottes in unserer Zeit – ein Gespräch über Aids, Widerstand und einen modernen Islam mit dem südafrikanischen Theologen Farid Esack in Zenith, Zeitschrift für den Orient, 1/2002.
13 Ebrahim Moosa, "The Debts and Burdens of Critical Islam" in Omid Safi, ed., Progressive Muslims: on Justice, Gender and Pluralism (Oxford: Oneworld, 2003), 125.

1967 on, in other words, since the disastrous defeat of the Arabs in the Arab-Israeli War, this religious layman occupied himself with Qur'anic exegesis. With ingrained scientific method and under the influence of philosophical dialectics, in 1990 he published his analysis entitled *The Book and the Qur'an: a Contemporary Interpretation* (*al-Kitab wa-1 -Qur'an: Qira'a Mu'asira*); within three months it had sold out in Damascus and was banned in Saudi Arabia.

In his writings Shahrour stresses that religious reform must precede democracy in Arab countries since religion there possesses a normative force. Democracy presupposes freedom of choice but Islam suppresses this freedom in its traditional form. For this reason, Shahrour is concerned with freedom in his modern reading of the Qur'an. His theory of freedom is based on the so-called "theory of limits". For Shahrour, God places limits on human beings in the Qur'an. When, for example, in Qur'an 5:38, it states that a thief must have his hand cut off, what is meant is that cutting off the hand represents the ultimate punishment – it is not, however, a punishment prescribed without any alternative. The thief could just as well be sentenced to some volunteering activity. Everything that falls between these two limits is allowable and a matter for laws which a parliament should determine. From this point, Shahrour bends the bow to democracy, for once the notion of freedom of choice has been made spiritual, everything else follows as a matter of course. He emphasizes that, according to his interpretation, the supporters of the death penalty are as much in the right as their opponents. Whatever sentence is finally applied is then a matter for a democratically elected parliament. With reference to the prescriptions on attire for women the theory of limits states that the upper limit consists in covering the entire body, the lower limit extends to the underclothes. Thus, everything that falls between the complete covering of the body, on the one hand, and going about in public in underclothes, on the other, is allowable.

At the core of Shahrour's critique stands al-Shafi'i (767–820), the scholar and founder of the school of law that bears his name. Al-Shafi'i put a stop to free decision-making because he responded to all questions by means of analogies to the life of Muhammad. According to

Shahrour, what was especially dire was that he shifted that which is forbidden, *"haram"*, into the foreground. This way of thinking was established over 1200 years ago in a reactionary period and it lives on today. At every street corner stands a shaykh who diffuses a sense of guilt. Every day religious television channels hammer into people's head that they are God's slaves. And yet, the word of God – and so the absolute law – says that you are free to choose. For Shahrour, the struggle against this way of thinking the true jihad. He seems to be conscious of just how difficult this is when he writes:

> I was fortunate to live in Syria. If I had not, perhaps what has happened to other thinkers in other Islamic countries would have happened to me as well; like Nasr Abu Zayd who lives in exile. Perhaps my fate would have been even worse. I am an engineer by training and I know that it is easier to construct a skyscraper or a tunnel beneath the sea, than to teach human beings to read the book of God with their own eyes. For centuries they have gotten used to read it through the eyes of others.[14]

Mahmoud Muhammad Taha's experience is an example of just how dangerous reform can be. This scholar, politician and Sufi, born in 1909 or 1911 in the Sudan, and who was the very exemplar of a moderate Islam, was condemned to death on a charge of having apostasized from Islam and hanged in 1985.

Taha's modern interpretation of the Qur'an defended democracy and the legal equality of men and women. The argument of this well-educated hydraulic engineer rested on the fact that the Qur'an was revealed to Muhammad in two stages, first in Mecca and then in Medina. Taha ascribed timeless significance only to the suras revealed in Mecca. He considered the Medinan suras, by contrast, to have been dictated by prevailing circumstances and so only valid for the seventh

---

14 Mohammad Shahrour, "The Divine Text and Pluralism in Muslim Societies," Muslim Politics Report of the Council on Foreign Relations 14 (July-August 1997), 8. http//www.quran.org/library/articles/shahroor.htm.

century. The two stages are differentiated by the fact that the Meccan suras were revealed at a time when the Prophet and his companions lived as an oppressed minority. In Medina, however, the Prophet established leadership and lived amongst both members of other faiths and heathen. Accordingly, in Taha's view, the Meccan suras are addressed to humankind at large. They are buoyed up by a spirit of freedom and equality. For Taha, they represent Islam in its perfected form, just as the Prophet lived it: summoning to belief through admonition and encouragement, not through threats. In his most important book, *The Second Message of Islam (al-Risala al-Thaniyya min al-Islam)*, published in 1967, he writes that the life of early Muslims in Mecca had been the most exalted expression of their religion. It consisted of worship, good deeds and a friendly coexistence with other peoples. In Mecca the Prophet preached tolerance, equality and individual responsibility for all men and women without discrimination on grounds of race, gender or social origin.

When the Prophet and his companions were persecuted and forced to leave Mecca, the message underwent a change. In Mecca the Qur'anic verses of peaceable persuasiveness predominate whilst those revealed in Medina are replete with rules, coercion and threats, and include the duty of jihad as well. For Taha they represent an accommodation to the actual reality of life in a seventh-century Islamic state in which there was no law but that of the sword.

The Medinan verses, which were addressed not only to Muhammad but also to the community of early believers, formed the basis of the sharia as it came to be developed by legal scholars in the following centuries. Taha designated it as the first message of Islam. Nevertheless, in his view, the elevation of the Medinan verses to a legal standard was not meant to be forever. God wanted the verses from the Meccan period, which represent the true ideal of religion, to be revived at a time when humankind had reached a stage of development in which they could accept and realize them. They would then usher in a renewed Islam based on freedom and equality. According to Taha, this second message is both higher and better than the first one, transmitted in the seventh century by a messenger who arrived from the future.

Living in the twentieth century, Taha believed that the time had
come for Muslims to receive this second message. In this way Taha
– who held the conviction that freedom as well as complete equality
between men and women was one of the fundamental principles of
Islam – opened up a method of Qur'an interpretation that shows a way
out of the crisis of modern Islam. The way he proposed allows Muslims
to strengthen their faith without having to live under inhuman laws. To
be sure, Taha could not succeed in promoting these ideas; he had to
pay for them with his life.

His ideas did not die with him but have been developed further by
'Abdullahi An-Na'im (b. 1946) who fled from his Sudanese homeland
in the 1980s after Taha, his teacher and companion, was killed. He now
teaches in the law faculty of Emory University in Atlanta. In the Sudan
he had served as the Executive Director of Human Rights Watch. Following in Taha's footsteps – whose work he has translated into English
– he has been involved in reform of the prevailing conception of the
sharia. In his book *Toward an Islamic Reformation*, An-Na'im advocates a revision of sharia that would be completely compatible with the
requirements of international rights and human rights. To this end he is
attempting to create a modern reconstruction of the sharia by interpreting the textual sources afresh. The sharia, he believes, is a body of law
that for a long time was quite progressive. In the nineteenth century,
however, it could no longer keep pace with reality. Muslims today,
therefore, have the task of calling the long-vanished humanistic ideals
of the sharia back to mind.

In An-Na'im's view the state and religion must be separated; insofar
as the state is secular by its very nature, the notion of an "Islamic state"
represents a contradiction in terms. On the other hand, religion and
politics cannot be separated. Upon being invited to Berlin in 2009 to
give the annual Carl Heinrich Becker Lecture – named after the great
orientalist and Prussian minister of culture – at the Wissenschaftskolleg,
An-Na'im directly addressed the secular fundamentalists in European
debates over Islam, informing them that the separation of state and religion was not a Western achievement. Whoever declares that enlightenment, modernity and individualism are Western achievements is

laying a trap for Muslims. It is as though the secularists telling Muslims that they cannot be modern unless they abandoning their religious identity. This is a colonialist way of thinking.

Why is an Islamic state a contradiction? Because, in An-Na'im's view, the principle of Islam is, at its core, individualistic. Only the individual believer can follow God's commandments; the state cannot be religious. Codification of the sharia by the state deforms the religious law; religious conformity cannot be state sanctioned without undermining the very meaning of religion. An-Na'im categorically dismisses the notion of an Islamic state. The unity of state and religion, the watchword of the Islamists, is not justified by the traditions of Islamic legal teachings.

Islam in and for Europe

Tariq Ramadan (b. 1962) is easily the most glittering figure in European Islam. He is as controversial as he is popular. He serves above all as a model for young Muslims. Many see him as the ideal type of the reformer; for others he is a wolf in sheep's clothing. The view of him in official quarters is equally contradictory. A strategy paper for the British government brought him into the discussion as a leader of Islamic reform in Europe; Notre Dame, the Catholic university in Indiana, appointed him in 2004 as chair in Religion, Conflict and Peacebuilding. But then the American department of Homeland Security withdrew his already approved visa on the grounds that his presence represented a danger to national security. His activity as a guest professor in Rotterdam's Erasmus University, as well as his role as advisor to the city of Rotterdam on multicultural matters, was terminated without notice by both institutions in August of 2009 on the grounds that Ramadan had appeared as a moderator in a broadcast extensively funded by the Iranian government. Since October 2006 he has been the Sheikh Hamad Bin Khalifa Al Thani Professor of Contemporary Islamic Studies at St Antony's College, Oxford.

For many, Ramadan represents a threat because he is who he is, namely, the grandson of Hasan al-Banna, the founder of the Muslim Brotherhood. Tariq Ramadan's father Said went into exile in Switzerland and founded an Islamic centre in Geneva. Tariq Ramadan was born there in 1962. In recent years he has become a leading spokesman for Islam in France as a result of his countless presentations, debates and books, and as an independent intellectual, neither belonging to the Muslim Brotherhood nor in thrall to it, as his critics charge. From his grandfather he has inherited, in particular, his charismatic magnetism as a speaker; in addition, because of his origins he has assumed a great religious aura of legitimacy in the eyes of many Muslims. His participation in the European Social Forum in 2003, the controversy that he stirred up with Jewish intellectuals in France, whom he scolded for narrow partisanship, in other words, bias – namely, for Israel – as well as, finally, his television debate in November 2003 with the then-Interior Minister Nicolas Sarkozy over the headscarf, all turned him in the end into an international media star.

Ramadan seeks out his public forum amongst secularized Muslim youth in the suburbs of Lyon, Paris and Marseille, on the one hand, and on the other, amongst liberal, left-wing intellectuals and opponents of globalisation, not least in the Arab world. This extreme divide gives him a distinct glitter. Thus, he is not a reactionary Islamist, as liberal, left-wing voices have labelled him for some time. Ramadan definitely wants change but in the internal Islamic culture clash over the two speeds of reform, he positions himself on the side of the Muslim immigrant class demanding change. This class clings fast to the conventional and is characterized by a traditional mentality. Ramadan writes:

> What should we do to effect a change in thinking? Condemn the scriptural sources and no longer belong to the Islamic world? Impose a so-called modern outlook and thereby be seen as "secularized" in our actions or, even worse, as defectors to "the enemy's" side? To be listened to by the West at the cost of losing the ear of the Muslim world? To be satisfied with an assumed modernity at the cost of no longer playing any role in a world that is foundering under oppression and sanctimonious religious justification?[15]

15 Tariq Ramadan, *Peut-on vivre avec l'islam? Entretien avec Jacques Neirynck*, 2d. rev. ed. (Lausanne: Favre, 2004), 22.

For Tariq Ramadan, reform begins at the point where it is recognized as imperative to interpret the Qur'an by means of human reason and to accommodate changed circumstances. But he means to remain faithful to its spirit. Ramadan too wants to consider the Qur'an in its historical context to find the possible bases for its application to other times and other places. Nevertheless, in his view, there is absolutely no latitude for interpretative reason whenever ritual practices ('ibada) are involved. For Ramadan, these count as timeless. But for that very reason, there is even greater latitude with regard to social matters (mu'amalat). Here the classical principle retains its validity: everything is permitted that the text does not expressly prohibit. This opens up a considerable space for progress and reform, and so too for legal education that keeps pace with the times and considers circumstances on the spot.

Ramadan has made a name for himself with his notion of Europe. In his book Muslims in the West (Musulmans d'Occident: construire et contribuer), he asks of Muslims to take part in the social and political life of their new homeland and to consider the non-Islamic countries in which they now live as their homelands. This is no foregone conclusion; traditionally, Muslims are permitted to stay in non-Islamic states only on an interim basis. But instead Ramadan tells Muslims in Europe: here, where you are, assume responsibility for your political and social destiny, bring yourselves in. In his book Western Muslims and the Future of Islam, he writes that the attitude of withdrawal is something to be avoided and that political activity is to be grasped as an arena for the expression of community interests. He declares forcefully:

> Today it is no longer a question as to what place Muslims in Europe occupy or will occupy. The question that interests us now is rather what contribution they can make to their current societies.[16]

He seeks to convey a positive attitude towards Europe to his listeners and his readers:

---

16 Tariq Ramadan, Muslimsein in Europa (Marburg: MSV, 2001), 277.

Muslims in the West can feel more secure amongst themselves –
something that the free practice of their religion requires – than
in certain so-called Muslim countries. This analysis could lead,
in conjunction with the criteria of security and peace, to the
conclusion that the designation *Dar al-Islam*, that is, the Abode of
Islam, is applicable to nearly all Western countries whereas for the
majority of Muslim countries it is scarcely applicable any more.[17]

To anchor the loyalties of Muslim citizens aright within the Western
secular democracies in which they live, Ramadan makes do with a
provisional design. In accord with the concepts of sharia, their very
presence in Europe already implies a moral pact. For this reason he
obliges Muslims to respect the prevailing constitution and the law that
it validates. This is the very minimum, to be sure, but it leaves something to be desired, for in Western democracies it is the case that the
law as made by human beings in parliament takes precedence over
God's revealed law. Here we come to the most ticklish point. Tariq
Ramadan is unwilling to make this concession; for him the sharia is
divine law once and for all. For this reason, there is no essential down-
grading of the sharia, for him, to a mere moral guideline; rather, certain
concessions are made temporarily, with regard to secular law. It is for
this reason that he can speak, for example, of a moratorium on stoning,
but not on its abolition.

He has been rebuked for this proposal, and reproached for not dis-
sociating himself from it. There have been demands for him to reject
sharia wholeheartedly. He has not done so however; for Ramadan, the
sharia is still God's law and no Muslim can claim that it is not. Accordingly, he refuses dissociate himself from sharia. Nevertheless, he does
seek to discover ways and means to reconcile elements of Islamic law
with human rights and democracy. According to Ramadan, corporal
punishments, the penalties for sin, the unjust regulations with respect
to women's rights, cannot be put into practice. The moratorium that
Ramadan has proposed is a meaningful and constructive idea. For

---

17 Ramadan, *Muslimsein in Europa*, 158.

many, however, it doesn't go far enough. Farid Esack, for example, argues for a far more radical procedure. Conversely, one might ask if it is not a mistake to demand that Muslims adopt Western ideas since this involves the risk losing of them losing their religious identity in the end.

Criticism as Self-Criticism

The fact is that reform must occur; many Muslim intellectuals are convinced of this, now, as in the past. In Islamic countries as well as in Europe, South Africa and the US, debates are being held about Islam in the modern world. There are sharp clashes over modern interpretations of the sources and a critical approach to the tradition. Instead of ascribing blame to the West for all developmental failures, a great deal of self-criticism is taking place. Sadiq al-'Azm, born in 1934, is the best example of this. Growing up as the son of a well-to-do family in Syria – whose reputation and status often protected him – al-'Azm earned his doctorate at Yale University and in 1963 began his teaching career at the American University of Beirut.

After the Arab defeat by Israel in 1967, al-'Azm called upon Arab states to practise self-criticism; a year later he brought out his *Critique of Religious Thought (Naqd al-Fikr al-Dini)*. He would become known as well for his criticism of Edward Said's conception of orientalism as well as for his intervention on behalf of Salman Rushdie. Al-'Azm composed petitions, collected signatures and tried to make *The Satanic Verses* available to Arab readers. This forced him to realize that only a minority of intellectuals was prepared to take a stand for artistic freedom. The reasons for this are many: a deep-seated anger against the West, which is held responsible for the political woes of the Arab world, together with a certain admiration for the Iranian Revolution that challenged a world power, the US.

Al-'Azm's 1968 book *Self-Criticism after the Defeat (al-Naqd al-DHati ba'd al-Hazima)*, which analyses the effects of the Six Day War on Arab nations, earned him both celebrity and hostility. In this book he launched vehement criticism against the Arab world, against its submission to authority, its religious dogmatism and against the role that

Arab regimes accorded to women. There existed no critical mass that could actually change the societies. Contrary to the prevailing opinion that the West is to blame for the stagnation of the Arab world, colonialism, imperial exploitation and the situation in Palestine, al-'Azm's argues that such opinions are merely pretexts by which Arab regimes preserve themselves, extend their repressive measures and squander the wealth of the region.

Sadiq al-'Azm once called his Arab compatriots the "Hamlets of the twentieth century" because, since the Arab renaissance of the nineteenth century, they have wavered between tradition and modernity, between Islam and secularism. After over 150 years they still haven't come to a decision as to which course they should adopt – and this drama, as with that of Hamlet, proceeds from one tragedy to the next.

The Algerian thinker, Mohammed Arkoun (1928–2010), who was born into a Berber family in Kabylia, was a similarly embattled critic. When he moved, at the age of nine, into a village near Oran, where French settlers lived, he experienced a shock. He became aware that as a Berber he not only belonged to an underprivileged minority but didn't have the same rights as an Arab. Moreover, he was unable to communicate within his own country; he would first have to learn Arabic and French.

Arkoun was strongly influenced by his uncle, who was connected to mystical Islam. From 1941 to 1945 he attended a school run by monks in which he became acquainted with Latin culture and literature, and studied the Early Church Fathers Augustine, Cyprian and Tertullian. Afterwards he studied Arabic literature in Algiers but also explored law, philosophy and geography. In the mid-1950s Arkoun enrolled at the Sorbonne in Paris. Life in France wasn't easy for him. Muslim intellectuals were often lumped together as rejecting the West. In their Algerian homeland, by contrast, they were seen as the fifth column of the enemy, as representatives of the imperialistic West. Arkoun remained in France where in 1971 he became Professor of the History of Islamic Thought at the Sorbonne.

Arkoun is critical of the development of Islamic thought that, since the thirteenth century, has led to a series of taboos. The notion of the "un-thought" plays a great part in his work. The task that Arkoun took upon himself entails thinking this previously "un-thought" in Islamic culture and expressing it in words. He views non-thinking as paralysed thinking; fixed convictions that make a critique imperative. In his main work, Critique of Islamic Reason (Pour une critique de la raison islamique), Arkoun attempts his own interpretation of the sources. To this end he draws on concepts and methods drawn from the disciplines of sociology and humanities. Thus, he brings structuralism, semiotics, structural anthropology, discourse analysis and post-structuralism into his own theories of Islam and Islamic reason. Arkoun demands a fundamental critique of central concepts – so-called theological constants, "the nature of the Qur'an", for example, or "the essence of Islam" which orthodox Islamic scholars defend as sacrosanct.

Nevertheless, his scholarly engagement is not restricted to a scrutiny of Islamic tradition. He wants to re-think Islam utterly in order to overcome the intellectual rigidity that he holds responsible for political and social misery.

> Up to the present, Islam has routinely rejected the liberal
> accomplishments of modern critical thinking. It has become
> entrenched in dogmatic isolation with an aggressive attitude towards
> that self-confident, all-conquering West, just as the peoples of
> the Muslim world have also in fact experienced, perceived and
> interpreted it.[18]

For this reason Arkoun strives for a radical reconstruction of both mind and society in the contemporary Islamic world. He argues for a change of perspective and demands a multiplicity of significations, in an attempt to counter the prevailing homogeneity and dogmatism. The politicization of Islam and the reduction of its message to questions of law and power were thus a thorn in his side. Whoever would

---

18 Loay Mudhoon, "Mohammed Arkoun: Kritiker der islamischen Vernunft," *Eurasisches Magazin*, 3/2/2011. http://www.eurasischesmagazin.de/ artikel/?artikelID=20110215.

claim nowadays that in Islam there exists no separation between the worldly and the spiritual spheres fails to understand that this status quo is based on the fact that politics has taken religion hostage, to disastrous effect.

Other thinkers that are concerned with a new critical approach to the Islamic tradition belong to this school of thought. Mohammed 'Abed al-Jabri (1936–2010) also set his sights on a new scholarly relationship with tradition; he called for the Qur'an to be interpreted Qur'anin such a way that it not stand in opposition to democracy and human rights. Furthermore, he too sought to introduce the findings of other disciplines into modern exegesis. Other thinkers alongside those already described should be mentioned, thinkers who devoted themselves early on to this undertaking. Already, by the 1970s, Sa'id al-Ashmawi (b. 1932) was making a distinction between religion and religious thought; Fuad Zakariya (1927–2010) established the relativity of each and every interpretation, and Hasan Hanafi (b. 1934) drew attention to the historicity of revelation. Muhammad Ahmad Khalafallah (ca. 1916–1998) had emphasized in his 1952 book, *The Narrative Art of the Qur'an* (*al-Fann al-Qasasi fi-1 -Qur'an al-Karim*) that the Qur'an can never be considered apart from those who received it but rather stands in a close relationship with those to whom it was addressed. Aisha 'Abd al-Rahman (1913–1998) showed that there are different possibilities for the interpretation of the Qur'anic revelation, for instance, the literary. Amin al-Khuli (1895–1967) wanted to return to the understanding of the Qur'an that those who first heard it had, that is, the Prophet's companions, in order to understand the history of the Qur'an's impact and set it in an historical context.

This school of thinkers, as it were, shows that a single theme stirs many intellectuals in the Islamic world, and has done so for a long time: a belief in the modern world. There are fierce disputes over a timely interpretation of the sources as well as over a critical approach to tradition. Even so, in contrast to radical Islamists, who have exploded into our consciousness in recent years, these thinkers and intellectuals have gotten only scant attention.

3

Nasr Hamid Abu Zaid: Who's the Heretic Here?

A Born Conqueror

Nasr Hamid Abu Zaid was born in 1943, two years before the end of the Second World War, in Tanta, a small village in the Nile Delta. His father named him Nasr, meaning "victory", because he was an optimist. He believed that the Allies would be victorious in the war. All of his friends, however, were for the Axis powers because the latter fought against England, the much-hated occupying power. Abu Zaid was born into humble circumstances. His father had a shop and because he had problems with his heart, the son had to help out from an early age.

The Muslim Brothers played an important role during Abu Zaid's milieu. They were very popular in the village, seen not so much by the inhabitants as a political party, but rather as a religious and charitable organization. They concerned themselves with social issues and children's education. Parents sent their children to the Muslim Brothers so they wouldn't hang around in the streets but learn something instead. Under the tutelage of the Brothers they were taught to understand the meaning of Islam. This was not religious indoctrination. On the contrary, in his autobiography *A Life with Islam*, Abu Zaid tells how religious notions of ethical values at that time were concerned with equality and ensured, for example, that no one went hungry. This view of religion with its emphasis on simple piety made a lasting impression on him.

His parents sent him to Qur'an school at the age of three. There, arithmetic as well as the Qur'an and the alphabet were taught so that the children could eventually attend elementary school. By the age of eight Abu Zaid knew the Qur'an by heart. Because of this, a ceremony was held for him in the village mosque. Later, he attended a private Christian school, since the school's director took pity on his father and loaned him the tuition fee. The close contact with different religions that he encountered there fascinated Abu Zaid.

> It was a Christian school that I, a child from a Qur'an school, attended in which my Muslim teacher of Arabic was called Mr "Jesus" and we Muslims had a common prayer room. Today many young people grow up in Saudi Arabia or Kuwait because their parents are guest-workers there. In these countries the notion is widespread that every non-Muslim is a *kafir,* an unbeliever.[1]

After secondary school Abu Zaid expected his father to enrol him in high school so that he could earn his diploma. He wanted to study at the Faculty of Arabic at Cairo University but his family didn't have the money and so his father sent him to an occupational school.

His father died just as Abu Zaid turned 14. Even before, in the long years of his father's illness, Abu Zaid had shouldered great responsibility; now he was the sole support of his mother and his five younger siblings. After he completed his training as a radio technician at the age of 17, he got a position in 1961 working for the police force's radio – a section of the Ministry of the Interior. He would remain there for 12 years and travel the entire country. Abu Zaid had to complete his probationary period in Cairo; coming from a village he had been completely overwhelmed by the city. He felt alone and he couldn't cope. His shift lasted from eight in the evening to eight in the morning.

---

1 Nasr Hamid Abu Zaid, *Ein Leben mit dem Islam* (Freiburg im Breisgau: Herder Verlag, 1999), 30.

Because he had so little to do, he read a great deal, reflected upon himself and carried on conversations with himself as a way of ordering his thoughts. Six months later he was posted to Mahella al-Kubra, a city that was similar to his hometown. He brought his mother and his siblings there where they remained until 1968.

In 1967, the year of defeat by Israel, Abu Zaid began to attend evening school. He had foreseen the defeat, he wrote, because a people that is not free cannot fight. By that time, his faith in Nasser and the revolution was already faltering. This was linked to the growing oppression and persecution that the Muslim Brothers were undergoing. Abu Zaid viewed them as pious men who had been pushed aside by the revolutionaries around Nasser who only wanted power for himself alone. The death sentence given to Sayyid Qutb further contributed to his estrangement from the Nasser regime. Abu Zaid was aware Qutb the author, a side that was less known to Islamists; he had written on the poetry of the Qur'an, for example. He described the Qur'an as a text that contains ethical, moral, spiritual and legal pronouncements, but at the same time being a work of poetic art which moves both reader and listener aesthetically. Qutb had been influenced by literary romanticism and he focussed on the psychological effect of the text. Abu Zaid admired him for his literary grasp of the Qur'an, and the execution of this Qur'anic scholar appalled him. He didn't hold Qutb responsible for the fact that his book *Milestones* served to legitimate armed conflict; nevertheless, he rejected Qutb's social and political model as totalitarian.

After graduating, Abu Zaid registered at the Faculty of Arabic. He even managed to be posted to Cairo. For years he divided his time between work and study. When he had to work in the morning, he went to the university in the afternoon; when he had to work in the afternoon, he went to school in the morning. For him the university was no ordinary place: "When I entered as a student in March of 1968," he wrote in his autobiography, "I wept."[2] Of course, he soon realized that university was different from what he had dreamt it was.

---

2 Abu Zaid, *Ein Leben mit dem Islam*, 94.

The university seem more concerned with simply processing students; the teacher read out his notes, often from a book, and the students wrote everything down. Frustrated by this, Abu Zaid began studying without a teacher. He began to read books on textual analysis because he wanted to be able to do more than merely report on the content of poems. In his third year he finally found what he'd been looking for: he was to be taught by the philosopher Hasan Hanafi, in whose classes students could actually debate the texts. Hanafi and Abu Zaid became good friends though Abu Zaid later criticized the philosopher strongly. Hanafi's approach to the Islamic legacy was too selective for Abu Zaid. According to him, Hanafi did not analyze the tradition. but instead painted it over afresh with his own notions. That was just what the Islamists did, to Abu Zaid, it's just that they used different colours.

Two other Egyptian scholars, along with Hasan Hanafi, made a particular impression on Abu Zaid. Amin al-Khuli, who had developed the literary approach to the interpretation of the Qur'an, was one of these. His methods provoked a scandal in 1947 when al-Khuli's student, Muhammad Ahmad Khalafallah – the second scholar whose influence on Abu Zaid was substantial – employed al-Khuli's principles in an examination of the Qur'an for his dissertation. Khalafallah sought to prove that in the Qur'an God did not provide historical facts but wished solely to transmit principles and values. Therefore, the Qur'an is also literature and far better understood if one tries to comprehend it by the methods of literary analysis. All the tools of modern literary scholarship may be employed: linguistic, philological, theories of historicism and even those of psychology.

At that time, literature represented Abu Zaid's greatest interest. He wrote poems in dialect and in classical Arabic, and he even won prizes for these. The language of the Qur'an, however, also riveted him. His relationship to the Qur'an as a literary text, as a text "whose aesthetic can stir the soul"[3], had begun early on. It was not so much the message of the Qur'an that most drew him, but rather, its linguistic order, its

---

3 Abu Zaid, *Ein Leben mit dem Islam*, 100.

inner music. Even as a child Abu Zaid had missed no opportunity to listen to a recital of the Qur'an. He enjoyed Qur'an recitation the way others enjoy a classical concert or an aria. When he came to the Faculty of Arabic he was already determined that he would work on the aesthetics of the Qur'an.

Abu Zaid wrote his Master's thesis on Qur'anic metaphor in the thought of the Mu'tazilites, an eighth and ninth century rationalistic school of thought that attempted to remove apparent contradictions between the Qur'an text and reason by invoking metaphor. Thereafter, the political situation in Egypt occupied him increasingly. It was in 1977, the year in which – as a result of a curtailment of subventions for basic foodstuffs, required by the International Monetary Fund – bread riots broke out. Abu Zaid couldn't afford a place to live; he couldn't get married. When he learned of a stipend, offered through his Faculty, he pounced on it and went to the US.

> I knew that I would have to learn English and become acquainted with Western culture to realize my scholarly goals. In any case I felt that in Cairo I was suffocating, inflation turned everything upside down and the political pressure kept growing day by day.[4]

Africa, America, Asia

Abu Zaid came to Philadelphia to study at the University of Pennsylvania. He counted among his positive experiences in the US the fact there one could demand one's rights even from someone who held a higher position than oneself. On the negative side, however, there wasn't much hospitality in the US. He remained there for two years and had occasion to be initiated into the discipline of hermeneutics, or textual analysis. He read Lévi-Strauss and de Saussure, he immersed himself in structuralism, and he discovered Gadamer's work. He realized immediately that he had found what he'd been searching for but at the same time that he had too little preparatory knowledge

---

4 Abu Zaid, *Ein Leben mit dem Islam*, 112.

to understand Gadamer. And so he studied the ancient Greeks, Schleiermacher, Wilhelm Dilthey and Martin Heidegger.

Many other thinkers followed and all at once Abu Zaid discovered their closeness to Ibn 'Arabi (1165–1240), the great Arab mystic. He began to read afresh his masterpiece, *The Meccan Revelations (al-Futuhat al-Makkiyya)*, in which the author interprets the Qur'an in a new way. By reading Ibn 'Arabi in conjunction with the works of Western scholars, Abu Zaid discovered the theme that was common to all these books: the relationship between the text and the reader. As he put it, he came to understand that language was never merely a neutral vessel:

> Gadamer asks where truth is. Is it in the I or in the world outside, in the reader or in the text? Or does it lie in their interaction? This is exactly how Ibn 'Arabi poses the question. He says that the truth changes with respect to whomever is regarding it. Often Ibn 'Arabi means by truth God Himself who changes under observation. What God is "objectively" cannot be understood by human beings. Human knowledge of God is inevitably subjective but at the same time it is dynamic and varies from one person to the next.[5]

Alongside hermeneutics, which would prove so influential to his own scholarly work, Abu Zaid became aware of Toshihiko Izutsu, a Japanese scholar of Islam, not especially well known at the time, who taught at McGill University in Montreal and who was investigating the conceptual world of the Qur'an. Izutsu had analyzed Qur'anic semantics and formed conclusions about the worldview of the Qur'an. Abu Zaid had always believed, as he writes in *A Life with Islam*, that only Arabs could understand the Qur'an. But now, in the United States, he was reading books in English by a Japanese scholar, who taught in Canada, and he was amazed both by his sensitivity to the characteristics of Qur'anic language and by the precision of his thought. He went to Montreal for the express purpose of meeting the Japanese scholar but the latter was

---

5 Abu Zaid, *Ein Leben mit dem Islam*, 117–8.

staying in Tehran at the time. Izutsu was also the reason why Abu Zaid later went to Japan. In any case, he never met him and the scholar left the letter that Abu Zaid wrote to him unanswered.

Two years later Abu Zaid returned to Cairo full of new ideas as well as longing for his students and his family. He didn't like life in the US very much:

> I'd found many friends, not so much because Americans are friendly but because I'm a friendly person...I always want everyone to like me. And so I love them and I show them my love.[6]

After his return Abu Zaid submitted his doctoral dissertation and began to teach at the university again. He also got married but almost nothing is known about his first wife whom he divorced after 12 years of marriage.

When Anwar al-Sadat had 1500 opponents of his policies arrested in 1981, among whom were many well-known intellectuals and highly regarded professors – together with anyone suspected of opposition – Abu Zaid had to leave the university too. He was transferred to the Ministry of Social Affairs but after a few months was allowed to return to the university on the grounds of personal hardship. Nevertheless, the university had changed fundamentally in the interval. The students seemed suddenly incapable of discussion or of entertaining new ideas; they were afraid to express an opinion. For this reason, Abu Zaid accepted an offer to teach as a guest lecturer at the University of Khartoum in the Sudan, where he encountered highly-motivated students. They restored his enjoyment of teaching and for this reason he later dedicated his book *The Concept of the Text* (*Mafhum al-Nass*) to them.

In 1984 Abu Zaid was invited to Japan as a guest lecturer and accepted the invitation unhesitatingly. He still had Izutsu's name in his mind and the possibility of getting to know a new culture attracted him. The two years that had been planned for Japan turned into four.

---

6 Abu Zaid, *Ein Leben mit dem Islam*, 121.

Abu Zaid especially valued his contact with the students, though he came to grief over the Japanese language. Even so, that didn't prevent him from exploring Japanese culture. He spent hours in Japanese theatres because he believed that there he could discern the inner movements of Japanese culture.

Separation from the Homeland

In 1989 Abu Zaid returned to Egypt. During his four years in Japan he had finished his book *The Concept of the Text* and had written the greater part of his *Critique of Religious Thinking* (*Naqd al-Fikr al-Dini*). Meanwhile in his homeland he had attained the rank of associate professor, directing his own special discipline – Qur'an and hadith studies – within the Faculty of Arabic. During his absence, the Islamic movement in grown in society and elsewhere. It controlled the student union and its presence was particularly in evidence in Arabic studies. In 1992, Abu Zaid's critique of Imam al-Shafi'i, the founder of the school of law named after him, appeared. In classes many students expressed a view of this traditionalist that deviated from that of their teacher. Abu Zaid blamed al-Shafi'i as essentially responsible for the petrification of Islamic thought.

In 1992, also the year of his second marriage, Abu Zaid's book *Critique of Religious Discourse* (*Naqd al-KHitab al-Dini*) appeared; in this he intervened in the conflict between the nominally secular Egyptian government and the Islamist opposition in the country. He critically analyzed the political and social roles of the groups and the individuals who saw themselves as religious leaders. His critique dealt with both the government-funded religious scholars and preachers as well as with the Islamist opposition. In his view it wasn't only the influence that the Islamists wielded in Egypt but also the strong social position that the traditionally oriented religious scholars enjoyed in their service to the state, that made it impossible for discussion to develop freely. Both groups had declared their own interpretation of the Qur'an as the only true one and reduced reason to silence – all in the interest of their own power. He delivered harsh judgments on the representatives of religious discourse:

Religious discourse in the end contradicts Islam itself since it denies one of its most important bases, reason, and believes that in so doing it confirms tradition. But in fact it negates tradition by denying its epistemological principles. Contrary to the propaganda of contemporary religious discourse, one cannot go back to Islam through the arbitration of texts, the consequences of which Islamic history attests to, but rather only by according to reason its former rank.[7]

It struck Abu Zaid as downright heathenish to claim that there is only a single valid interpretation of the Qur'an – namely, one's own. This act of self-divinization, this making one's own understanding of the text absolute, accords badly with the principle of monotheism that is central to Islam. This critique led to lively discussions between Abu Zaid and his students, and especially the Islamist students, but for the time being it had no further consequences. In 1993, however, his application to become a full professor was turned down on the grounds that he was a heretic.

There were three documents involved. Two endorsed his application; however, the university followed the minority vote of 'Abd al-Sabur Shahin that Abu Zaid's work displayed shameless lies, perverse ideas, Marxist and atheistic notions, as well as the most loathsome contempt for the fundamental principles of religion. When Shahin, a professor of philology and a popular preacher, repeated Abu Zaid's alleged views on Islam in a Friday sermon, raging articles and caricatures appeared in the Egyptian press. One portrayed a fat man who was stabbing a Qur'an from which blood flowed. Such a caricature is deadly in a society in which the majority can neither read nor write. The first threatening letters began to arrive; the situation escalated. Abu Zaid could teach only under police protection.

For Abu Zaid this was all symptomatic. The rejected application reflected the lamentable condition of Egyptian universities. The spread

---

7 Nasr Hamid Abu Zaid, *Islam und Politik: Kritik des religiösen Diskurses* (Frankfurt: Dipa-Verlag, 1996), 65.

of a backward-looking Islam affected teaching; suddenly teaching was dominated by a fear of the religious. The universe was divided into things that were prohibited by religion and things that were permitted. Once, as he reports in his autobiography, when he was discussing a love poem in a lecture, an 18-year-old girl stood up suddenly and said that love poems were prohibited in Islam:

> Instead of explaining the structure of the poem, suddenly I had
> to provide a legitimation of poetry in Islam; I had to qualify the
> statements introduced against poetry and put them in context; I had
> to sink to a level unworthy of a university – the level of *permitted*
> and *prohibited*. And so you sink deeper and deeper and deeper. It
> can easily be imagined what would happen in my Qur'an courses if
> I were to say: the Qur'an is a product of its culture.[8]

Abu Zaid was in Tunis when news reached him that a suit had been filed to force his marriage with Ebtehal Younes to be annulled. Neither he nor his wife could believe it, and after the process began in their absence, they believed that the matter would be quickly thrown out when they returned to Egypt. Their lawyers confirmed them in this opinion; a compelled divorce was simply not possible, was ridiculous. And yet, in Egypt there was a legal basis for such an annulment; this is the principle of *hisba*, according to which every Muslim has a duty to promote the good and forbid the bad. The complainant based his case on this principle. The principle of *hisba* makes it possible for an outsider, for someone not personally affected by a case, to file suit in court if he considers the interests of the community at large to be affected. The interests of the community at large were affected in this case since it is not permissible for a non-Muslim to be married to a Muslim. If he is an apostate the marriage is a violation of God's laws and, thus, against the interests of the community at large.

Perhaps Abu Zaid had even had a presentiment of what would befall him when he published his critique of Egyptian religious discourse in

---

8 Abu Zaid, *Ein Leben mit dem Islam*, 147.

1992: "One can raise up resistance against the rule of men," he wrote, "but the battle against the rule of the theologians, inasmuch as it is declared to be disobedience and heresy against God's rule, brings the charge of unbelief, atheism and heresy down on one's head."[9] One year later, when the scholar was accused of apostasy from the faith, he stated to the *Middle East Times*, with a certain gallows humour, "Every researcher is happy to see how his ideas become reality."[10]

On June 14, 1995, the judgment was delivered: the marriage of Ebtehal Younes, Professor of Romance Languages at Cairo University, and Nasr Abu Zaid was annulled. The shock was certainly huge, but when Abu Zaid recounted it he spoke above all of the support that he received from the dean of his faculty, his colleagues, his students. There were even expressions of solidarity in the Egyptian media. One newspaper alluding to Egyptian divorce law wrote that it makes it difficult for women to obtain a divorce while the only woman in Egypt who wants to remain with her husband is divorced.

The couple did not submit to the divorce decree but instead went into exile together. In Holland, first in Leiden, then in Utrecht, Abu Zaid was offered a position. From 2004 on he occupied the Ibn Rushd Chair of Humanities and Islam at the University of Utrecht. He made visits to Egypt only as a private citizen; though always expecting an apology from the authorities, it never came. He lived with his wife in Leiden where he wrote books, taught Western students, gave his opinion on Islam in Europe, attended conferences and received prizes. But he missed his homeland more than anything: "Egypt, which I am so mad at, is my homeland, it is my love, it is my mother. How could she allow this?"[11] In a remarkable irony of fate, Nasr Hamid Abu Zaid died on July 5, 2010, in his native country.

---

9 Nasr Hamid Abu Zaid, *Naqd al-khitab al-dini* (Cairo: Dar Sina, 1992), 81.
10 Steve Negus, "Professor charged with apostasy," *Middle East Times* 6, 12/7/1993.
11 Abu Zaid, *Ein Leben mit dem Islam*, 177.

God's Word

Every attempt to develop a new hermeneutics of the Qur'an is contested, as Abu Zaid once said, comparing himself with Mahmud Mohammad Taha. That went for his attempt too. A central idea in Abu Zaid's work is that a dialectical relation exists between the Qur'an's text and those to whom it is addressed; only someone who investigates the historical context in which the Qur'an was revealed can grasp its meaning. Only then can it be determined whether this verse or that one deals with a universally valid commandment or with a rule that was relevant only for a specific situation. For this reason, in his book *The Concept of the Text* Abu Zaid presents a text-critical approach to the Qur'an by investigating it like any other text – by means of semiotics, philology, hermeneutics. He describes the goal he set himself as follows:

> I want to know the nature of the Qur'an; its structure; its historical
> background, to be able to introduce a hermeneutical approach. This
> is what I'm concerned with in my work. Maybe we can know the
> context. Understand the context. We might learn how important
> the context is for its interpretation. Just what has always been
> done in Qur'an interpretation. And maybe that will lead to a better
> understanding of the situation in which we Muslims live.[12]

Abu Zaid distinguishes between the human experience of the divine revelation and the conditions that prevailed in its time. And he empha-sizes the distinction between religion and religious thought. Many interpreters would present their religious thinking as religion itself:

> Religion is a collection of historically determined religious texts
> whereas religious thinking is made up of the human strivings
> to understand these texts, to interpret them and to extract their
> meaning.[13]

---

12 Nasr Hamid Abu Zaid, Interview with the author, 1999.
13 Abu Zaid, *Naqd al-khitab al-dini*, 185.

By reading the Qur'an as a literary text and subjecting it to a historical and critical interpretation, Abu Zaid shakes up some basic dogmas.
His merit lies less in the attainment of his own particular interpretation
of the Qur'an, but rather in his way of bringing right before the reader's
eye how utterly imperative it is to interpret the Qur'an, as well as in
showing that throughout the course of history wholly different interpretations have existed.

In this, the decisive issue for Abu Zaid is how the influence of
Qur'anic exegetes, who have often been motivated by their own interests, can be avoided. In his youth he had often observed how the
meaning of Islam could be manipulated. In the 1960s and 1970s quite
disparate interpretations of Islam, all irreconcilable with one another,
were drummed into people by official agencies. In the 1960s, the dominant religious discourse stressed that Islam was a religion of social
justice. The leading scholars of al-Azhar University, Egypt's most influential religious authority, spoke solely about Islam and socialism in
their sermons and writings. Then, when the government veered in the
1970s towards a liberal economic policy, Islam was abruptly reinterpreted as a religion that protects private property.

These contradictions prompted Abu Zaid to occupy himself more
closely with the interpretative methods of traditional Islamic theology. He came across the rationalistic school of the Mu'tazilites who
introduced the concept of metaphor into Arabic rhetoric at the beginning of the ninth century. The Mu'tazilites interpreted verses that they
considered ambiguous or unclear as metaphorical. When Abu Zaid
looked into the dispute into which the Mu'tazilites entered, on account
of their methods, with their opponents, it became clear to him that the
Qur'an was already, in the earliest centuries of Islam, a battleground
of fierce intellectual and political struggles; indeed, the doctrine of the
Mu'tazilites had itself arisen out of social and theological confrontations between various groups. While the Umayyad caliphs legitimated
their absolute rule with the theological notion of predestination, the
Mu'tazilites, who insisted on human free will, fought against Umayyad
dominion and doctrines with their own brand of Qur'anic interpretation.

The intellectual adversaries of the Mu'tazilites were the traditionalists who clung to a literal interpretation of all Qur'anic verses. All the divine attributes, all the eschatological images, of which the Qur'an speaks, have to be taken literally. One example is the Qur'anic statement that God is seated upon a throne. For the Mu'tazilites it was inadmissible to take this statement literally; for them this was anthropomorphism. They held that human beings, by virtue of the duty imposed upon them by God to use their reason, were obliged to think about just what might be meant by such a statement. To be sure, many adversaries of the Mu'tazilites also did not take literally the so-called "Throne Verse" or other verses in which God's face, for example, or His eyes or His hands are mentioned. Ibn Hanbal (780–855) claimed that the anthropomorphisms in the Qur'an were to be taken as literally true but without asking how.

For Abu Zaid yet another example of the multiplicity in Qur'anic interpretation is found in the writings of the philosopher Ibn Rushd (1126–1198). This thinker, who is better known in the West as Averroes, developed the Mu'tazilite system even further. For Averroes the Qur'an possesses three levels of meaning: first is the outer poetical form, by which the masses are addressed; second is the argumentative form, which is meant for theologians; and third is the inner dimension, that applies to philosophers.

Ibn 'Arabi, to whom Abu Zaid devotes his dissertation, takes this theory yet further. Ibn 'Arabi, the grand master of Qur'anic exegesis and arguably the most fascinating hermeneuticist whom the Islamic world has produced, wrote in his *Meccan Revelations* that each person finds in the Qur'an what he strives to find. The Qur'an has something to say to everyone, be he peasant, philosopher or mystic. Ibn 'Arabi distinguishes four levels of meaning and so circumvents the traditional juristic dichotomy of ambiguous and unambiguous verses. He concentrates on the inner meaning of the verse which he viewed as accessible only to initiates. Ibn 'Arabi made a forceful impression on Abu Zaid with his insight into the relativity of all human knowledge.

It was clear to him that interpretation of the Qur'an is never an innocent undertaking. He was increasingly convinced that it was necessary first to ascertain the nature of the text to be interpreted and to investigate the rules that govern its study. For as long as it remains unclear how the text lends itself to exegesis, and where the limits of interpretation lie, the text can be forced to serve as a mouthpiece for any ideology whatsoever.

> It holds good for any interpretation that it must seek to understand the text in its original context. That isn't easy. If I read the Qur'an today I carry the legacy of its entire history of interpretation along with me from the Prophet's Companion Ibn Abbas up to the television preacher Shaykh Sharawi. To lay the Qur'an bare of these accumulated layers of interpretation requires scholarly efforts that are eschewed by many. They prefer to pick out one citation here and another one there in order to have the Qur'an say what they themselves want to say.[14]

Underlying Abu Zaid's endeavor is, of course, the doctrine that the Qur'an is God's word, that it was revealed to the Prophet Muhammad in clear Arabic over a period of 23 years. He is thus in agreement with the definition that has been accepted by all Muslims regardless of their theological and cultural differences over the entire history of Islamic thought. Nor does Abu Zaid deviate from this dogma, even if he is accused of that over and over again by his adversaries. Nevertheless, he distinguishes three aspects within this framework: God's word (*kalam Allah*), the Qur'an, and revelation or inspiration (*wahy*). According to him, these three aspects are not distinguished from one another in modern Islamic discourse. In classical theology, by contrast, there was an awareness that each of these three aspects denoted something particular.

From this starting point Abu Zaid poses the question as to what exactly God's word is. He finds a Qur'anic answer in verses 18:109 and in 31:27. These verses emphasize that God's word is infinite and inexhaustible: "If all the trees on earth were pens and all the seas, with seven more seas besides [were ink], still God's words would not

---

14 Abu Zaid, *Ein Leben mit dem Islam*, 87–8.

run out." But if God's words cannot be limited, Abu Zaid concludes, the Qur'an as a text is nevertheless of limited scope for the Qur'an clearly represents only one specific manifestation of God's word. True, the Qur'an refers to itself in many passages as God's speech and this appears to confirm that God and His word, the Qur'an, are one. For Abu Zaid, however, it creates a number of complicated theological questions if we regard God as a speaker. In what sense, therefore, does the Qur'an contain God's word, and how do the linguistic expressions of the Qur'an relate to the message that Muhammad received from God?

Here Abu Zaid broaches a central theological question – perhaps the single most important question of Islamic religion, and one of primary importance for any reform of Islamic thought. Islamic theologians in the Middle Ages had held debates at a very high level over this very question. In the ninth century, the Mu'tazilites had initiated a dispute over whether the Qur'an as God's word is eternal, as God Himself is, or whether it had been created by God. The Mu'tazilites did not accept the notion of the Qur'an's eternity. Instead, they believed in the createdness of the Qur'an, since there can be no second eternal existence alongside God. That would contradict God's oneness (tawhid), the single most important Islamic principle of all. The Mu'tazilites conceived of God as absolutely transcendent, as One who is accessible to human reason only in His oneness, uniqueness and eternity. How could some second eternally existing being coexist with Him?

Furthermore, the Mu'tazilites could not accept that God's word had existed for all eternity for another reason: to whom would it have been addressed? If someone speaks, he addresses listeners; hence, God first spoke after He had created the world and encountered possible auditors in the angels and in human beings. The Mu'tazilites tended to the view that the Qur'an was created and, therefore, that it came to be in this world over the course of time. For a time the caliph al-Ma'mun (786–833) enforced the doctrine of the Qur'an's createdness as authoritative. Even so, those who held the opposite opinion refused to accept that God's word was something created. In the end the conflict was settled politically and the doctrine of the Qur'an's eternality became the mainstream Sunni belief. It is precisely here that Abu Zaid, who endorsed the Mu'tazilite position, stands apart from Sunnis – as well as, indeed, from Shi'ites.

In *Muhammad and God's Signs* he quotes a Qur'anic passage that is central to this debate (verses 43:2–4):

> By the clear Book!
> We have made the Qur'an in Arabic
> so that you may understand.
> It is with Us in the 'Mother of Scripture',
> sublime, wise.

What today is sometimes translated as the 'source of the Book' is *umm al-kitab*, which in Arabic means literally, 'Mother of the Book'. This verse comes close to the interpretation that there is a sort of book or word of God that is eternal and with God. This is how most Sunnis today read this passage. But it is also possible to read it metaphorically. In this case *umm al-kitab* would mean "God's knowledge". This is the reading that Abu Zaid follows.

The meaning of the expression *umm al-kitab* is linked with the question about the extent to which the Qur'an actually contains God's exact words. This too is a question that was much disputed in early theology. Eventually the view prevailed that in the Qur'an God's word has been translated into human language or that God's word was translated by the angel Gabriel into human language.

> Up to the present day, and possibly even especially today, there have been believers who understand the Qur'an in an even stricter sense as God's Word, in effect, as if God had uttered exactly these words. The more widespread this view is the less compelling it is. You only have to think of the implication: did God maybe speak Arabic?[15]

15 Nasr Hamid Abu Zaid, *Mohammed und die Zeichen Gottes* (Freiburg im Breisgau: Herder Verlag, 2008), 71–2.

According to Abu Zaid, one point above all contradicts this view. If the Qur'an contains God's word in His precise wording, then Muhammad really didn't accomplish anything very special. He merely received God's word and proclaimed it. Of course, that does not agree with the Muslim conception of Muhammad's achievement. As the one to whom God's word was addressed, Muhammad had access to the revelation in manifold ways, as the Qur'an proves unambiguously. In Abu Zaid's opinion, this has to alter the idea of what "God's word" signifies.

What exactly then did Muhammad receive? That he did receive something stands beyond all doubt for Abu Zaid. Tradition calls what Muhammad received a message not made up of human speech but rather *wahy*. Following from this, the second decisive question that Abu Zaid poses is, what exactly is *wahy*? This term is of central significance for most of the thinkers presented here.

In Western Islamic studies *wahy* is sometimes translated as inspiration, sometimes, less aptly, as revelation. According to Tilman Nagel, the verbal form may be translated as "to inspire" or "to imbue". Navid Kermani has shown that *wahy*, originally and fundamentally, indicates nothing more than a form of communication that is somewhat less clear than everyday speech. Thus, a poet's inspiration can equally be called *wahy*; this goes back to pre-Islamic Arabic usage that applied in numerous contexts, some of which have been retained until now. In pre-Islamic poetry *wahy* occurs also in the sense of "to make indications", with the hands or eyes, for example, but also as a synonym for "writing".

The Qur'anic usage of *wahy* is also manifold; it isn't only prophets who experience *wahy* but also angels, ordinary human beings, animals (16:68) and even the earth and the heavens (99:5, 41:12). The demonic whisperings of Satan are a form of *wahy* too. Basically it can mean any of God's communications with a human being; whether these come directly or indirectly from an angel, they can equally be designated as *wahy*, and the same holds for the revelations of the prophets who preceded Muhammad. The scholars of Islam Theodor Nöldeke and Friedrich Schwally have observed that:

...by the word *wahy*, revelation, Muslims designate not only the Qur'an but every one of the Prophet's inspirations, every divine command to him, even if these words were not proclaimed as Qur'anic.[16]

They allude here to the inspirations of Muhammad called *hadith qudsi*, that is, the words of God reported outside the Qur'an. The scholar Suyuti (d. 1505) distinguishes four types of *wahy*: firstly, *wahy* at the ringing of bells; secondly, by inspiration from the Holy Spirit into Muhammad's heart; thirdly, through Gabriel in human form; and lastly, directly from God, either when one is awake, as happened in Muhammad's Night Journey, or in dream.

Other scholars add yet another six types. Essentially, however, two basic forms can be distinguished, which the Islamic scholar Tor Andrae identified as the auditory and the visionary. A revelation is auditory in which there is a voice that speaks either into the ear or into the heart of the Prophet. The oft repeated word *qul* "speak!" in the Qur'an presupposes *wahy* through the sense of hearing. But the Qur'an also mentions visions. Tor Andrae considers these less clear-cut; their meaning "often has a mysterious symbolic depth which the soul intuits rather than clearly grasps."[17]

Thus, God imparts His message either directly or He reveals Himself to humans indirectly through a messenger. But in the Qur'an even direct revelation has two forms. The first is what the scholars have called *ilham*. This is accomplished wordlessly. Such is the case with the angels and with the mother of Moses who was instructed by God to keep her son quiet. Another form of direct revelation is the "speech behind the dividing wall", as occurred to Moses, the only person who was privileged to have God speak directly to him.

---

16 Theodor Nöldeke, *Geschichte des Qorans*, Vols. 1 and 2 revised by Friedrich Schwally (Leipzig 1909), 1919.; vol. 2 by G. Bergsträsser & O. Pretzl (Leipzig 1938), One-volume reprint (Hildesheim 1961), 21–2.
17 Tor Andrae, *Muhammad: Sein Leben und sein Glaube* (Göttingen: Vandenhoeck & Ruprecht, 1932), 39.

Traditional scholars are in agreement that God did not communicate directly with Muhammad but, rather, used an intermediary, the angel Gabriel. Gabriel makes use of *wahy*, non-verbal communication, and from this we may conclude, according to Abu Zaid, that *wahy* is not synonymous with God's speech. Hence, *wahy* cannot be equated with the Qur'an. Today, of course, many Muslim and non-Muslim scholars do equate them.

Does God Speak Arabic?

For Abu Zaid, this issue is linked with the question of what it means when the Qur'an repeatedly emphasizes that it has been revealed "in plain Arabic". This can hardly mean that God speaks Arabic for according to the Qur'an Islam is one and the same message that all prophets have preached since the beginning of the world.

It means that God takes the language of people into consideration to whom He sends His message. This is why it says in verse 14:4, "We have never sent a messenger who did not use his own people's language to make things clear to them". Accordingly, Abu Zaid doesn't consider it very likely that the Qur'an represents God's word exclusively and that this word is hitched to the Arabic language. Otherwise Arabic would have to be deemed a sacred language.

In his view there are three aspects of the Qur'an that must be distinguished: its content, its language and its structure. The attribute of divine applies only to the source of the Qur'an. That becomes clear solely through the history of its emergence. The Qur'an was originally transmitted orally; everywhere in the Islamic literature it is stated that Gabriel imparted verses to the Prophet at each and every revelation which Muhammad then later recited to his companions. These verses or passages were compiled into chapters and given a written form in part. On this too, the Islamic sources are absolutely unanimous. After the Prophet's death these chapters were finally collected, arranged and written down in book form.

If it be said that the Qur'an is God's actual word, then there are also linguistic aspects to be considered. Arabic script, at that time differed from modern Arabic; in the latter, points and diacritical marks give the vocalization of a word and add to the clarity and unambiguity of the word's meaning. When the Qur'an was first put into written form, only the consonants were recorded. The first manuscript of the Qur'an, commissioned by the caliph 'Uthman, was basically not a readable text; it was rather a notation that served as an aid to memory in recitation.

In order to avoid misreadings, vowels were eventually indicated in their short form with different signs above or below the corresponding consonants. A great significance attaches to these "reading aids" since they created clarity amongst undifferentiated variants. In early Arabic, however, these were not yet customary; this system of vocalization was first added later in the Qur'an commissioned by 'Uthman. Abu Zaid discusses this problem extensively in *Muhammad and the Signs of God*.

Tradition reports further that already in Muhammad's earliest community there were differences of opinion about how a particular expression should be pronounced. One person favoured this pronunciation, another that, at which point both went to Muhammad and asked him which of them was right. Muhammad listened to the version of one of them and stated that it was correct and he then listened to the other and declared that that too was right. He explained the matter by saying that it is still God's message just as long as something that is forbidden is not made into something that is permitted and something permitted into something forbidden. Abu Zaid here cites the historian and legal scholar al-Tabari (839–923) who reports this in the introduction to his Qur'an commentary because this ambiguous information has confused people. But for Abu Zaid the principle is clear: nothing should be altered in the contents but Muhammad did sometimes allow one word to be replaced by another word to facilitate understanding.

Given that the Qur'an was revealed bit by bit and piece by piece he reacted to the needs and demands of the community. Because he responded to the questions of the community, the Qur'an slowly developed a legal character. It therefore reflects the dialectical circumstances of God's word and human interests. This is one of Abu Zaid's central points:

In this very complicated process of dialogue there are attempts to persuade, polemics and contradiction. In the Qur'an itself it is quite obvious that Muhammad's entire following also played a large part. There are such statements as "They have asked you", "You say to them". For this reason I am convinced that we ought not regard the Qur'an simply as a text but as a collection of speeches. But at every speech we have to see who is really speaking. And who are the auditors? What kind of speech is in question? It's not merely a matter of returning to the historical text but to its complex structure as well. By such an approach to the Qur'an, we understand it better, as well as what actually happened at that time. Not least in this process is the question as to whether the form and manner of speech in our time might reveal something or whether it is simply bound to the historical context of revelation. To make this distinction is no casual matter because it isn't at all easy sometimes to identify the individual speeches.[18]

When the Qur'an became canonical a new arrangement of the verses and chapters arose that no longer corresponded to a chrono-logical order. Even different speeches, revealed in different historical situations, were combined. Thus, out of the recited Qur'an a book (*kitab*) came into being.

For Abu Zaid, this attests that the original word of God in its incom-prehensible absoluteness, that is, before it found expression in Arabic, is holy and divine; however, its manifest expression is not. This is the same whether one holds to the Mu'tazilite doctrine of the "created-ness of the Qur'an" or not. The logical conclusion is always the same: the Qur'an that we read and interpret is not identical with the eternal word of God. The Qur'an that human beings now have before them is, Abu Zaid says, a message that God conveyed to humans through the Prophet Muhammad, a human being himself. But since God, as

---

18 Stefan Orth, "Historische Kontext stärker berücksichtigen: ein Gespräch mit dem Islamwissenschaftler Nasr Hamid Abu Zaid," *Herder Korrespondenz*, 7/2008, 341.

the "Sender" of the Qur'an, cannot be the object of scholarly investigation an analysis of the cultural and historical context of the Qur'an offers the only approach to a discovery of His message. Consequently, the Qur'an that is decoded in the light of its historical, cultural and linguistic context must be newly interpreted with regard to the cultural and linguistic context of today's interpreter. In this way we arrive at the interpretative multiplicity that constitutes Islamic history.

Just because Islam's message must be valid for the whole of humanity regardless of time and place, there must be a multiplicity of interpretations. And yet, because they remain convinced that the Qur'an is God's exact expression, many Muslims resist a historical approach to reading the Qur'an. Even so, that should not alarm us, Abu Zaid says:

> My belief in God's revelation and in the prophethood of Muhammad is not in the least shaken by the fact that I see in the Qur'an the result of a divine inspiration rather than the exact words of God.[19]

Just because Abu Zaid does not see God's exact verbal expression in the Qur'an, his interpretation of the Qur'an opens up possibilities for the social and political reforms that he believes are desperately needed. Hence, the Qur'an must not be enlisted as an authority for everything that is commanded and forbidden. One must no longer ask how it stands in relation to democracy, human rights or the freedom of the press.

Disaster Politics

Abu Zaid regrets that a dogma has arisen according to which the Qur'an's authority goes beyond belief to encompass all the domains of society and of knowledge. For him its religious, spiritual and ethical dimension is central. He explains this vividly when he reports on his own personal experiences with religion. In his childhood in the village, belief motivated people to act justly and well. It was the real reason

---

19 Abu Zaid, *Mohammed und die Zeichen Gottes*, 76.

why people assumed responsibility and created something of a social balance. People lived their faith without talking about it much. Today by contrast, he writes, people are speaking all the time about religion while the values that it handed down were absent from Egyptian society:

> In the village belief was made up of rites and ethical standards, not of the state and the law... The principle by which people acted was: al-din 'ibadat wa-mu'amalat – "religion consists of ritual obligations and of actions". God may forgive negligence in obligations but not people's evil deeds even if he to whom you have been unjust forgives you. God can forgive you for not praying but He does not forgive you for stealing from someone else... Since the core of religion lay for us in people's deeds there was no scandal in the village if someone did not pray. People might ridicule him and make jokes about him but nobody called him a heretic. If someone didn't fast during Ramadan people found excuses for him; it was said that he worked hard or didn't feel well. People didn't approve of it but they tolerated it. But unjust deceitful behavior was not forgiven. The Islam that I got to know during my childhood consisted of religious duties, the observance of which was a private matter, as well as of actions that had consequences for other human beings and for society and that therefore were not private matters.[20]

The problem for Abu Zaid lies in the fact that the principle 'ibada wa-mu'amalat, as well as the fact that religion is made up of ritual and deeds, has been steadily reinterpreted in the twentieth century. In the 1940s "rites and deeds" was turned into "belief and law" ('aqida wa-shari'a) by Shaykh Shaltut, the famous Grand Imam of al-Azhar University. The fundamentalists then interpreted 'ibada wa-mu'amalat as "religion and state" (din wa-dawla) and claimed that the state was necessary to strengthen religion. Hence, for them, there could be no belief in the absence of an Islamic state.

The catchphrase whereby Islam is a union of religion and state

---

20 Abu Zaid, Ein Leben mit dem Islam, 50–1.

corresponds neither to the doctrines of Islam nor to the actual course of history; Abu Zaid emphasizes this and he quotes the theologian al-Amidi who wrote in the twelfth century: "We now want to treat the question of government and the caliphate which do not belong amongst the principles (usul) of belief." The choice of a ruler occurred according to the rules of society; it is not stipulated in the Qur'an. Accordingly, the conflict over the succession to Muhammad was political, not religious. Abu Zaid is certain that it is better if religion is not the state:

> Where religion is the state the danger arises that it will be identified with all the inadequacies [of the rulers] or, as in Iran, with state crimes.[21]

Religion should have as little to do with politics as possible. Thus, the failings of democracy in Islamic societies have many causes, to be sure – social, cultural, political, both domestic and foreign – but all that has very little to do with Islam. It is for this reason that Abu Zaid is critical of both the opponents and the supporters of democracy who use Islam to justify their position. As an example, Muslim democrats point out that Islam is familiar with shura "consultation" and they often quote verse 42:38:

> those who respond to their Lord and keep up the prayer; conduct their affairs by mutual consultation; give out to others of what We have provided for them.

Thus, whoever wants democracy says that Islam stands for democracy because it supports shura; whoever does not want democracy says that Islam supports not democracy but shura. Everyone finds what he is looking for in the text; everyone uses the text as a quarry. Abu Zaid reproaches both groups for ignoring the context and the meaning of the verses. Shura is neither identical with democracy nor is it Islamic law; it is not an Islamic political system but rather, the practice of

---

21 Abu Zaid, Ein Leben mit dem Islam, 56.

the pre-Islamic tribes for whom it was customary at the time that the leader engage in consultation with the other members of the tribe. And so when the Qur'an speaks of the *shura*, as Abu Zaid notes, it is speaking of something already in existence. The verse is not law; it is a description.

> All of this is interesting but it doesn't answer the question of how we can bring about a democratic system nowadays. The *shura* doesn't give us much help since we no longer live within a tribal unit. The organization of political life, the social system, the structure of the state are not religious matters. They are to be arranged in terms of our experiences, our reason and the will of the citizenry. Even as I say this I know very well how the knee-jerk objection will sound: whoever separates religion and politics separates religion from society. But that is neither compelling nor logically conclusive. This objection is an expression of a confusion that prevails amongst many Muslims and almost all Islamists. They equate the state and society.[22]

Abu Zaid spots another misunderstanding in the assumption that the existence of an Islamic state today is bound up with the establishment of sharia. The Qur'an proclaims laws, so the Islamists explain, and in order to be able to apply these, a state that is defined and aligned religiously is necessary. Hence, there is a tendency to regard the least part of the Qur'an that has juristic relevance as its authentic message. Abu Zaid is critical of the fact that all other verses drop into the background. The Qur'an is thus transformed into a legal text. But in fact, it is an all-encompassing religious and spiritual prophecy that contains, among other things, a series of legal prescriptions that have no need of political power to be put into effect. Their application depends on the conviction of the individual human being. For Abu Zaid, no religion needs to be assigned to the authority of the state and the power of its branches to make its principles and standards operative. Belief is a matter between God and the believer, he says, and

---

22 Abu Zaid, *Ein Leben mit dem Islam*, 62.

so, it unambiguously contradicts all Islamists. Whoever makes belief a matter for the state mistrusts the individual and in the end God Himself who in the Qur'an gave man the choice either to believe or to turn away from Him. The Islamist mistrusts God's trust in the individual.

Here too Abu Zaid stands starkly apart from contemporary Islamists who believe that people should be compelled, by force if need be, to comply with Islamic regulations and who allow them no freedom of choice in matters of faith. It is this emphasis on the individual levels that exist between a person and his God that Abu Zaid wants to rescue from the Islamists for humanity. Because of this he regards the conjunction of state and religion not only as non-compelling but as even dangerous for the believer. In a case in which the individual believer has an understanding of his religion or of his God that deviates from the understanding that the state has, then that believer cannot practice his faith. Abu Zaid fears that in such a state – and examples such as Iran prove that his concern is justified – only the religious understanding of the rulers will be accepted. All other interpretations and viewpoints will be considered heresy. Such a state is turned into a church, as the example of the Islamic Republic has shown before our very eyes. Abu Zaid laments that Islamists want to spoon-feed people to be certain that they obey God's laws.

> It is every Muslim's responsibility to obey God's laws; it's not the responsibility of the few who are in power. Perhaps the majority will agree on a law that runs counter to Shari'a. Perhaps the majority will come to an agreement on a policy that is not in accord with Islamic principles. That is a justifiable concern. But it is not justifiable to take the power of decision from people because of this concern. There is no limited or halfway democracy.[23]

Precisely because Abu Zaid rejects all suppression of freedom of expression, he even gave his support to Shahin, that assessor who unleashed the entire campaign against him with his charge of heresy

---

23 Abu Zaid, *Ein Leben mit dem Islam*, 64.

and who himself was accused at the end of the 1990s with heresy because he sought to harmonize the Qur'anic account of creation with the theory of evolution.

If Abu Zaid put great value on the separation of religion and politics, that doesn't mean that he failed to act as a political critic himself. He had blunt words of criticism for the Egyptian government under Mubarak which claimed to combat the Islamists. He considered the would-be democracy in Egypt a farce: choice was not free, the parties were not equal, the ruling party had legitimacy only because the president was one of its members. Abu Zaid frequently called the Egyptian president Mubarak a dictator and when the Islamists reviled him as a pharaoh, he thought it justified.

Abu Zaid did not spare the West in his criticisms either; in this he was like most intellectuals in the Islamic world. He reproached the West for supporting dictatorial regimes in the Islamic world and for having only their own advantage in mind by so doing. On the one hand, the military putsch in Algeria met with approval, but on the other hand, not a word was uttered about abuses of human rights in Saudi Arabia, whereas the non-vassal states of Sudan and Iran were pilloried. Abu Zaid accuses the West of playing along with the games of the dictatorial regimes in the Arab world, supporting them out of fear of Islam and, therefore, of being complicit in the destruction of democratic process in the region. This Islam, that inspires such fear in the West, is, nevertheless, an illusion, a fabrication, according to Abu Zaid.

Scholarship: The Personal is Political

Abu Zaid was a scholar whose personal experiences cannot be separated from his research. He said, for example, that he was unable to differentiate between his personal attitude towards women, his interpretation of the Qur'anic statements about women, his belief in the equality of man and woman, and the personality of his mother. She taught him to believe in God as a creator who tolerated no injustice between the sexes.

When Abu Zaid spoke about the woman question he always set it in its socio-political context. Thus, he explained that the woman question was raised by conservative Muslim authors in the course of the economic crisis and growing unemployment. True, the revolution of 1952 had assured women of access to educational institutions and the employment market, but the ensuing economic and developmental policies had foundered. Instead of identifying the real causes, namely, the absence of an economic policy, it was suddenly asserted that women were to blame for unemployment because they had taken jobs away from men. The solution suggested was to send women back home. In Abu Zaid's view, Muslim thinkers were thus offering a solution to a political and economic problem that was, in fact, highly political, even though they claimed that it was based on religion. When it became obvious to him that the game was being played with marked cards, he began to study the Qur'an with regard to the question of women and he ascertained that one of the Qur'an's fundamental concerns was the emancipation of women. The Meccan suras themselves are manifestos of equality. In the Qur'an's account of creation (verse 4.1) it says:

People, be mindful of your Lord Who created you from a *single* soul and from it created its mate and from the pair of them spread countless men and women far and wide!

This verse must be understood as a summons to Muslims to establish equality. However much Abu Zaid may identify the Qur'an as a literary text he does not reduce it to its poetical elements. For him, now as before, it is a book of guidance even with respect to questions of gender.

What then is Islam for Abu Zaid? For him it is at once very simple, but it also constitutes a way of life that is far more comprehensive than all theology and all ritual.

A Muslim is someone at whose hand and tongue people are safe. Everyone is a Muslim who deals considerately with his fellow man and with the universe and who strives to leave a good mark behind.[24]

Perhaps this is what led him to the project *Libforall*. The abbreviation stands for "Liberty for All", that is, freedom for all. This internationally linked project was founded in Indonesia. It sought to strengthen mysticism as a counterweight to legal Islam and to orthodox Wahhabi Islam that is rigidly fixated with the wording of the Qur'an, proclaimed as law. In opposing them, Abu Zaid and his fellow colleagues at Libforall interpreted those Qur'anic verses that appear violent and inhumane by explaining that people had misunderstood the Qur'an and its truth. Libforall formulated it thus:

> Those who view Islam as a religion of fanatics are often unfamiliar with its inner dimensions, as revealed by the great mystics, who have illuminated the Path of Love and inspired traditional Muslim societies with their wisdom and tolerance.
>
> Even today, Sufi (mystically-inclined) Muslims are in the forefront of the battle against extremist ideology – unafraid to oppose the hijacking of Islam by those who claim to speak for God on behalf of *all* Muslims.[25]

Shortly before his death, Abu Zaid said to his wife that it was in Indonesia, which he visited near the end of his life, that he had glimpsed the smiling face of Islam.

When Mubarak was overthrown in February of 2011, many of Abu Zaid's friends regretted that he had passed away before having had the chance to participate in a social movement that demonstrated peacefully, and whose watchwords were freedom, common decision-making, constitutionality and democracy. Many of his students will have marched in the forefront. The seed that Abu Zaid and others had sown

---

24 Abu Zaid, *Ein Leben mit dem Islam*, 207–8.
25 "Background," Libforall, http://www.libforall.org/background-islamic-mysticism-and-tolerance.html

had now sprouted in a peaceful revolution – or at least many perceived it as so.

Abu Zaid's absence is felt in Egypt today. He would have been an important voice in organizing the transition to a civil and democratic society and could have voiced his conviction that religion is not an obstacle to democracy and that human rights are the common property of all humankind which have no need of religious legitimation.

4

Fazlur Rahman: From the Qur'an to Life and Back Again to the Qur'an

A Traditional Scholar

Fazlur Rahman (i.e., Fazl ur-Rahman Malik), one of the most important voices within the discussion of the reform of Islamic thought in the twentieth century, was born on 21 September 1919 in the province of Hazara, now located in Pakistan. His father, Mawlana Shihab al-Din, was an *'alim*, a religious scholar, and it was from him that Rahman received an education in the classical disciplines of the Islamic sciences, namely, in *tafsir* "exegesis", hadith "traditions of the Prophet", *fiqh* "jurisprudence", *usul al-fiqh* "theoretical jurisprudence", *kalam* "theology" and *falsafa* "philosophy". After receiving his high school diploma he attended Punjab University in Lahore and earned both a bachelor's and a master's degree in Arabic literature.

Subsequently Rahman went to Oxford where he wrote his dissertation on the Persian philosopher Avicenna (980–1037). After receiving his doctorate he taught Islamic philosophy at the University of Durham in Great Britain from 1950 to 1958. He soon realized, however, that while the philosophers were certainly very clever in their arguments, "nevertheless their God remained a bloodless principle – a purely intellectual construct lacking in power and passion."[1] Accordingly he

---

1 Ebrahim Moosa, "Introduction" to Fazlur Rahman, *Revival and Reform in Islam*, edited and with an introduction by Ebrahim Moosa (Oxford: Oneworld, 2000), 5.

turned to theology and, in particular, to those religious thinkers – such as al-Ghazali (1058–1111), Ibn Taymiyya (1263–1328) and Shah Wali Allah (1703–1762) – who had created a synthesis between their expertise in jurisprudence and theology. In 1958 Rahman accepted the position of assistant professor in Canada at McGill University's Institute of Islamic Studies. He stayed there for three years until, at the instigation of General Ayyub Khan, the then-president of Pakistan, he went back to his homeland. Ayyub Khan wanted him to be the director of the Islamic Research Institute that had been founded, according to Rahman, to advise the government on its religious policies. These were to be based on Islamic principles, as interpreted, however, by Rahman and his colleagues, and suited to changing conditions in the modern world.

Above all the Institute was to lend intellectual support and backing to Ayyub Khan's project of modernization. Pakistan, founded as a homeland for Muslims, was from the outset torn between the traditionalistic Islam of the populace and the modern Islam of the intellectual and secular elite. For the president, it was important to introduce modernization without bringing the traditionalists down on his head. With his traditional Islamic scholarliness, and because of his longstanding contact with the West, Rahman appeared to be one of the few candidates equal to this challenge.

In his new position Rahman glimpsed a possibility of reforming the religious establishment and, in particular, its educational system – for Islamic reform can only begin with education. In this way, he began to train young academics to approach the Islamic tradition from a critical perspective. In the journal *Islamic Studies,* published by the Institute for Islamic Research, Rahman gave his opinions on all the actual issues in Islamic thought, for example, on the position of the individual, or on the effects of modernization upon religion. He also took on questions addressed to him from a Western angle. Hence, he wrote that Islam is seen in the West as a religion that emphasizes the community but not the individual. Even so, he turned again and again directly to a Pakistani readership and, in particular, his opponents among the clergy. He declared directly to them that if the state of Pakistan were not to solve the problems that arose between Islam and modernity, secularization would inevitably come about.

An essential part of the mandate given to him by Ayyub Khan consisted of providing policy makers with practical suggestions concerning every kind of Islamic query. This ran the gamut from the prohibition on interest to the alms tax and family law. On all of these points Rahman adopted a liberal outlook which quickly brought him into conflict with the traditionalistic religious establishment. The most vehement opposition, which arose over the issues of women's rights and reform of family law, came from the conservatives. The resentment of Ayyub Khan's adversaries discovered an ideal target in Rahman; for them he symbolized the worst aspects of the modernization project: religious and social reform.

In this way, the scholar caught between the two factions; he became a pawn in the power struggle between the president and the mighty religious establishment. To attack the government's readiness to reform, the opposition seized on the architect of this reform and demonized him. Deeply rooted traditionalism together with the illiteracy of the masses intensified the problem incrementally. When hysteria began to reign, and after Rahman began receiving death threats, he decided to resign from his position.

The specific occasion for these threats was the translation into Urdu of Rahman's book *Islam*. He was reproached for having claimed that the Qur'an is not divine – an allegation that was not, in fact, true. Rahman and the Justice Minister S.M. Zafar held a press conference in response to the public outcry. So charged was the situation that the justice minister, who had pledged his complete support to his vilified colleague during the press conference and had stated that he found "nothing objectionable" in his formulations, urged the journalists afterwards to strike out the words "nothing objectionable". For the politicians it was a calculation of interests: politics versus principles. Rahman was sacrificed to politics.

At this point Rahman left Pakistan with his wife and children and resumed his academic life in the West. He was offered a professorship for Islamic thought at the University of Chicago where he remained until his death in 1988. Amongst his students was Michael Sells, currently Professor of Islamic History and Literature at the Divinity School of the University of Chicago. Earle H. Waugh, another of his students, paid tribute to Rahman's life, thought and influence, as well as his significance with regard to Islam in America, in an essay and a monograph. In Waugh's view he was an utterly new phenomenon on the landscape of the American university because he firmly opposed the neutral secularism of scholars. Waugh writes about Rahman, his teacher:

> Fazlur Rahman brought with him a rigor of mind and heart that could be objected to but which could not be rejected. Equally appalled by sloppy scholarship among Muslims as among his students, he represented a tough-minded Islamic scholar that demanded self-criticism before all else. Certainly, he would not compromise on the essentials of Muslim belief, as his many studies testified, but he did not object to the claim that there were other ways of engaging Islam than those validated by Muslim history.[2]

In Chicago he also played an important role in the formation of Muslim doctoral candidates. These came mostly from Turkey and Indonesia and because of this, his ideas were particularly widespread there afterwards. His students Mehmet Aydın, Mehmet Dağ and Alparslan Acıkgenc made his thought available in Turkey through translation. Aside from Turkey he has been achieved acceptance nowadays in Indonesia, though less so in Arab countries and in Iran. All his major works have been translated into Turkish and Indonesian. Rahman had a considerable influence on the so-called "Ankara School" that emerged in the mid-1990s at Ankara University and that from 1996 on propagated its ideas through the scholarly theological journal *Islamiyat*. His regular visits to Turkey, together with his publications, provided the initial catalyst for new thinking at the theological faculty in Ankara.

---

2 Earle Waugh, "The Legacies of Fazlur Rahman for Islam in America," *American Journal of Islamic Social Sciences* 16/3 (1999): 31.

One representative of this school is, for example, Ömer Özsoy, a professor of theology who has been teaching in Frankfurt am Main since 2007 and whom Felix Körner, who has dealt extensively with the Ankara School, calls a "Fazlur-Rahmanist".

That Rahman has been only partially accepted in the Arab world may have to do with the fact that many Arabs, even today, have little confidence in the abilities of non-Arab thinkers and intellectuals, despite the fact that many non-Arab thinkers played a leading role in early Islamic history. Tabari (839–923), for example, and Zamakhshari (1074–1144), who were both Persian, give us the most outstanding examples in the realm of Qur'anic studies. Because of this mentality, the influence of non-Arab scholars remains limited, even though the most innovative ventures in Islamic thinking are undertaken by them today, as Abu Zaid once affirmed in a note of self-criticism.

The German academic community has hitherto scarcely accepted Rahman. There has been no dissertation on the Pakistani thinker in the German-speaking world, despite the fact that the quality of his writings – in comparison, for example, with those of Muhammad Shahrour on whom three PhD dissertations have appeared in recent years – certainly does not fall short of these but in fact, in the opinion of many, far surpasses them.

Many of his former students have since attained high academic positions in their native countries; so, for example, Nurcholish Madjid, for example, taught as Professor of Islamic Studies in Jogjakarta until his death in 2005 and, like Rahman, motivated by his faith as a Muslim, linked scholarship with a dedication for the betterment of society. His efforts were taken up and further developed in the US as well. The best-known examples of here are Amina Wadud and Asma Barlas who applied his ideas with respect to Qur'anic interpretation based on gender equality. Others fervently acknowledge the influence of his ideas. This is so, for example, for the reformist thinker Farid Esack who calls him "one of the profoundest thinkers of the century"[3], as well as Ebrahim Moosa who writes:

---

3 Farid Esack, *Qur'an, Liberation and Pluralism* (Oxford: Oneworld, 2002), 11.

Though I was not Fazlur Rahman's student I consider myself to be someone who has benefited greatly from his writings and his ideas.[4]

Unlike Abu Zaid, Soroush and Shabestari, Rahman never consciously adopted the analytical approaches of Western thinkers. Even though he spent the major part of his academic life in the West, his interests lay exclusively with Islamic thought. The Islamic world was always his frame of reference; he regarded it as his mission to explicate tradition and renewal to a Muslim public above all. For this reason, Rahman, who read German and French, took a rather critical stance vis-a-vis Western study of Islam, which he continually confronted. Apart from a few exceptions – Kenneth Cragg, Toshihiko Izutsu, Angelika Neuwirth and Josef van Ess – few scholars met with his approval. He reproached most of those who dealt with the Qur'an for being concerned only with certain closely defined aspects. They never viewed it in its entirety, in its unity, and never sought to investigate it in its own terms and, as a result, had not understood it.

Rahman's writings encompass a broad spectrum, proceeding from Islamic philosophy, with which he had begun his career, and extending far beyond. Amongst his countless articles there are those on the reform of Islamic education, on Qur'anic hermeneutics, on hadith criticism, on the early developments of the Islamic intellectual tradition, the reform of Islamic law, and Islamic ethics. In his scholarly work he was concerned with striking a balance between reason and revelation and finding an answer to the question: how can Islam, with its cultural, religious, political and ethical heritage, deal with a world that is ever modernizing and changing?

The Decline of Muslim Societies

Rahman was convinced that the decline of Muslim societies did not begin originally with the encounter between the Muslim and Western worlds in the nineteenth century, as Muslims mostly believe, but in

---

4 Moosa, "Introduction" to Rahman, *Revival and Reform in Islam*, vi.

fact occurred much earlier. In his view, the so-called pristine Islam, formulated as orthodoxy and later identified with Sunni Islam, has been lost. Sunni Islam may claim to be the original Islam but for Rahman it is a deviation from pure Islam. He dates what he calls the tragic turn away from the Qur'an to the moment when the formation of Sunni orthodoxy occurred, in other words, with the emergence of Umayyad rule. In his view, the advent of a dynastic rule had the most deleterious effects on Islam.

The first step therefore had to involve a historical critique of the theological and legal developments in Islam. It seemed essential to Rahman to indicate the rejections that took place among the various areas of the Islamic sciences: theology, exegesis, jurisprudence and the worldview of the Qur'an. The Qur'an had nothing to do with what the other disciplines made of it after the event. In particular, the jurisprudence and political philosophy of Islam lost their connection with the ethics of the Qur'an – for Rahman something of central importance – and this led to fundamentalism and stagnation.

As a Sunni, Rahman had a great fondness for the Mu'tazilite conception of prophecy and the nature of revelation and these, along with history, formed the most important components of his own Qur'anic hermeneutics. The Mu'tazilites had developed a theory of rational ethics based on the notion that good and evil can be discerned only by the use of reason, that is, without the aid of revelation. Consequently, primary or general ethical truths about good and evil are rationally discernible by means of intuitive reasoning. In Rahman's view, mankind needs revelation solely for carrying out its obligations to secondary ethical truths.

Other things about the Mu'tazilites fascinated him even more. He was convinced by their notion of the Qur'an's createdness, and so, he contradicted contemporary Sunni mainstream belief. His sharpest critique took on the ideological adversaries of the Mu'tazilites, the theological movement of the Ash'arites. More than anything else, he considered this tenth century school's doctrine of predestination to be truly pestiferous. In his view, one had to take responsibility here and now for one's deeds. The Ash'arite position struck him as a mutilation of the Qur'anic message which, in his opinion, regards the human person as a free and responsible individual.

As a reformer Rahman had great models. He esteemed modern Islamic renewers such as Muhammad 'Abduh and the Indian Ahmad Khan (1817–1898) because they had developed an awareness of the necessity for reform and change, but he also praised key figures of fundamentalist Islam, such as Hasan al-Banna and Abu al-A'la Maududi (1903–1979). They had resisted the excesses of Islamic modernism and had protected Islam from secularism. True, he criticized them for lacking any method and for offering ad hoc solutions to ongoing problems. In his opinion the fundamental questions of methodology and hermeneutics had not been correctly addressed by Muslim thinkers.

The chief problem for him was the decline of Islamic intellectualism. To overcome this, in Rahman's view, a new way of interpreting the Qur'an was needed. He believed that a fresh interpretation of Islamic methodology in the light of the Qur'an was a prerequisite for any reform of Islamic thinking. In particular, he was concerned with a Qur'an-centred ethics that rested on two pillars: a theory of prophecy and the nature of revelation together with a grasp of history. The theory of prophecy would form the basis of a theory of Qur'anic interpretation which was made up of two steps or a double movement. It was first of all imperative to study the context in which the Qur'an was proclaimed; in this way it would be possible to understand the original message. From this, the principles and values which the Qur'an promulgated as norms could be inferred. The question is, therefore, how these norms might have an enduring relevance for the Islamic community without becoming anachronistic:

> In building any genuine and viable Islamic set of laws and
> institutions, there has to be a twofold movement: First one must
> move from the concrete case treatments of the Qur'an – taking the
> necessary and relevant social conditions of that time into account –
> to the general principles upon which the entire teaching converges.
> Second, from this general level there must be a movement back to

specific legislation, taking into account the necessary and relevant
social conditions now obtaining.[5]

Rahman criticizes any attempt at exegesis that treats the Qur'an as a
series of isolated verses and thereby fails to convey any understanding of
the Qur'anic worldview. Muslims have not understood that the Qur'an
is a unity and instead have taken an atomistic approach. Moreover, this
fragmentary treatment of the Qur'an has increased in modern times.

It was for this reason that he wanted to develop an Islamic meta-
physics based squarely on the Qur'an. Only if the metaphysical part
is rightly understood can a coherent reconsideration of the Qur'an's
moral, social and legal message become possible. Rahman's goal was
to rescue the moral core in order to formulate a Qur'an-centred ethics.
He complained that Muslim scholars had never attempted an ethics
of the Qur'an. But no close study of the Qur'an could avoid its ethical
passion. Its ethics form its essence and they also form the requisite
connection between theology and law. True, the Qur'an tends to con-
cretize the ethical, to clothe the general in a specific paradigm and
to convert the ethical into legal or quasi-legal prescriptions. But it is
precisely a token of its moral passion that it is not content to stay with
generalizing ethical prescriptions but is eager to translate them into
actual paradigms. The Qur'an always illustrates the goals and principles
that are the essence of its laws.

The Dictation Theory

Rahman's theory of prophecy represents a radical shift away from the
orthodox Sunni account of revelation, which he found unsatisfying,
terming it the "dictation theory". The dictation theory reduces the
Prophet's role in revelation to that of a recipient of God's message
which he – rather like a tape recorder – repeated exactly just as he
had received it. For Rahman, however, revelation (*wahy*) is something

---

5 Fazlur Rahman, *Islam and Modernity: Transformation of an Intellectual Tradition*
(Chicago: University of Chicago Press, 1982), 20.

more complex. That the Prophet was the recipient of God's final verbal revelation is not at issue but he tries to go further to delineate the creative process that was effected in the Prophet's mind by the revelation. He believes that the source of this creative process surpasses what human beings can understand. On the other hand, this process does take place in the mind of the proclaimer. Thus he comes to the conclusion that it is his word in the usual sense in that it involves a psychological process. But it is also the revealed word inasmuch as its source lies beyond his reach.

Since "word" is not the same as "sound" for Rahman there is no real contradiction in saying that the Qur'an is the word of the Prophet as well as the word of God. In his opinion, an organic relation exists between feelings, ideas and words. During inspiration, even during poetic inspiration, this relation is so consummate that feeling-idea-word becomes a whole and possesses its own individual existence.

According to Rahman, during the process called *wahy* – a word whose translation as "revelation" is somewhat unsatisfactory – ideas and words come to be born in the Prophet's mind. To be sure, their source cannot lie in his mind, as the Qur'an explains, because these ideas and words are so novel. For this reason, Rahman says, they must derive from a source beyond. He wishes to distinguish the character of the divine *wahy* from poetical, mystical or other forms of creative thinking or from artistic creation. Even if these appear psychologically similar, the Qur'an has a wholly different rank by virtue of its moral content.

In his view *wahy* is the result of a meeting of two spheres, that of the created and the uncreated world. The Prophet was indeed inspired by the divine but his own world is clearly mirrored in the linguistic result of this encounter. Hence, in the Qur'an the expectations, fears and anxieties of the Prophet and his community are reflected. The fact that the revelation mentions things that personally befall the Prophet cannot be ignored. As one example he cites verses 80:1–3:

He frowned and turned away
when the blind man came to him.
For all you know he might have grown in spirit.

Decades later, what Rahman here terms "encounter" Abu Zaid would designate as the dialogic relationship between Muhammad and his milieu. Rahman saw this aspect of the connection between the Prophet and an event that occurred as something that had been completely neglected in Islamic theology. The revelation came from God but at the same time, the location of the revelation was the Prophet's heart. Rahman thought it a great mistake that no significance was accorded to this.

Moreover, the science of the *asbab al-nuzul* (poorly rendered as "bases" or "occasions" for the "sending down" of revelation), one of the oldest of all the Qur'anic sciences, had been neglected increasingly over the course of time. In Rahman's opinion, in order that the Qur'anic instructions might be applied to as many situations as possible. Precisely here, however, as Rahman affirms, the *asbab al-nuzul* bear witness to the close relationship between the revelation and its social and cultural context that must once more be made plain.

The Qur'an as Ethical Guide

For Rahman the Qur'an is not a book of law at all. He was quite critically opposed to this currently prevalent view amongst Muslims. The Qur'an stands as a guide for people, with the Prophet as a moral reformer for humanity. People should live in accord with the ethical rules of the Qur'an and not attempt to extract laws from them. Legal directives constitute only a very small part of the Qur'an and relate to a particular situation in a particular context.

Furthermore, in his opinion, the Qur'an's ethical and legal instructions operate on two levels, that of the ideal and that of the so-called "share". The ideal was the goal towards which believers should fundamentally strive but that was not necessarily attainable at the time of revelation. By contrast, what Rahman calls the level of the share denoted what was attainable in the Prophet's time. His close connection with his environment and its problems implied that the Qur'an did indeed address specific problems in their specific situations but on the other hand, that it had reference to the ideal. In concrete terms this means that the Qur'an first sought to change whatever at that time lay in the realm of the possible. Ultimately, however, it pursued a much higher goal.

For example, the Qur'an did not abolish polygamy, which was permitted in the time of the Prophet. Even so, it was stressed that a man should marry only one woman if he could not do justice to more than one wife. That means, moreover, that however much the man might try, he might not be able to treat several wives justly. For Rahman, the Qur'an had formulated an ideal, monogamy, that was nevertheless adjusted at one and the same time to seventh century circumstances, hence polygamy was allowed. The legislation made no claim to be everlasting but took society as it then existed as its point of reference. Finally, the Prophet wanted people to move towards the ideal and turn it into reality. To be sure, over the course of Islamic history many of the Qur'anic pronouncements were held up as the ideal even though they had a descriptive rather than a normative character. Examples of this are the *hadd*-penalties, i.e., the punishments for transgressors, such as amputation of the hand for theft, and family law.

Still, what is the ideal? For Rahman it is unequivocally social justice. This is why in every generation there should be reflection on just how this ideal can best be realized. He emphasizes that all the Qur'anic teachings should be viewed as directed towards the creation of equality. Accordingly, Islam's goal cannot be attained as long as there is no freedom from all forms of exploitation – social, spiritual, political and economic. To attain this an ethics is required. And yet, ethics has not been one of the disciplines within the Qur'anic sciences in Islamic history. All the writings on ethics were based exclusively on Greek and Persian sources. For Rahman the basis for the ethics that needs to be developed is *taqwa* (usually translated as "fear of God" but probably better understood as "awe of God" or "awareness of God"); by this he means the ability, as well as the requirement, to make the distinction between good and evil. This is not a matter of the legal question about what is permitted and what forbidden, on which Muslims today are so fixated, but about the moral core.

The People of the Book

The integral approach that Rahman's mode of interpretation represents is very clearly revealed in his handling of the question about the Qur'an's attitude towards believers of other faiths. Alongside the question of women's rights, he regards this question as the central challenge for Islamic thought in the modern age.

As is well known, there are pronouncements in the Qur'an about Jews and Christians; the so-called Sabians are also mentioned. In Islamic history these religions were indeed recognized as "religions of the Book", a notion that was extended to Zoroastrianism and Hinduism as well, but whose adherents were not accepted as of equal value. This is reflected even today in the law of many Islamic states: Jews, Christians and Zoroastrians are free to practice their religion but are nevertheless second-class citizens. A series of rights available to Muslims are unavailable to them. This is the case, for example, in the Islamic Republic of Iran.

Furthermore, it is still disputed in Islamic theology as in mainstream Islam who the so-called *kuffar*, "unbelievers", in the Qur'an are. Whereas in Islamic history for the most part only polytheists were seen as such, today radical groups include Jews and Christians in this category as well. Moreover, there are differing notions as to just how the Qur'an stands in theological terms to the *ahl al-kitab*, "people of the book", i.e., Jews, Christians and Zoroastrians. Do they have a share in divine truth? Will they find some sort of redemption? Are they souls who have strayed and who should be brought back to the right path? Or are they really Muslims without knowing it?

Rahman tries to answer these questions in his book *Major Themes of the Qur'an*. The fact that religions as such differ not only from one another but also comprise subgroups within them is a theme he notes repeatedly. But the Qur'an also offers a solution in his view: humanity was one but this unity was shattered through acceptance of the divine message brought by the prophets. He deems it a divine mystery that the prophets' messages formed a kind of turning point; if God had willed He might have led humanity along a single path. He cites verse 2:213:

Mankind was a single community,
then God sent prophets to bring good news and warning,
and with them He sent the Scripture with the Truth,
to judge between people in their disagreements.
It was only those to whom it was given
who disagreed about it after clear signs had come to them,
because of rivalry between them.
So by His leave God guided the believers to the truth
they had disagreed about.
God guides whomever He will to a straight path.

And verse 11:118:

If your Lord had pleased, He would have made
all people a single community,
but they continue to have their differences.

And verse 10:19:

All people were originally a single community,
but later they differed.
If it had not been for a word from your Lord,
the preordained judgment would already have been passed
between them regarding their differences.

This is why the Qur'an speaks in the Meccan period of Jews and Christians as sectarians but later of the communities of Jews and Christians. Moreover, they had been invited to accept Islam but now were acknowledged as an exclusive community. Rahman attempts here, in conformity with his own methodology, to imagine the circumstances of the revelation. He puts himself inside the Prophet's perspective: he withdrew his original request and came towards the Jewish and Christian communities with a new attitude. He acknowledged them. Rahman cites Qur'an, verse 2:113, as evidence:

The Jews say, "The Christians have no ground whatsoever
to stand on", and the Christians say, "The Jews have no ground
whatsoever to stand on", though they both read the Scripture,
and those who have no knowledge say the same.
God will judge between them on the Day of Resurrection
concerning their differences.

And verse 2:111:

They also say, "No one will enter Paradise unless
he is a Jew or a Christian".
This is their own wishful thinking.
Say, "Produce your evidence
if you are telling the truth".

And verse 2:120:

The Jews and the Christians will never be pleased with you
unless you follow their ways.
Say, "God's guidance is the only true guidance".
If you were to follow their desires
after the knowledge that has come to you,
you would find no one to protect you from God or help you.

For Rahman the Qur'an's response to the exclusivist claims of the
Jews and the Christians is absolutely unequivocal. Right guidance is
not the responsibility of communities; it is God's responsibility. Hence,
no community can claim to be exclusively chosen and justified. The
entire tenor of the Qur'an is opposed to chosenness. Rahman cites
verse 2:124 to this effect:

When Abraham's Lord tested him with certain commandments,
which he fulfilled, He said,
"I will make you a leader of men".
Abraham asked, "And will You make leaders

from my descendants too?" God answered,
"My pledge does not hold for those who do evil".

And verse 2:134:

That community passed away.
What they earned belongs to them,
and what you earn belongs to you:
you will not be answerable for their deeds.

In complete accord with this firm rejection of exclusivity and chosenness the Qur'an accepts the fact that there are good people in other
communities.

The believers, the Jews, the Christians, and the Sabians –
all those who believe in God and the Last Day and do good –
will have their rewards with their Lord.
No fear for them, nor will they grieve.   (2:62)

The Qur'an even makes this statement many times:

The believers, the Jews, the Sabians, and the Christians –
those who believe in God and the Last Day and do good deeds –
will have nothing to fear or to regret.

Here Rahman distances himself from traditional Muslim exegesis.
The great majority of Muslim commentators have been desperately
occupied with misunderstanding the obvious meaning of this verse;
they maintain that by Jews, Christians and Sabians is meant those who
have become Muslims or else those Jews, Christians and Sabians who
lived before the coming of the Prophet. Rahman calls both interpretations nonsense; the verses say unequivocally that all people who
believe in God and the Resurrection and who do good will be saved.
As for the claim of Jews and Christians that the next world is for them
alone, the response of the Qur'an is to say:

Any who direct themselves wholly to God and do good
will have their reward with their Lord.

(2:112)

One aspect of the logic that all who do good and believe in God
and the Resurrection are to be acknowledged is, of course, that the
Muslim community be also acknowledged by members of other faiths.
According to Rahman's reading of verse 5:48, the Qur'an gives its final
answer in this context to the complex of problems in a pluralistic world:

We sent to you [Muhammad] the Scripture with the truth,
confirming the Scriptures that came before it,
and with final authority over them:
so judge between them according to what God
has sent down. Do not follow their whims,
which deviate from the truth that has come to you.
We have assigned a law and a path to each of you.
If God had so willed, He would have made you one community,
but He wanted to test you through that which He has given you,
so race to do good: you will all return to God
and He will make clear to you the matters you differed about.

Rahman also addresses the question as to why there are so many
religions and societies. The value of this pluralism resides in the fact
that they should compete with one another in doing good. The primary
message which he distilled from the Qur'an within the framework of
his double-movement theory, is that plurality is something willed by
God.

Each community has its own direction to which it turns:
race to do good!

(2:148)

The essential matter is to do good; verse 2:177 expresses this:

Goodness does not consist in turning your face
towards East or West.
The truly good are those who believe in God
and the Last Day, in the angels, the Scripture and the prophets;
who give away some of their wealth, however much
they cherish it, to their relatives, to orphans, the needy,
travellers and beggars, and to liberate those in bondage;
those who keep up the prayer and pay the prescribed alms;
who keep pledges whenever they make them; who are
steadfast in misfortune, adversity, and times of danger.
These are the ones who are true,
and it is they who are aware of God.

The Muslim community in Medina, which is lauded (2:144) and
praised as the best of humanity (3:110), enjoys no guarantee "of automatically being God's favourite".[6] It must first act well. In verse 47:38
Muslims are even warned that God can withdraw His love from them:

You are called upon to give in the cause of God.
Some among you are ungenerous; yet whoever is ungenerous
to this cause is ungenerous to himself.
Indeed, God does not need you, but you need Him.
If you pay no heed, He will replace you by others
who shall bear no resemblance to yourselves.

Apart from Judaism and Christianity, Rahman did not make any concrete statements about other religions. Unfortunately, we don't know
what his theological opinions were on the Ahmadiyya who were persecuted in his native Pakistan. The Ahmadis consider themselves Muslims
but this is widely disputed. According to this latter view, the founder
of their community of faith, Mirza Ghulam Ahmad (1835–1908), who
saw himself as a renewer, was a heretic, for he even made the claim of
being the promised Mahdi at the end of time.

---

6 Rahman, *Islam and Modernity*, 167.

For Muslims in the Indian subcontinent the Ahmadiyya movement poses a serious theological challenge. Nevertheless, when Rahman declares that it is the deciding factor that one believe in God and the Resurrection and do good, then they too, at least theoretically, must have earned his acceptance. In his above-cited *Major Themes of the Qur'an* he does not deal with them, which is understandable enough given that post-Islamic religions do not crop up in the Qur'an. But he did criticize the ban on the Ahmadiyya in Pakistan in 1974, which he attributed to pervasive and negative Saudi influence.

The subject of the believers of other faiths was not the only one that Rahman considered utterly misunderstood. In connection with Islamic penal law he was convinced that the pertinent passages in the Qur'an had been knowingly misinterpreted. Here too, he believed, the jurists had represented an interpretation from the outset that completely runs counter to the Qur'an. Thus, the term *hadd* means a "limit". It denotes a boundary, a barrier, that one should not cross, as verses 2:229–230 make utterly clear:

> Divorce may be pronounced twice, and then a woman
> must be retained in honour or allowed to go with kindness.
> It is unlawful for husbands to take from them anything
> they have given them, unless both fear that they may not
> be able to keep within the bounds set by God; in which case
> it shall be no offence for either of them if the wife ransoms herself.
> These are the bounds set by God; do not transgress them.
> Those that transgress the bounds of God are wrongdoers.
> If a man divorces his wife, he shall not remarry her until
> she has wedded another man and been divorced by him;
> in which case it shall be no offence for either of them
> to return to the other, if they think that they can keep
> within the bounds set by God.
> Such are the bounds of God.
> He makes them plain to men of understanding.

Notwithstanding this, Islamic law uses this term to designate a fixed punishment for consumption of alcohol, mugging and the like. Even in the earliest second-century legal literature the notion is reported in the sense of a Qur'anically-determined punishment. Thus, yet again, the misinterpretation of the Qur'an stands at the centre of the argument. But how can one arrive at a correct understanding? Through the double-movement theory, according to Rahman. And it is precisely here that criticism of Rahman begins.

Reception and Criticism

Mehmet Paçacı, a member of the Ankara School who was born in 1961, subjects the double-movement theory to a critical examination. If understanding the Qur'an requires an understanding of it in the context of Muhammad's times, Paçacı asks, how can we be so sure of comprehending the past? How can one know with any certainty what norm lies concealed behind this or that Qur'anic directive? Can one confidently state that it is to be applied nowadays in this way rather than that? True, in his 1996 essay "The Qur'an and I – how historical are we?" Paçacı does accept Rahman's characterization of the Qur'an as an ethical handbook as well as his double-movement theory. Even so, Paçacı regards the situation of the interpreter differently. In his view, it is possible to speak of a correct application of the Qur'an today only if one possesses a correct understanding of the present. But since every reader stands fixed in a specific historical situation that is thereby limited he cannot know the present totally.

For this reason Paçacı introduces the notion of "pre-understanding" into the methodology of Qur'anic interpretation. In contradistinction to Fazlur Rahman, who believes that an objective grasp of history is possible, he recognizes that every consideration of the Qur'an proceeds from a specific perspective. Finally, he constructs a synthesis of the thought of Gadamer and of Fazlur Rahman (who had rejected Gadamer, stating that if he were right, his double-theory could not work). Paçacı sees this differently. Like Gadamer, he sees the exegete in a system of coordinates of time and space while with Fazlur Rahman he discovers the universal principles that underlie the Qur'an. Paçacı does not relinquish Rahman in accepting Gadamer.

The Ankara School thus developed Rahman's approach further and it worked through possible objections to it. Its members do not practice some sort of avant-garde theology in an ivory tower without a wider effect. Rather, the theologians form a school as well in that they educate Turkey's younger generation of theologians. Every year some 100 students, male and female, complete their studies at the Ankara faculty and afterwards are active as teachers of religion, as imams and as officials in the Turkish religious authority. Furthermore, theology in Turkey is of worldwide significance in new intellectual approaches to Islam. Its ideas have been taken up by students in Central Asia and the Balkans, all of whom read Turkish. In the Persian and Arabic-speaking, however, world they have not yet attracted significant attention, even though they have much to offer that is both exciting and novel. As Abu Zaid put it: "What is new comes from the peripheries".

In response to the call for a study of theology like that in the West, Turkish officials set development in motion in 1948. In 1949, a faculty of theology was brought into being based upon a modern scholarly model at the newly founded University of Ankara; today it stands as the parent faculty of all the educational institutions of theology in Turkey. Since the faculty does not use the term "Sharia" in its title, and so does not put jurisprudence, formerly of huge significance, at its centre, but instead identifies itself with "theology" (*ilahiyat*), as is common in the West, its founders were sending an unmistakable message. They wanted a modern institution in which the professors would not pass on handed-down knowledge to the students but would rather teach them independent thinking. By the end of the 1940s Muslim theology was being practised in conjunction with such critical disciplines as empirical psychology, sociology, and history. Even non-Muslims such as Annemarie Schimmel taught the history of religion there. Other important advances came from such now-retired professors as Mehmet Said Hatiboğlu and Hüseyin Atay. Furthermore, during their studies students were expected to spend a certain amount of time in Europe or the US in order to experience Western influence. Islamic theology should thus be practised as a scholarly discipline; so neutral and objective should it be that Ömer Özsoy, who came to prominence at this faculty (and who today is decisively engaged in the establishment of Islamic theology in Germany), still flinches when he hears that this discipline should now be practised as a normative science from an internal perspective, in other words, that a Muslim subjective approach should be introduced.

Certainly Ömer Özsoy has been strongly influenced by Rahman; yet, he also draws a line between himself and Rahman. As a result, in an effort to distinguish *what* the Qur'an means to say from *how* it says it, he takes the sunna far more into consideration than Rahman does. Like Abu Zaid, toward whom the Ankara School was highly receptive, he wishes to regard the Qur'an in its interplay with reality, that is, with the history of its first auditors. For Özsoy, anyone who reads the Qur'an as a text, as a self-contained system that can be understood on its own terms, can only read it wrongly. Only when one considers how Muhammad and his milieu reacted to the revelation, and how the Qur'an, in turn, entered into their reactions, is it possible to understand its message. For it is not text but *discours,* speech, as Özsoy puts it with reference to Paul Ricoeur. In this way Özsoy avails himself of a term for describing a complex reality, a term, moreover, that Abu Zaid in his last years considered more suitable for conveying what the Qur'an really is.

Ömer Özsoy agrees expressly with Fazlur Rahman that it is possible to interpret a past set of circumstances. But like Paçacı, he holds that every interpretation of one's own present is nevertheless riddled with errors. Here it becomes clear that what his Turkish students preach today is no longer unadulterated "Fazlur-Rahmanism". Even so, the Pakistani scholar has left his mark on Turkish thinkers – who alongside the Iranians are credited with the greatest originality of all modern theologians – in an unmistakable way. And for that reason he will also mark Islamic theology in Germany with his stamp.

5

Amina Wadud: Inside the Gender Jihad

A Muslim by Conviction

This daughter of a Methodist pastor was born Mary Teasley in Bethesda, Maryland, in 1952. She grew up with five brothers and one sister in a country where there was a marked awareness of injustice. The idea that God might be connected with oppression was foreign to her, she has said. "As a minister my father taught me to understand the close connection between freedom and faith, God and righteousness."[1]

She describes her father as very devout and calls him her spiritual mentor. Her mother, whom Wadud describes, by contrast, as oppressive and violent, nevertheless held the family together. Wadud developed a great passion for reading early on but her giftedness wasn't supported by her family. It was a teacher who first discovered her talent and brought her to a good school in Boston. As an Afro-American she personally experienced the period when segregation was outlawed. As a black in a white-dominated Boston high school she learned what it meant to be black in America. So she decided to study in Pennsylvania "to have more black people around me."[2] During the Civil Rights Movement, as well as the Black Power Movement, to which she also belonged, she fought for recognition of human rights. Among other

---

1 Amina Wadud, Interview with the author, 25/9/2012.
2 Amina Wadud, "On Belonging as a Muslim" in Gloria J. Wade-Gayles, *My Soul is a Witness: African-American Women's Spirituality* (Boston: Beacon Press, 1995), 260.

things she took part with her father in Martin Luther King's famous march to Jackson.

Wadud is someone who had to endure great pressure – as a black woman in a society in which the superiority of whites was assumed, as well as a poor person in a society that confuses material comfort with values, and lastly, as a woman in a society in which women are still discriminated against, despite the sexual revolution. Even so, she was aware of her own strength very early on: "As the descendant of a slave woman it was clear to me that in everything I had a choice. I became a vegetarian. I became a Muslim."[3] Her conversion took place shortly before she learned that Matt Cox, her great-great-great-grandfather on her mother's side, had been a Berber. While it was meaningful to learn of this connection she didn't take it as determining. Wadud is a Muslim by her own choice, not by birth. Unlike other converts who defend their decision before their former milieu and want to establish themselves in their new community of faith, so that they tend towards apologetics and exaggeration, Wadud is delightfully unconstrained in her religiosity.

Before she became acquainted with Islam – by accident when she was 20 years old – she was a Buddhist, lived in an ashram and practised meditation. She has always been very interested in God, in human nature, in morality and spirituality, she says.[4] At that time an acquaintance took her along to the neighborhood mosque where she lived and pressed her to utter the *shahada*, the Islamic avowal of faith. She wanted to increase women's share in the community, Wadud wrote later in her book *Inside the Gender Jihad* (which is also a reckoning with conservative Islam). It seems that she converted to Islam "just for fun". On the other hand, Islam with its radical promises of equality for all races has been, since Malcolm X and the "Nation of Islam", a viable option for Afro-Americans. The convert, who took the name Wadud (one of the 99 "most beautiful" names of God and which

---

3 Amina Wadud, *Inside the Gender Jihad: Women's Reform in Islam* (Oxford: Oneworld, 2007), 7.
4 Wadud, Interview with the author, 25/9/2012.

means "the Loving One who wants justice") expected more freedom from her new religion. Today she says that her hopes that her life would change for the better with her conversion to Islam were naïve. She imagined that it would be easier to be a part of the Muslim community. This has caused her trouble, she explains, alluding to public reactions that she has encountered because of her commitment. Her adversaries have abused her as a "devil with a head scarf" or as a "feminist fundamentalist".

Why Islam?

The Qur'an gave her the decisive push towards a genuine, inward turn to Islam. Here she found herself again, she felt understood – with her love of nature and her questions about the next life. However unconsidered her conversion may have been, nevertheless, a thoroughgoing intellectual encounter with Islam followed rapidly. As a convert, Wadud brings not only a special awareness shaped by her identity but a spirit of critical scrutiny as well. As a result, her views often offer refreshing new insights into the Qur'an's teachings. Her family background may have been decisive for her. She was familiar with discrimination because of her race, but she had also learned how to defend herself.

> For those who have been born into Islam and gender-apartheid, there may be situations in which many patterns of thought are tolerated, even if they are oppressive. Of course I didn't have this background and accepted nothing that wounded my dignity. On the other hand, I'd already learned how to fight in a racist America.[5]

After 1972 Wadud studied meanings for the self as presented in the Qur'an, as well as the possibilities of interpretation, especially for female identity. In her view, the Qur'an confirms woman's equality, even if current practice in Muslim countries runs counter to it. In her scholarly work Amina Wadud concentrates particularly on the Qur'an

---

5 Wadud, Interview with the author, 25/9/2012.

as the authoritative reference-point for all Muslims, and less on the sunna, the collection of the Prophet Muhammad's words and deeds, to which such feminists as Fatima Mernissi and Nawal el-Saadawi have devoted their attention. With her claim that Muhammad's pronouncements have no validity nowadays if they run contrary to the Qur'an, she wishes to establish a Qur'anic basis for gender equality in Islam. If the countless publications on women in Islam overwhelmingly focus on women's conditions in various Islamic countries, Amina Wadud has been the first to put the representation or concept of women in the Qur'an at the centre. This brings her to the question: can the situation of women today in Islamic countries be called Islamic, that is, as willed by God? For Wadud this entails tracking down ideas of equality in the Qur'an and wielding them in what she terms "the gender jihad". Qur'anic legitimation serves her as a means to challenge Muslims' notions about women and to reform them.

More than 15 years passed between her conversion and the start of her scholarly career. After she completed her BA in education she went for two years with her then-husband and her newborn child to Libya. There she was brought face to face with the numerous prohibitions that were couched in the name of Islam. Wadud did not accept these; she began to question whether Islam really expresses such notions about women. She began to study the primary sources. Upon her return she enrolled in the MA programme in Middle Eastern studies at the University of Pennsylvania, with the intention of getting to the bottom of her question. In 1986 she began research on her dissertation which she also pursued at the University of Cairo. In Cairo she attended lectures both at al-Azhar University, the intellectual centre of the Sunni world, as well as at the American University of Cairo.

In the course of her studies her instructor's teaching methods frustrated her more and more. She wanted not only to know what a given term or a given sura meant but also to look for herself at the exegetical literature. She wanted to analyze and discuss; she wanted to read the Qur'an with her teacher, not merely listen to his explanations and learn by rote. In an effort to persuade him to read the Qur'an with her, she demonstrated to him that, on the basis of the Qur'an, it does not say that women ought not to study it. Wadud showed him that a critical engagement is not some Western approach but an essential component of Qur'anic study. The submission to God's will (*islam*) that the Qur'an demands doesn't mean blind adherence but a human being's free choice by virtue of his nature as "a representative of God, not a marionette."[6] Wadud describes what the Qur'an wants from people as "engaged surrender".

Amina Wadud has five children from two marriages; her youngest daughter was born in 1989. At the beginning of the 1990s she divorced for a second time and afterwards raised her children herself. After completing her doctorate in 1988 at the University of Michigan in the fields of Islamic Studies and Arabic, her first posting took her to Malaysia where she accepted an assistant professorship at the International Islamic University. She formed a friendship there with the well-known human rights activist Chandra Muzaffar who now directs the Just World Trust, an NGO that promotes interreligious dialogue and which is based in Kuala Lumpur. In Malaysia Wadud also played a considerable part in forming the organization Sisters in Islam. This group, today an influential NGO, wished to move the theme of women and gender equality more strongly to the forefront and fight against discrimination. An acquaintance with the women who still form the core of Sisters in Islam today offered Wadud the opportunity of becoming an activist. Activism plays a central role, together with scholarship, in her life. Wadud strengthened Sisters in Islam by introducing Qur'an-based arguments for equality. Only by so doing could they counter the charge that their demands ran contrary to Islam. In collaboration with other women from this circle she published writings in which she provided evidence that gender equality is supported in the Qur'an. One publication from 1991 bore the provocative title *Are Muslim Men Allowed to Beat their Wives?* Up to the present the organization still proceeds in accord with Amina Wadud's hermeneutical starting-points. On its home page it says:

---

6 Wadud, *Inside the Gender Jihad*, 23.

Through the expertise of mufassira [an expert in tafsir, 'interpretation'] Amina Wadud, the group engaged actively in a model of Qur'anic hermeneutics that examined the socio-historical context of Revelation as a whole, and that of particular Qur'anic verses. The group examined the language of the Text and its syntactical and grammatical structure, and it looked at the Text as a whole to understand its worldview.[7]

In an essay that appeared in a Festschrift published in 2012 in Amina Wadud's honour, two of the founders of Sisters in Islam describe the outstanding role that Amina Wadud played on their behalf and that of the organization. It was like a gift from God when the two of them, Zainah Anwar and Rose Ismail, learned that Wadud was in Kuala Lumpur. They had asked the question how it could be that God is considered just and yet is so unjust to women. They suspected that much of what was peddled as Islamic commandments or Qur'anic pronouncements wouldn't hold up to scrutiny. But they didn't know Arabic, so they invited Amina Wadud to tell them more about the Qur'an in a private study circle and to read it with them. That was the start of, by far, the most successful women's NGO in the Islamic world – and it remains so today. Many of the laws disadvantaging women have been changed in recent years thanks to its activity. Amina Wadud brought about a shift in awareness on the part of thousands of people by making them aware of her own God-given rights. Zainah Anwar and Rose Ismail write:

Amina may not realise the full extent of her contribution to SIS – but we know that she gave us the means to fight for a just Islam. And that has made all the difference.[8]

---

7 "Home page,"Sisters in Islam, http://www.sistersinislam.org.my/page.php?35.
8 Zainah Anwar & Rose Ismail, "Amina Wadud and Sisters in Islam – A Journey towards Empowerment" in Kecia Ali, Juliane Hammer & Laury Silvers, eds., *A Jihad for Justice: Honoring the Work and Life of Amina Wadud* (Austin: University of Texas Press, 2012), http://www.bu.edu/religion/files/2010/03/A-Jihad-for-Justice-for-Amina-Wadud-2012–1.pdf, 72.

In 1992 Wadud also published her trailblazing work *Qur'an and Woman* in Malaysia; she couldn't find a publisher for it in the US. The book first came out in the UK in 1999. Since then it has been translated into Turkish, Persian, Arabic and Indonesian as well as into various European languages though it is prohibited in many countries, such as the United Arab Emirates.

Also in 1992, Wadud was appointed professor at the Virginia Commonwealth University where she taught until her retirement in 2008. From 1997–8 she was a fellow at the renowned Harvard Divinity School. In 2006 her markedly autobiographical book *Inside the Gender Jihad* appeared. Following her retirement, Amina Wadud continued her teaching as a guest-professor at the Center for Religious and Cross-Cultural Studies at Gadjah Mada University in Jogjakarta, Indonesia. In addition to this, she taught as a guest-professor in various universities in the Islamic world. In the summer semester of 2015 she will be guest-professor at the Akademie der Weltreligionen at the University of Hamburg. In 2007 this Islamic scholar, who was depicted in the TV documentary *The Noble Struggle of Amina Wadud*, received – among her numerous other prizes – the Danish Democracy Prize. A grandmother several times over, she lives near Berkeley, California.

She doesn't always don the headscarf, but does so especially when she wants to be heard amongst conservatives, as she reports. Furthermore, she sometimes wears it because she's not immediately recognizable as an Afro-American when she does so. With the headscarf she can pass as a South Asian too. The public is more respectful towards her, in this case. In any event, in her reading of the Qur'an she finds no religious obligation for women to cover themselves. For her, the headscarf is nothing more than a form of cultural expression.

Female, Muslim, Black

Wadud is quite aware of the difficulties to which her programme of reform faces. She writes that Qur'anic exegesis isn't enough to effect a change in relations between the sexes; a movement is needed like that which led to the abolition of slavery, a citizens' movement.

In *Inside the Gender Jihad* Wadud describes both her positive and her negative experiences within the Muslim community as well as within the academic profession; for a long time she was the only scholar of Islam with a headscarf teaching in the US. Even there, where she taught, she observed an attitude of rejection towards Islam amongst scholars of religion. She faults Islamic studies in the West for not believing Muslims capable of a scholarly consideration of Islam. While they allegedly lack objectivity, the Christian or Jewish scholars of Islam don't, of course; it's as though the discussion over orientalism had never occurred. "Western post-modern domination of theological and religious discourse", Wadud writes, "is another form of cultural imperialism."[9]

But Wadud also criticizes her supposed allies in the fight against conservatism. For one thing, women were marginalized and excluded even in progressive discussion; for another, they were only being used and no one was interested in their own views. In *Inside the Gender Jihad* Wadud describes how she was invited to a conference on Islam and civil society in South Africa in 1994. No one had informed her that she was to hold Friday prayer in the Claremont Main Road Mosque in Cape Town. She was outraged that the decision had been made over her head.

Wadud fought also on another, broader front. Afro-American Muslims often feel patronized by Muslim immigrants. Wadud addresses this paternalism, which even veers toward racism, quite openly in Muslim communities in the US. This racism is all the more depressing and absurd for many Afro-American Muslims since many of them converted in order to escape from racism. A controversy broke out in this context during a conference in Toronto at the beginning of 2005 after she said, in a discussion following her presentation, "I am a nigger and you will just have to put up with my blackness."[10] Later she added that

---

9 Wadud, *Inside the Gender Jihad*, 64–5.
10 Tarek Fatah, "I am a nigger, and you will just have to put up with my blackness". Professor Amina Wadud confronts her hecklers in Toronto. 11/02/2005. http://najat-fares-kessler.blogspot.de/

the topic of racism amongst Muslims in the USA should receive more attention in scholarship as well as in political discussions in the US. In her outburst at the time many things came out that had long been held in, states her close friend Omid Safi. Whenever she says something that doesn't suit her audience it is said that she doesn't know her Qur'an, her Islam – and that, of course, she doesn't know Arabic at all. This reaction goes back to one fact and one fact alone, that she is a black woman. If Khaled Abou El Fadl says the same thing, as he does on many subjects, this does not happen.

> What's amusing – if only one is committed to laughing so we don't
> cry – is when male scholars (Abdullahi an-Na'im, Khaled Abou El
> Fadl, etc.) say essentially the same thing, the objections are usually
> phrased as: "Dear Ustadh, I beg to differ with you." There is both a
> male privilege as well as a "brown privilege" (not to assay anything
> about white privilege) compared to Amina's position as an African-
> American female scholar. Amina has had to bear this burden at a
> daily level, and has done so for decades with a level of dignity that
> is both ultimately unfair and undeniably remarkable.[11]

When she was asked in an interview about her outburst that had attracted much attention, Wadud explained, "Yes, I am a nigger. Only in the instance that people think that I am unaware of the internalized standpoints and politicized racist hierarchies within the Muslim community. I regard my blackness as one of the qualities that has given me the strength to confront other -isms."

For some, Amina Wadud has become a courageous reformer and freedom fighter; for others, she is a heretic or at least, not to be taken seriously as a theologian. In the academic world she is criticized for being too personal in her statements about Islam, and her interpretation

---

11 Omid Safi, "Walking with Amina" in Kecia Ali, Juliane Hammer & Laury Silvers, eds., *A Jihad for Justice: Honoring the Work and Life of Amina Wadud* (Austin: University of Texas Press, 2012), http://www.bu.edu/religion/files/2010/03/A-Jihad-for-Justice-for-Amina-Wadud-2012–1.pdf, 228.

of Islam. But she believes – certainly playing deliberately on Carol Hanisch's famous essay – that the personal is political.

Her involvement on behalf of gender equality in Islam with the support of Qur'anic exegesis is continually misunderstood by Muslims as a fundamental critique of the whole religion. For all that, her critique is aimed only at those who speak for Islam, in the name of Islam. Maybe, according to her, they aren't willing to concede that, as a woman, still more as one with an African background, and as an American convert, she wants more than what they are prepared to give her. The Muslim community took its revenge on her. It demanded that Virginia Commonwealth, her university, give her the sack. "There are five mosques in Virginia. They are so at odds with one another that they can't agree on how to celebrate the most important Muslim holiday together but they are at one in their rejection of my person."[12] To be sure, the university didn't give in, but Wadud left on her own accord.

The hardest lesson that she had to learn was that there was no place for her in the mainstream Muslim communities. But on learning this she found herself. One doesn't have to belong to something, she says, one only has to belong to God. That gives her peace and it is how she understands the statement that a human being, every human being, is God's representative (*khalifa*). She translates the term into English as "agent", which is somewhat unusual; she uses it in the sense of someone who acts responsibly on God's behalf. And as such, as a *khalifa*, a Muslim may not stand by and watch if he sees injustice. Wadud has made Fazlur Rahman's approach her own; it has left its stamp on her indelibly. True, she never studied with the Pakistani scholar; she met him only once at a lecture and never got to know him personally; however, Rahman influenced her through his writings. In Rahman's view, Islam is taking part in the construction of a just social order. For Wadud women's equality must be part of that.

When she led a public Friday prayer it made her world-famous. In March 2005, she prayed in New York at a Friday prayer in a mixed community of some 100 participants. Of course, women had already

---

12 Wadud, Interview with the author, 25/9/2012.

occasionally led the Friday prayer; in South Africa Amina Wadud had also served as the chief celebrant in a Friday prayer. Even so, the Friday prayer in New York was something new; normally women only lead other women in prayer. Even the call to prayer came from a woman – a further breaking of taboo. Men and women travelled from Kentucky and Michigan, and even from Turkey and Egypt, to take part in the widely publicized historic occasion. The event was sponsored by the Muslim Women's Freedom Tour under the direction of Asra Nomani, a journalist and women's rights campaigner well known in the US, by the progressive website Muslim Wake Up! and by members of the Progressive Muslim Union. Since the three mosques in New York that had been approached did not want to allow a Friday prayer to be led by a woman imam, a woman prayer-leader, it was switched to the Synod House, an Anglican church. An art gallery that had stood ready to house an event of revolutionary significance for the entire Muslim world in its rooms withdrew the offer after it had received a bomb threat.

Though only a handful of demonstrators protested in front of the church, there was an outcry throughout the Islamic world. While American Muslims – which, in U.S. parlance, refers to Afro-Americans – feared a schism between the religious beliefs of Muslim immigrants and the more liberal and modified U.S. Islam of their children and grandchildren, conservatives in Egypt and Saudi Arabia suspected an American conspiracy to discredit Islam. 'Abdelaziz al-Shaykh, the grand mufti of Riyadh, announced that anyone who defended Wadud's action was rebelling against God's law. Mohammed Sayyed al-Tantawi, the grand shaykh of Egypt's al-Azhar University – hence, the supreme religious authority of Sunni Islam – declared that women may only lead other women in prayer but may do only if no men are present. The popular television preacher Yusuf al-Qaradawi spoke on al-Jazeera, branding the action as un-Islamic and heretical. The Egyptian paper al-Masa' reproached Wadud in capital letters on its front page, stating "She besmirches Islam", and an Egyptian female law professor went so far as to accuse her of abandoning Islam.

A spectacular precedent was set in the case of the intellectual Farag Foda which demonstrates just how dangerous such propaganda can be. Early in the 1990s a popular preacher said of him that people must take the matter into their own hands if the state failed in its duty to put him to death as an apostate. A few days later Farag Foda was dead, stabbed by a fanatic on a public street.

Wadud's defenders waded vociferously into the dispute. The Progressive Muslim Union asserted that neither the Qur'an nor the sunna contained any prohibition against women leading prayers in mixed congregations. The Prophet had even supported the practice explicitly. And the influential Egyptian mufti Shaykh 'Ali Gom'a was quoted on the Al Arabiya network saying that a Friday prayer led by a woman for a mixed congregation was to be allowed as long as the community was in agreement about it. To buttress his position the Mufti brought in both the exegete Tabari and the mystic Ibn 'Arabi who had seen the matter in just this way. The reformer Gamal al-Banna, the brother of the founder of the Muslim Brotherhood, offered a similar opinion. Against the argument that men could be seduced by a woman who prayed in front of them Nasr Hamid Abu Zaid countered that anyone who wants to gaze at a woman's behind should go to a nightclub. The scholar called Wadud's violation of taboo an important step for American Muslim women, for women in the Islamic world and for their struggle for justice in matters of gender; he considered the question as to whether women might lead the prayer as actually rather marginal.

According to Amina Wadud such a prohibition exists only on the part of Islamic orthodoxy; no proofs for it can be found in either the Qur'an or the sunna. By her act she wanted to encourage women in particular towards Friday prayers for mixed congregations under women's leadership. To be sure, she hadn't counted on such media attention – for weeks she got 40 requests for interviews a day but refused them all – nor had she expected that the topic would be manipulated in this manner. For this reason she would lead such prayers henceforth only within a small circle.

Amina Wadud had to be placed under police protection because of the numerous threats that followed this event; she was able to teach her students during that semester only by video. When she's asked today what the result of her action was, she says that the notion that women might lead the Friday prayer before mixed congregations still represented only a minority opinion but that the number of its supporters had risen. Thus, the Muhammadiyya, with 30 million members – the second largest Muslim organization in Indonesia – had recently decided to let women take part in leading the prayer under certain conditions. In the meantime, other local mosques were arranging for women to lead the prayer on a regular basis. These tiny steps forward were becoming more common. It could be the start of something that she had always fought for, namely, that the participation of women in religious positions of authority come to be seen as normal.

She is right. Things do change, and so do people. They may be small changes but they happen. A nice example of this was a memorial service in honour of Nasr Hamid Abu Zaid that took place in June of 2011 in the Kulturwissenschaftliches Institut in Essen. An entire array of reformist thinkers were invited to a conference entitled: Islamic New Thinking. His friends and colleagues wanted to commemorate him by continuing what he stood for: new thinking. The get-together was supposed to begin in a small group with a prayer of commemoration. As a cleric, Mohammed Shabestari was asked whether he would give the prayer. He excused himself; he couldn't take part in the first meeting because he had an appointment. However, he proposed Amina Wadud, since of all those present she had the most beautiful voice. Furthermore, there were plenty of men present, among them, such as 'Abdolkarim Soroush, Farid Esack, 'Ali Mabrouk, Osman Taştan, 'Abdulkader Tayyob – in other words, a wide range of blacklisted theologians. Nevertheless, as though it were the most self-evident thing in the whole world, Shabestari – who in the 1960s had endorsed Ayatollah Khomeini's call not to grant women the vote – suggested a woman out of all those in attendance.

Gender in the Qur'an

Over the long term her writings have contributed far more than such publicly effective appearances as the Friday prayer in New York to a change in the situation of women. Khalel Abou El Fadl, professor of Islamic law at the UCLA School of Law, writes in his impressive introduction to *Inside the Gender Jihad* that men and women haven't yet grasped the fact that patriarchy is an affront to both Islam and morality. In his opinion, Wadud's merit lies precisely in having demonstrated the truth of this. The great feminist researcher Margot Badran asserts that she has unleashed a revolution with her book *Qur'an and Women*. Wadud's breakthrough in Islamic thought at the start of the 21st century is comparable with that of Muhammad 'Abduh at the start of the last century. The law professor Madhavi Sunder considers her a revolutionary woman philosopher – less because she has interpreted the Qur'an on her own from a feminist perspective than because she has also taught ordinary women how to do the same.

Wadud's exhortation to study the Qur'an for oneself had a strong influence on women in various contexts. The Malaysian context has already been mentioned; in Gambia she induced Isatou Touray, who had been circumcised at the age of 11, to read the Qur'an herself. To her considerable astonishment Touray discovered that circumcision of women's genitalia is nowhere mentioned there; meanwhile, 75 percent of all girls in Gambia are circumcised because men believe that that is written in the Qur'an. After learning this Touray founded the Gambia Committee on Traditional Practices. Now, when the Committee states that the Qur'an does not require the circumcision of female genitalia, the scholars of Islam cannot contradict it. As a result they have stopped producing arguments in favour of this practice. Recourse to the Qur'an makes it easier to move against the practice of genital mutilation. In 2007 several organizations publicly condemned circumcision and Isatou Touray was chosen as Gambian of the Year.

Wadud's numerous studies revolve around one theme: the conceptualization of gender and gender-relations in the Qur'an. For before new ideas can be accepted in the Islamic world, their legitimacy within the sphere of Islamic thought must be shown. That comes down to the Qur'an alone. That is why this female scholar of Islam interprets the Qur'an – a fact that is rare indeed. The only woman, alongside Wadud and Asma Barlas, who practiced a truly comprehensive exegesis, was the Egyptian Aisha 'Abd al-Rahman in her *al-Tafsir al-bayani li-1 -Qur'an, or "Explanatory Commentary on the Qur'an"*. Other Islamic feminists such as, for example, Riffat Hassan (b. 1943), who taught religious studies at the University of Louisville until her retirement in 2009, made many statements in agreement with Wadud about the Qur'an although she has not published any study of on the Qur'an of her own. The absence of women in the field of exegesis is surprising, all the more so since classical Islamic scholarship recognized many women.

The objective of Wadud's Qur'anic research is to discover how the text may best be read and, especially, how a female voice might be discerned within it. Wadud thoroughly concedes that any reading is always informed by a certain subjectivity. For her, reading is an interpretative act and she wants to expose the relationship between Qur'anic exegesis and the exegete. In this she concentrates on what the Qur'an says, how it says it, what is said about the Qur'an, and who says what about the Qur'an. To this has been added in recent years an interest in what is not said, that is, the interpretation of omissions in the Qur'anic text. Wadud basically complains that the Qur'an is confused with its interpretation and that some interpretations are viewed as sacrosanct and beyond criticism.

Wadud sees the traditional method of exegesis as atomistic. It proceeds from the beginning to the end of the Qur'an, verse by verse. The attempt to work out the overriding themes or the connections between individual verses and suras is, however, rarely undertaken. A process of linking similar ideas, syntactical structures, principles or themes with one another, is practically non-existent. While traditional exegetes read the Qur'an as a kind of stone quarry, they neglect to bring out the fundamental ideas that are inherent in the Qur'anic message. The result of this is that certain statements are generalized. So, for example, many of the restrictions to which women are subject are based on the assumption that solutions which are formulated in the Qur'an for a specific case are universally valid principles.

Wadud takes women's dress as one example. In this matter the Qur'an gives a general directive: modest dress is best. But Islamic law elevates the Qur'anic definition of what counts as modest dress in the seventh century to an everlastingly valid principle and claims that the headscarf alone conforms to this. Wadud holds that in the Qur'an it is a matter of a descriptive, not of a normative, statement. To make the headscarf part of a universally valid legal code is to universalize the cultural and economic conditions that prevailed in the Arabian Peninsula in the seventh century and which led to a certain conception of modesty and decency. Hence, a cultural peculiarity is presented as the Qur'anic message which is thereby automatically qualified unless all cultures have the same conception of modesty. For Wadud it is imperative to understand that the Qur'an teaches the principles of modesty and decency but does not pack these principles full of concrete instances.

The scholar thus brings out the particular context in which certain of the Qur'an's prescriptions were revealed. It is her conviction that the Qur'an's message must be central. It – not the prescriptions in their details – should be worked out and stand at the centre of faith. To this end she proposes a hermeneutics of *tawhid*. *Tawhid* is the principle of God's oneness in Islam. God is one, as it says in the *Fatiha*, the opening sura of the Qur'an. On this basis, the Qur'an has a timeless message: the principle of justice and equality. Wadud wants to show that the idea of unity pervades every part of the Qur'an.

To this end, for example, she investigates the language of the Qur'an in detail with regard to the sura in which an account of creation occurs. This is complicated, however; for our purposes here, Wadud's interpretation of verse 4:1 is given in order to clarify what is at issue. To convey the most exact possible account of the content, the translation by Rudi Paret, the standard translation in use in German studies of Islam, is cited first. The words inserted in parentheses are those that bear on Wadud's interpretation. Next the corresponding Arabic version, here transliterated, is provided so that the references may be clearer. Finally the English version appears on which Wadud draws in her exposition.

O people! Fear your Lord, who created you from (*min*) a
single soul (*nafs*) and from (*min*) it its fellow (*zawj*)
and who out of them both (brought forth) many men and
women and spread them (over the earth)!

Arabic original:

Ya ayyuha n-nas ittaqu rabbakum alladhi
khalaqa-kum min nafsin wahidatin wa-khalaqa min-ha
zawjaha wa-baththa minhuma rijalan kathiran wa-nisa'an.

The English translation by Wadud with her emphases:

And *min* His *ayat* (is this:) that He created You (humankind)
min a single *nafs*, and created *min* (that *nafs*) its *zawj*, and
from these two He spread (through the earth)
countless men and women.

The verse contains the basic elements of the Qur'anic version of
the origin of humanity, the creation of Adam and Eve. Wadud considers the four core-words *ayat*, *min*, *nafs* and *zawj*, but in particular the
words *min*, *nafs* and *zawj*. If, like the exegete Abu al-Qasim al-Zam-
akhshari (1074–1144), relying on the Biblical version of the account,
one understands Arabic *min* (the second *min* in the verse) in the sense
of an extraction, then the superiority of the man is assumed. This *min*
in effect conveys the idea that the first created being was perfect and
complete. Consequently, the second created being, a woman, is not
perfect since she was extracted out of a whole.

But if conversely *min* is translated as "in" or "in the same way" the
verse takes on a completely different meaning: "...and in the same
way He created..." In fact, *min* can be understood so, as comparison with other verses, e.g., 42:11 and 30:21, shows. This can also be
shown on the evidence of other translations. Paret's translation of verse
30:21, "and of His signs is that He created wives for you, out of yourselves..." has a patriarchal ring; by contrast, in the Persian translation
of the Qur'an by Jalaloddin Mojtabavi, 'Abdolmohammad Ayati and
Baha'oddin Khorramshahi a gender-neutral wording is used: "He has
created *hamsar* for you in the same way as you were created". The
word *hamsar* in Persian, that has no grammatical gender, is used for a
male spouse as well as for a female one. Although the three translators

could have used the Arabic loan-word *zawja* (female spouse), they decided on the gender-neutral term. In the Persian translation, Paret's "out of yourselves" for *min anfusikum*, becomes "in the same way as you yourselves are". In Hartmut Bobzin's German translation of the Qur'an that appeared in 2010, we also read, "You people! Fear your Lord who created you out of *one* soul and created its counterpart therefrom..." (his emphasis). These examples show us that the verse can indeed be differently understood, as Wadud claims.

Unfortunately, exegesis has followed Zamakhshari's interpretation, who enjoys great esteem because of his meticulous linguistic commentary; however, in this instance, according to Wadud, he was clearly influenced by the Bible. Her translation does not, however, throw any light on the most important words of the verse, i.e., *nafs* and *zawj*. Wadud holds that *nafs*, which really means "self", is always used in the Qur'an for mankind, in other words, for the common source of humanity. The word is grammatically feminine and so adjectives and other words have to correspond to the word in the feminine. But as for the concept, *nafs* is neither feminine nor masculine, she says, for it forms an essential part of both men and women. This is why *nafs* could also be assigned modifiers in the masculine. In fact, grammatical gender doesn't always correspond to actual gender; the German word for "girl", *das Mädchen*, for example, is a neuter noun. Wadud quotes Fazlur Rahman, her teacher, on this point:

> The term *nafs* which later in Islamic philosophy and Sufism came to mean soul as a *substance* separate from the body, in the Qur'an means mostly 'himself' or 'herself' and, in the plural, 'themselves', while in some contexts it means 'person' or the 'inner person', i.e. the living reality of man-but not separate from or exclusive of the body. In fact, it is body with a certain life-and-intelligence center that constitutes the inner identity or personality of man.[13]

---

13 Amina Wadud, *Qur'an and Woman: Rereading the Sacred Text from a Woman's Perspective* (Oxford: Oxford University Press, 1999), 19.

Wadud believes that according to the Qur'an, God never proposed to begin creation with the male. There's not even any reference to Adam as the beginning of mankind. In her opinion the Qur'anic version of the account of creation does not acknowledge gender at all. To support this further she turns to an explication of the word *zawj*. *Zawj* is generally used in the Qur'an to denote "spouse" or "partner" or "spouses". It's the term used in the second part of the creation story and which is customarily taken to indicate Eve. Nevertheless, *zawj* is grammatically masculine and so is used with verb and adjective in the masculine. Of course, the concept of *zawj* is neither masculine nor feminine in the Qur'an. Plants (55:52) and animals (11:40) are denoted by this term as well as humans. Wadud suspects that this lack of univocity caused such commentators as Zamakhshari to have recourse to the Biblical contents of the creation story where it is stated that Eve was created out (*min*) of Adam's rib.

After closer study of the Qur'anic use of *zawj* she concludes that everything in creation has a partner, is one of a pair: "everything in creation is paired."[14] As proof she also cites verse 51:49: "And of everything We created a pair". In her view, there are, of course, some differences with respect to nature, characteristics and functions but the two constitutive parts are so shaped that they fit together. With allusion to Toshihiko Izutsu's *God and Man in the Qur'an: the Semantics of the Qur'anic Weltanschauung*, a work that has become hugely important for Muslim scholars, she writes, "Each member of a pair presupposes the other semantically and stands on the very basis of this correlation."[15] Accordingly, a man is a husband only in relation to a wife. The existence of the one is presupposed by the existence of the other. With regard to creation, the quote "and of everything We created a pair" means that the counterpart of every created thing is part of the plan. From this Wadud draws the conclusion that the creation of both the original parents is irrevocably and originally linked one with the other. Hence, both of them are essential at one and the

---

14 Wadud, *Qur'an and Woman*, 21.
15 Wadud, *Qur'an and Woman*, 21.

same time. She cites other verses (51:49, 43:12, 36:36) to prove that all created things are paired and that this is a mutual necessity. This brings Wadud to the following gender-neutral translation of verse 4:1:

> O Mankind! Be careful of your duty to your Lord Who
> created you from a single *nafs* and from it created its *zawj*,
> and from that pair spread abroad (over the earth) a
> multitude of men and women.[16]

Other interpreters, including the aforementioned Persian translators, come to a similar reading of the verse, as well as, for example, Nasr Abu Zaid who writes:

> There is no indication in the Qur'an that woman was created out of man, as is written in the Bible. Later, Muslim interpreters drew on the Old Testament and explicated the verse in a Biblical sense but in the Qur'an itself one searches in vain for the idea that woman was created out of man's rib. In the Qur'anic story of creation both sexes are given equal status. The division of the soul into a pair does not produce any superiority of one over the other. We discover still more still more remarkable aspects when we consider the linguistic level that is neglected by many because they do not treat the Qur'an as a text that is subject to the rules and methods of textual analysis. The Qur'an belongs among the earliest of all Arabic texts in which men and women are explicitly addressed. In the old Arabic poetry the addressee is exclusively male.[17]

What Does the Qur'an Say to Us Today?

Along with a new way of reading of this sort, the main challenge for every new generation of Muslims, according to Wadud, lies in

---

16 Wadud, *Qur'an and Woman*, 22.
17 Nasr Hamid Abu Zaid, *Ein Leben mit dem Islam* (Freiburg im Breisgau: Herder Verlag, 1999), 83.

spiritually internalizing the fundamental principles stated in the Qur'an and putting them into practice in relation to one's own society. This is so because the concrete application and formulation of these principles vary with respect to social and cultural conditions and they change over time. That this kind of transformation hasn't occurred very often in history she attributes to the fact that exegetes have not understood that the content and the context of the Qur'an form a unity. Hence she writes:

> In the realm of gender conservative exegetes read explicit Qur'anic
> reforms of existing historical and cultural practice as literal and
> definitive statements about these practices for every place and time.
> I want an interpretation that views these reforms as what they were.
> They created a precedent with regard to an ongoing development in
> the direction of a just social order.[18]

By this she means the following: when it says in the Qur'an, for example, that a woman's testimony counts for half as much as that of a man, that does not imply that woman's testimony counts for half as much as a man's in today's world. Rather, it implies that the Qur'an improved women's status, since prior to this, their testimony didn't count at all. Other improvements in women's living conditions include the acknowledgment of personal rights as well as the prohibition on killing newborn girls. Wives, formerly seen as a husband's property, now had rights to property, inheritance, education and divorce. Thus a reform was initiated that was in women's interest. In her view this call for reform in the Qur'an should be carried on further. One shouldn't keep clinging to the fact that in the Qur'an it says that a woman's testimony counts for half as much as a man's. What matters is the spirit, not the letter. The letter merely reflects the context.

Here again conservative exegesis cries out that she treats the historicization and contextualization of the Qur'an message in accord with an inadmissible transference of the methods of Biblical research

---

18 Wadud, *Qur'an and Woman*, xiii.

to the Qur'an. Nevertheless, in the spirit of Fazlur Rahman, Wadud counters that the Qur'an emerged within a specific social and historical background and as a response to it. It is God's response, by way of Muhammad's mind, to a historical situation. To be sure, neither of these was or is seen by orthodoxy in this way. Wadud here distances herself decisively from the conservative mainstream.

Furthermore, she criticizes the fact that over the course of history only men have interpreted the Qur'an. Women and women's experiences were systematically excluded. But no complete understanding can develop of what it means to be a Muslim in this way. In Islam men and women are equal, Wadud states, and yet they differ from one another. Their experiences, therefore, are also different. Even so, this is elided in traditional *tafsir* (Qur'anic exegesis) because men have taken it upon themselves to declare to women what it is to be a woman: "Men not only determine what it means to be a Muslim but also what it means to be a Muslim woman."[19] For Wadud this not only impairs their dignity as human beings but also runs counter to the Qur'anic designation of men and women as *khalifa*, as God's successor or trustee. The meaning of creation, she states, is expressed in verse 2:30: "See, I am going to put a viceroy (*khalifa*) on the earth".

This term and its corresponding concept form two further, and central, points of departure in her approach to the Qur'an. It is her conviction that men and women have an equal obligation to *khilafa*, successorship or trusteeship. In conformity with the Qur'anic worldview the fulfilment of this trusteeship is the *raison d'être* of human existence. But by not allowing women to become complete personalities, one also disallows their capacity of becoming *khalifa*. One thereby takes away the possibility of their fulfilling the responsibility that God has imposed on all human beings. But since in the Qur'an, she continues, no essential distinction is formulated that bears on the worth of man and woman, women should also not be subject to more limitations than men. By taking the Qur'anic perspective on human creation as a basis it is possible to develop a rational Islamic ethics. Nevertheless,

---

19 Wadud, *Inside the Gender Jihad*, 96.

if women are denied a voice – as part of the text and in response to it – there can be no Islamic ethics.

Wadud is not concerned with pointing out mistakes in patriarchal exegesis but she does want Muslims to recognize what it leaves out. She is certain that women will develop an authentic Muslim identity if they are paid heed. This in turn may lead to their greater participation and involvement in religious life. Thus, as a scholar of Islam she wants a *tafsir* that is based on justice between the sexes. First of all she maintains that what has been left out of the text is not necessarily identical with God's will. This distinction between divine speech and its worldly realization isn't new; the Qur'an itself makes it. But over the course of history Islamic communities have exchanged God's revelation for their own notion of God's revelation. This attitude, she believes, obstructs new readings of the Qur'an and allows conservatives to depict disagreeable critics of *tafsir* as critics of the Qur'an itself. They are safeguarding their hegemony on religious knowledge, produced by a small number of male scholars in Islam's earliest period. True, not all such thinkers have been hostile to women but over time this point of view came to predominate. It is just for this reason that Wadud's distinction between God's speech and its annunciation through human beings is so important. She holds that interpretation is subjective and incomplete where traditional *tafsir* is concerned – a fact that Muslims often overlook. By paying heed to this she is in a position to liberate the Qur'an from misogynistic interpretations and to take a stand on one interpretation or another. This viewpoint is not necessarily contradictory; the Qur'an itself summons us to read it with the best intentions.

Wadud sees the Qur'an as a text in history. Accordingly, Qur'anic teachings must be explicated in connection with the social and historical context that Islam set out to reform. In a quite similar way Mahmud Muhammad Taha attempted to infer general principles from the Qur'an. In his opinion, to be sure, the distinction between the universal and the particular is itself a part of revelation. For him the general and binding prescriptions were revealed in the Meccan period while the more particular ones were part of the revelation in Medina. In Medina,

Muhammad was not only a founder of religion but a statesman and this is embodied in the suras that were revealed there.

Wadud rejects this division of the Prophet's career; instead, she sees a textual and historical continuum in the revelation. Moreover, not all the Meccan suras are universal in nature, nor are all the Medinan suras particular or time-bound. In her opinion the problem can only be resolved by hermeneutics, through a model that derives fundamental ethical principles for future developments and legal considerations by according the more general pronouncements priority over the more specific. This is where her interpretation of the technical term *asbab al-nuzul*, usually translated as "occasions of revelation", comes in. Wadud prefers the rendering "reasons for revelation". Understood in this way, specific occasions are *causes* of revelation. By trying to understand the reason for a particular revelation Wadud wants to grasp the context but without basing a Qur'anic principle on this single context. Rather, the Qur'an should be contextualized; the very fact tells people that the revelation took place within history. At the same time she doesn't want the Qur'an to be understood as a historical document but rather, as a moral history the goals of which are super-historical and transcendent, such that its temporal setting does not lessen either its significance or its effects. Ultimately it should provide universal guidance and instruction. Historical details serve to elucidate universal concepts so that the reader can understand their relevance with regard to his or her own life.

In Wadud's opinion the paramount objective must be to move away from the literal and comprehend the spirit of the Qur'an. To this end she gives an example from Islamic history: after the caliph 'Umar had won a war, he abstained from taking booty even though the Qur'an explicitly permitted this. He based his decision on the fact that this would not be right, since the defeated populace was in a perilous state. In this case, Wadud noted that 'Umar had quite consciously not adhered to the actual letter of the Qur'an but to its spirit, according to which righteousness should be practiced. Nowadays, however, anyone who thought or acted in this way would be branded a heretic. One could proceed according to verse 4:34 which permits men to beat their wives. It is valid to say NO to the text when it cannot be brought into accord with one's own conception of righteousness. She writes:

> I have personally come across passages where what the text says is simply utterly inappropriate or unacceptable, no matter how much interpretation you use on it.[20]

For this reason Wadud resorts to the ethical principles of the religion that are not discoverable through the Qur'an alone. But what are the ethical foundations, what is the spirit of Islam? For Wadud the answer to the question is unequivocal. For her, righteousness, equality and dignity are the God-given rights of every individual, whether male or female.

Perspectives of Islamic Feminism

Over time Wadud's studies have come to be considered standard works of Islamic feminism; they serve as a foundation for reform-minded believers from Indonesia to Egypt. She herself is regarded as easily the most prominent representative of Islamic feminism, even though she rejects the term, preferring the designation "pro-faith activist", or, "pro-belief activist" for herself. She remains convinced that God's summons is directed to men and to women equally. The goal therefore must be to do away with patriarchy, not to fashion new hierarchies. And if Wadud doesn't sanction the term "Islamic feminism", neither does she see any contradiction between Islam and feminism – in contrast to many critics of Islamic feminism. Amongst the latter are many Western or Western-oriented Muslim feminists who believe that the two cannot be reconciled, pointing out Islam's misogynistic character. But the same opinion is held as well by many Muslim men who regard the notion of equal rights for men and women, or even an identification with human rights, as a Western concept that is for that very reason incompatible with Islam. Because feminists with a Western orientation also hold the view that the problem is inherent

---

20 Wadud, *Inside the Gender Jihad*, 192.

to religion itself and so plead to keep religion out of the discussion, Muslim women face the choice of either remaining faithful to Islam or of aligning themselves with human rights. For many women this dichotomy was insoluble.

It is to Wadud's credit that she offered a solution to the majority of Muslim women who have fallen prey to this dichotomy. She says:

It has taken a long time before we could be in the position to formulate a reconciliation between Islam and human rights. That both to remain true to Islam and to align oneself with human rights can work is based on awareness of a national identity as well as upon the conviction that we women must make our own contribution to the interpretation of Islam. That means even to take part as well in the explication of Islamic textual sources. In doing so we will be frequently misunderstood. Either we'll be placed in the Islamists' corner or we'll be accused of secular tendencies.[21]

Islamic feminism is distinguished from the conventional women's movement only in that it offers Muslim women the alternative of taking issue with Islam in order to create an awareness that men and women have equal value. In fact, today Islamic feminism is a broad-based movement. The idea of promoting equal rights with the help of the Qur'an has taken hold. The notion of reconciliation between Islam and human rights is new, to be sure, and yet, according to Wadud, the number of Muslims who believe in this is growing steadily.

Above all, the number of Muslim women who are following in Wadud's footsteps is constantly increasing. One of her concerns was to make women's voices more powerfully present in Qur'anic studies. At least in the US, this is the case, as well as in South Africa, where Sa'diya Shaykh, who teaches religious studies in Cape Town, acknowledges Wadud as her spiritual and intellectual mentor. In the Festschrift for Wadud, expressly published as a so-called "web-writing", as a way

---

21 Amina Wadud, Interview with Taz.de, 2011, http://www.taz.de/1/archiv/digitaz/artikel/?ressort=ku&dig=2011%2F08%2F17%2Fa0115&cHash=fdea1cb346/

of better facilitating its diffusion, there is alongside such sections as "Readings" and "Inspirations" another section designated as "Continuations". Essays are included here by women who bring this female voice into the open. Hina 'Azam is professor of Islamic Studies at the University of Texas in Austin. She writes about gender and sexuality in Islam, and especially about rape in classical Islamic law as well as about sexuality, marriage and veiling in contemporary literature. Kecia Ali, who feels closely allied with Wadud's endeavor, is a professor at Boston University. The titles of her books are programmatic: *Sexual Ethics and Islam: Feminist Reflections on Qur'an, Hadith and Jurisprudence* (2006) or *Marriage and Slavery in Early Islam* (2010).

Of course, there is criticism too, even from other reforming thinkers. For example, Abu Zaid thinks that to perceive the Qur'an only as a text falls short:

> This means that the Qur'an depends on the ideology of its interpreters: for a Communist the Qur'an reveals Communism, for an Islamist the Qur'an is a highly Islamist text and for a feminist it is a feminist text...What I have in mind is the dimension that is inherent in the structure of the text and which is disclosed in the process of communication. An awareness of this horizontal dimension is practicable only if we shift our conceptual framework from the Qur'an as text to the Qur'an as discourse.[22]

Amina Wadud responds to the charge that she reads her own ideology into the Qur'an by saying that, in any case, every reading is subjective. The Muslim community has always manipulated the text:

> We must now simply acknowledge that it has always been done and accept the responsibility of agency in doing so openly and in consultation with the community ... I have already argued significantly that the text *can* be interpreted with egalitarianism in

22 Nasr Abu Zaid, *Reformation of Islamic Thought: a Critical Historical Analysis* (Amsterdam: Amsterdam University Press, 2006), 98.

mind; I now propose a step that some consider as beyond even that. *We are the makers of textual meaning.*[23]

This is an unusual idea, to say the least, and an especially far-reading one. It accords a great deal of subjectivity to the interpretation of the subject which, however, must be agreed upon by the Muslim community. It will bring the unavoidable reproach of "anything goes" down upon itself. Moreover, it's an open question as to whether the community can agree on something and what the criteria might be for determining what conforms to the egalitarian spirit of the Qur'an and what does not.

Amina Wadud's importance in current discourse is not only based on the ready answers she always has but also on the effect that she exercises on the thought and action of many contemporaries. Her decisive contribution to Sisters in Islam has already been described, but even in the US her role has been significant. In the Festschrift in her honour, for example, Mohammed Fadel describes how she was the first person capable of providing answers to his questions. As a Muslim raised in the US he'd experienced how his neighborhood mosque had become a battleground of utterly conflicting views on the theme of Islam and gender. The opinions of many members of the community repelled him, nor could he reconcile them with the Islam that had been presented to him in his childhood. They quoted supposed sayings of the Prophet as well as Qur'anic verses to shore up their misogynistic views and he could not counter them. He began to have doubts about his own Islam. That changed when he read Wadud's *Qur'an and Woman*. Now he was able to reconcile the values that America had inculcated in him with his religion. For him, a "perplexed person", Wadud became a guide. Fadel, who teaches Islamic law at the University of Toronto, is today by no means in agreement with all of her arguments and shows of proof and, yet, she blazed a trail that led him to the discovery of his own identity.

Nimet Şeker would probably agree. This doctoral candidate at the graduate school of Islamic theology, set up by the Mercator Foundation

---

23 Wadud, *Inside the Gender Jihad*, 189.

to educate the younger generation of scholars that Germany needs today, wanted to write her dissertation on Amina Wadud and Asma Barlas. Today she is critical of the methods of both. Both of them have failed to do justice to their own methodological approaches and too often they neglect the context of revelation. Furthermore, they are frequently inattentive to linguistic subtleties. Nimet Şeker has taken it upon herself to prepare her own investigation of the verses pertaining to sexual equality which, well beyond the Islamic feminist premise that sexual equality can be inferred from the Qur'an as a norm, adopts a linguistic perspective as its justification. Şeker thinks through the methods recommended by Wadud and Barlas for historical contextualization of the Qur'anic directives revealed on the status of the sexes and develops her own new hermeneutical approach. Through an aesthetic hermeneutics of the Qur'an as well as a "hermeneutics of hearing", which views the Qur'an not as a text but as a sung recitation, she investigates figurations of femininity in the early Meccan suras which point to God's attribute as creator. Wadud's pioneering text has thus been instrumental with regard to the construction of an Islamic theology in Germany.

6

Asma Barlas: As Though Only Men Were Objective

A Eurocentric View of Islam

That the suppression of women stands in contradiction to the Qur'an is also Asma Barlas' credo. Like Amina Wadud, she interprets the Qur'an as a liberating text that can show women a way out of suppression – under specific conditions:

> The meaning of the text cannot be understood on its own terms. Everyone must give it a meaning. In this regard I note that the Qur'an has been interpreted exclusively by men for 1400 years, and always within a patriarchal society.[1]

Born in Pakistan and now living in the US, she has achieved fame there through her book *Believing Women in Islam*. Asma Barlas, born in 1950 to a Westernized family, has English as her first language. This was usual for members of her social class. She spoke Urdu, which she learned as a second language, up to her twelfth year of school, with household servants and members of lower social classes.

Today, having spent 30 years in the US, she can hardly speak – and still less write – Urdu, a fact that she regrets. This forms her criticism

---

1 Asma Barlas, Interview with DW. http://www.dw.de/dw/article/0,,1919362,00. html

of the post-colonial education her social class received: by reducing Urdu to the status of a second-class language, they became estranged from their own culture. Her parents had grown up in colonial India and thought that they had made the right choice. As a result Barlas attended a Catholic school run by nuns. In a recent essay about the labyrinth of racism she writes that this education instilled in her an image of the world and her place in it as a Muslim woman that was both anti-Islamic and Eurocentric. Only much later in her life did this become clear to her.

Barlas completed her BA in English literature and philosophy in 1969 at the Kinnaird College for Women in Lahore. In 1971 she got an MA in journalism, also in Lahore. From 1976 until 1982 she was in the diplomatic service as a head of division in the Pakistani Foreign Ministry until a nasty incident led to her dismissal: in revenge for divorcing her husband, he gave her diary to Zia-ul-Haq, the head of state – in it she had called the latter "Casper". After her dismissal she got a position as co-editor and columnist for the newspaper *The Muslim* but even so, in 1983 she had to leave the country; she felt that her security had been compromised by the incident.

In the US, where she went with her son, she received political asylum and in 1986 she completed further study at the University of Denver with an MA in International Studies. She earned her doctorate there as well in 1990 with a dissertation on *State, Class and Democracy: A Comparative Analysis of Politics in Hindu and Muslim Society in Colonial India, 1885–1947*. Subsequently, her scholarly career in the US underwent a rapid rise. In 1991 she was assistant professor at Ithaca College in New York; in 1997 she became associate professor, and in 2004, F she became a full professor. Since 2006 she has been director of the Center for the Study of Culture, Race and Ethnicity at Ithaca College. In 2008 she was the holder of the renowned Spinoza Chair at the Faculty of Philosophy at the University of Amsterdam. She has received numerous awards for her books.

Though her research interests have changed over the course of her life the theme of ideology and power has formed the common denominator of all her books. An interest in Islam, reflected in the 2002 book

Believing Women in Islam: Unreading Patriarchal Interpretations of the Qur'an, led her next to a consideration of Western power directed against Muslims: *Islam, Muslims and the US* appeared in 2004; and in 2008, her Spinoza lecture at the University of Amsterdam, dealing with the Western view of Islam, was published as *Re-Understanding Islam*.

Barlas' book on the Qur'an was translated into numerous languages. Furthermore, she presented the book's theses at various conferences in the US and around the world. She excited lively interest in it especially in Indonesia, Egypt and Pakistan, as well as in Europe. The name of Fazlur Rahman crops up again and again in her book *Believing Women*, where she adopts his "double-movement" approach. Asma Barlas shares not only a native country with Fazlur Rahman, which drove them both into exile. She came upon his work almost accidentally, but was immediately fascinated by his "logical, rational and persuasive approach, and his criticism of religious knowledge."[2] It quickly became clear to her that he had a deep love of Islam which, however, did not prevent him from adopting a critical intellectual standpoint towards his religion. "I would say that it is this critical awareness, steeped in love for Islam, that we both share."[3]

According to Barlas, her book emerged through a constant dialogue with Amina Wadud, who even read the manuscript. She adopted some of the Afro-American's arguments; many of her theses are also similar. But Barlas is more systematic than Wadud. She proceeds in a more scholarly way whereas Wadud's approach is sometimes more associative in effect. This also leads Barlas to cite much that has already been written on the subject. One wishes sometimes that she would rely more on her own judgment and write in a more strongly normative than descriptive way. Were it not for her passionate and lively style her book would certainly appear somewhat dry.

Asma Barlas dedicated *Believing Women in Islam* to her father Iqbal Barlas, who has always been supportive of her work, and to her

---

2 Asma Barlas, Interview with the author, 28/8/2012.
3 Ibid.

second husband Ulises Ali Meijas with the dedication: "with much love, especially because he has undertaken the journey to Islam."[4] Meijas, an American of Mexican origin, is Professor of New Media at the State University of New York at Oswego. Barlas has a son from her first marriage who was born in 1973, is married to an American of Turkish origin, and has two children.

The Patriarchal Interpretation of the Qur'an

In *Believing Women in Islam* the scholar criticizes the traditional male reading of the Qur'an. As a result she explores the masculine perspective on the Qur'an, on the one hand, and, on the other, she offers her own, anti-patriarchal interpretation. She is concerned with presenting the varied perceptions of the holy text and states:

> We can read the Qur'an as an anti-patriarchal text. In fact, I make the bolder claim that Qur'anic epistemology is inherently anti-patriarchal...To me Qur'anic epistemology is anti-patriarchal because it is based in a view of God who is neither father nor son nor husband nor man nor male and nor even created. This God is therefore beyond affinity with males and hatred for females.[5]

The fact that the Qur'an has not been regarded as a product of its culture is not, in Barlas' view, the result of a wrong interpretation of this text. Accordingly she has quite a different approach from that of Abu Zaid. For her the problem is not that the text emerged in a dialogue with its environment and so reacted only to existing conditions but is rather how a human being makes the text his own.

---

4 Asma Barlas, *Believing Women in Islam: Unreading Patriarchal Interpretations of the Qur'an* (Austin: University of Texas, 2002), xvi.
5 Asma Barlas, "Un-reading Patriarchal Interpretations of the Qur'an: Beyond the Binaries of Tradition and Modernity," (presentation to the Association of Muslim Social Scientists, Conference on Islam: Tradition and Modernity, Toronto, November 4, 2006).

Barlas' engagement with the Qur'an was occasioned less by schol-arly curiosity than by personal need. She began to think about herself and about the Qur'an because many years before, in her Pakistani homeland, she had come to realize that as a woman she had virtually no rights at all.

> I became ever more sensitive to the fact that the overwhelming majority of Muslim women with marital difficulties could be thrown out of their houses by their husbands and have their children taken away. There exists a whole series of oppressive practices against women that for me stand in the deepest contradiction to what the Qur'an teaches.[6]

Many women would suffer from this situation but only a few women would inquire further into what is presented to them as a Qur'anic commandment. They do not have the confidence in themselves to read the Qur'an for themselves. Barlas marvels at this diffidence and this fear. For a long time feminists have issued the challenge to resist this male monopoly. In the 1980s Fatima Mernissi was already calling on women to become specialists themselves in Qur'anic studies. Only by so doing might women squarely defy men who peddle their version of Islam as *the* Islam.

For this reason Barlas believes that a strengthening of awareness in Muslim women is imperative and that a struggle for their own rights is unavoidable. Muslim women, she believes, require greater access to alternative interpretations of religious thought. In the United States where she lives she contributes to this herself through her writings. But she stresses that she is not a scholar of Islam, but rather, a student of Islam; she studies the religion as a Muslim. In the introduction to *Believing Women* she strongly emphasizes her motivation as a believer: to strive through knowledge towards service to God.

Sound human reason tells her that the practices that lead to the sup-pression of women which are legitimated by Islam stand in opposition

---

6 Barlas, Interview with DW.

to both the Qur'an and its spirit; so too does her image of God. If one assumes that God is not unjust to His creatures, then His word too cannot preach injustice (*zulm*) towards His creatures. Why would He be unjust to women but not to men? It cannot be godly to deny full humanity to women, Barlas argues. Therefore, from a purely logical standpoint, something or other must have gone awry in interpretation. For God's most important quality, His most significant attribute, is justice. All Muslims believe this.

As a matter of fact a God who commands not to do *zulm*, that is, not to transgress the rights of others, cannot endorse *zulm* towards women. Those who benefit from the patriarchy may not call it *zulm* but women perceive it as such. Thus, the Qur'an cannot endorse *zulm* without falling into contradiction.[7]

Hence, there is a connection between divine ontology and discourse. Muslims need not concur in the definition of *zulm* to recognize how incoherent it is to assume that God could teach *zulm*, that a just God could preach injustice, Barlas says. Nevertheless, Muslims who say that God is just read injustice into His word.

For Barlas the cause for the emergence of this sort of interpretation lies in history. The most important texts of exegesis and law were produced in the first centuries of Islam, in a period therefore that was strongly marked by misogyny. Since the text was frequently confounded with its commentaries the impression arose that the text itself was misogynistic.

The Imam al-Shafi'i, roundly scolded by reformers, for Barlas too stands at the midpoint of her critique. This prominent legal scholar – so runs the reproach – prioritized the hadith, that is, the traditions of the Prophet, over the Qur'an. Furthermore, the consensus of the scholars and of the religious thinking that was current in al-Shafi'i's time (the 8th and 9th centuries) came to be canonized. Exegesis and hadith were given precedence over the Qur'an and scholarly consensus was given precedence over *ijtihad*, the independent determination of legal

---

7 Asma Barlas, "Re-understanding Islam: a Double Critique," *Spinoza Lectures* (Amsterdam: Van Gorcum, 2008), 21.

judgments. In addition, the interpretations of passages dealing with women were formulated in accord with prevailing social norms and values. Negative views crept into the discourse via the hadith. Those hostile to women were preferred to those favorably disposed to them.

Barlas has doubts about the soundness of these hadiths; she agrees with Fazlur Rahman who stated that the hadith were not so much history-*writing* as history-*manufacturing*. This is why Rahman also pleaded for hadith criticism as one of the most important aspects of modern study of the Qur'an.

Here is where research must be undertaken, here is the source of much wrong, Barlas expostulates. So says a hadith: obedience to a husband is akin to obedience to God. And yet, that is nonsense; the Prophet himself did not treat women this way. His wives discussed things with him, they disagreed with him, he requested their opinion and their counsel. Muhammad was not misogynistic. Such traditions were invented by men who wanted to safeguard their dominion over women. Nevertheless, generations of women have believed that the statements attributed to Muhammad really came from him.

Since it is hard to figure out which traditions really go back to Muhammad, Barlas repudiates the usual exegetic process *in toto* that consists of interpreting the Qur'an by means of the hadith. To be sure, this does work in certain instances. Thus, for example, the Prophet never beat his wives and it is reported that he directed other men not to beat theirs. If the Prophet be taken as the first interpreter of the Qur'an – in this case, verse 4:34 – and the most important point of reference, something might be gained, at a first glance, on behalf of women. But conversely such ideas as the creation of Eve out of Adam's rib or punishment by stoning go back solely to the hadith. Barlas writes:

> These are all un-Qur'anic or anti-Qur'anic ideas and practices. This is why it creates more problems for women than it solves if one draws on the Sunna and the Hadith to interpret the Qur'an.[8]

---

8 Barlas, "Re-understanding Islam: a Double Critique", 14.

To be sure, conservatives and even some feminists maintain that it is a dangerous tactic to reject the hadith or put it in doubt. To her, however, it seems just as dangerous and even theologically capricious to accept hadiths that undermine the Qur'an on the grounds that they are canonical. For Muslims there is no canon more crucial to defend than the Qur'an. Barlas also queries how the hadith came to be established. The community of interpreters grew ever more authoritative than the Qur'an itself. That interpretation of the Qur'an took precedence over the Qur'an strikes Barlas as an act of arrogation. The Qur'an itself warns against confusing it with its interpretations.

Islamic Feminism?

Barlas doesn't describe herself as a feminist, nor does she wish to be described as such. But she is aware of how much she owes to feminism and to feminist thinking. Nevertheless, in her opinion it must be made clear what the concept of feminism may be:

> For example, the notion of feminism suggests that it is a matter of emancipatory discourse. But as we know, the Western forms of feminism are still co-responsible for empires, wars and colonialism and along with this, for the oppression of many women.[9]

Furthermore, she is critical of the notion of feminism for its origins in a secular context:

> One of the reasons why I am against feminism is that most Muslim feminists are fundamentally secular and have little in common with me. At best, they remain hostile to the entire project of a new interpretation of the Qur'an.[10]

---

9 Asma Barlas, "Der Koran neu geselen," *Islam und Gesellschaft* 6, Friedrich-Ebert-Siftung Politische Akademie, Berlin (May 2008), 5. http://library.fes.de/pdf-files/akademie/berlin/05440.pdf.
10 Ibid.

Because she was formed by a very specific education and grew up in another culture, she represents an approach that is alien to many feminists. Until there is some clarity within the Muslim community as to what may be understood by feminism, she would simply say: I am a believer, to which she adds critically:

> Furthermore, and here I come to my second point, if we want Muslim women themselves to become stronger, why should we then not respect their right to call themselves what they want? If we don't want to call the project of equality and liberation feminism, why can't that simply be accepted? In my opinion, to call someone a feminist is not so transparent or nuanced or helpful as it might seem to be at first glance.[11]

But she also takes up the other side and criticizes the attacks of certain secular feminists against those who argue from an Islamic standpoint. On this she takes a position in an academic debate about the phenomenon of "Islamic feminism" that began in the year 1994. At that time Afsaneh Najmabadi, the Iranian-born professor of history and women's studies at Harvard University, described the struggle for equality by the Iranian journal for women *Zanan* "Women" as Islamic feminism. Further still, Najmabadi stated that the effort to improve the legal and social status of women could be a common denominator for both secular and religious feminists.

At this Najmabadi was shouted down by a group of Iranian left-wingers who, in Najmabadi's view, ought to enter into dialogue with Islamic feminists. Haideh Moghissi, also of Iranian origin and a profes-sor of sociology at York University in Toronto – and who has a Marxist background – argued that, "It has become fashionable to speak sympa-thetically and enthusiastically about the reformist activities of Muslim women, and to insist on their independence of thought." All of a sudden every politically active Muslim woman is an Islamic feminist, "even though their activities might not even fit the broadest definition

11 Barlas, "Der Koran neu geselen," 6.

of feminism". Moghissi criticized "these apologists for the Islamic government", arguing that the term feminism was being used in a false and irresponsible manner.[12]

In the 1990s this view was especially prevalent among Iranians in exile; among those who dealt with Iran as scholars a tendency arose that considered the term "Islamic feminism" a contradiction in terms. Iranians in exile declared that there could no improvement in women's rights as long as the Islamic Republic existed. A struggle within the system would weaken the goals of feminism and only help fundamentalism to continue.

Barlas intervened in this no-holds-barred debate when in 2003 she reviewed Moghissi's book *Feminism and Islamic Fundamentalism: the Limits of Postmodern Analysis*, published in 1999. She found that Moghissi's perspective on Islamic feminism rested entirely on her own negative experiences as an Iranian woman with regard to Islamic fundamentalism. Barlas reproached Moghissi for her strident tone and for confusing Muslims with Islam itself when she characterized them as patriarchal and oppressive while – in good Marxist fashion – classifying all those who thought otherwise (read: Muslim women) as backward and in need of liberation. The message was that the image of Islam offered by Iran is not Islam and those Iranians who are critical of the regime should stop presenting their experiences of an Islamic state to the world at large as normative Islam. They were setting themselves up as star witnesses for Islam even though the Islam that they had known represented nothing but a perversion of itself.

As a Muslim Woman in the USA

In questionnaires virtually every second American voices a negative opinion about Islam. One in three Republicans identifies Barack Obama as a Muslim, a synonym for being un-American. Muslims complain that the Republicans, and especially the Tea Party, have made Islamophobia a component of their political agitation. They make use

---

12 Haideh Moghissi, "Women, Modernity and Political Islam" *Iran Bulletin*, no. 19–20 (Autumn/Winter 1998), 42.

of fears, traumas and ignorance for their political game. In every election year a surge in anti-Islamic emotions is palpable.

Despite the worsening situation since 9/11, Asma Barlas values her new homeland which in many parts of the Islamic world is viewed as the very embodiment of an anti-Islamic culture; for many Islamists in her former homeland it is seen as "the great Satan". In the US she has numerous possibilities for advancing her research that would not be available in a repressive country such as Pakistan.

For this reason she strives, even today, to have some effect on the politics and the society of Pakistan. She regularly writes articles for the *Daily Times Pakistan* in which have had titles such as "About Democracy" or "Islam, Women and Equality" but also with the question as to how one becomes a Muslim authority in the USA. In addition, she gives her opinion on current topics as well; she is infuriated, for example, in one commentary over the fact that schoolgirls should wear the veil in order to combat an all-pervasive moral decline, stating:

> In a true Islamic society men wouldn't assume that morality lies in how women dress but in how they view women and behave towards them.[13]

Although she has come to appreciate the freedoms that America gives her, she is often astounded by how little Americans know about Islam and the Near East. She considers this disastrous given the interests that America has in the region. When she started teaching at Ithaca College on the Near and Middle East she realized that most American students barely understand the politics of the Middle East. One cause for this, she realized, lay in the students' ignorance about Islam.

This ignorance is one of the reasons why Asma Barlas, the political scientist, began to also deal with Islam from a scholarly perspective. Politics in the wake of 9/11 provided another reason. Since then, she has emerged as a critic of American foreign policy as well as of the laws which have been passed in the US since 9/11, within the framework

---

13 Asma Barlas, "Morality: for women and girls only," *The Daily Times*, Pakistan, January 14, 2003.

of Homeland Security. It was for this reason that the influential com-
mentator Robert Satloff, writing in *The New York Times*, called her "a
voice that speaks against us".

In her view as a scholar, George W. Bush and the US administration
used 9/11 as a pretext for establishing American hegemony everywhere
in the world. The US government has the deaths of thousands of civil-
ians in Afghanistan and Iraq on its conscience. Furthermore, the measures taken in the US as a result of its war on terror – racial profiling,
surveillance, pre-emptive imprisonment and secret courts, for example
– were aimed especially at Muslims. Moreover, these lasting hostilities
were launched throughout civil society. She herself, like many other
Muslim academics, was attacked by reactionary "watchdog groups"
who equate criticism of Israeli politics with hatred for America and
anti-Americanism.[14] While many regard these developments as tragic
but inevitable consequences of the events of September 11th, Barlas
believes that 9/11 simply brought an ever-present fear of, and aversion
to, Islam to the surface:

> Just like colonial masters most non-Muslim Americans also think of
> Muslims that "they are unpredictable", that "one never knows with
> them…". And like colonized people themselves, Muslims are never
> characterized as individuals but must be immersed in a nameless
> collective.[15]

Liberation Theology

Barlas knows, of course, that a new hermeneutics of the Qur'an cannot
end patriarchy; however, it is still important. A connection exists
between what we read and what we think that the texts say as well
as between how we think about women and how we treat them. A
connection also exists between reading sacred texts and liberation.
Nevertheless, a reading that liberates must possess legitimacy:

---

14 Asma Barlas, "Muslims in the US (I)," *The Daily Times*, Pakistan, June 17, 2003.
15 Ibid.

If such readings are unsuccessful in bringing about a radical
change in Muslim societies, it can still be affirmed with certainty
that no meaningful change can be introduced into these societies that
does not derive its legitimacy from the teachings of the Qur'an. This
is a lesson that secular Muslims everywhere will have to learn to their
sorrow.[16]

She has in common with other women who place the Qur'an at the
centre of their struggle for equality the fact that they all cast the motif
of male predominance, historically read into the Qur'an for ages, into
question. They strive to lay bare all the possibilities of liberation that
the Qur'an offers and to do so by elucidating its position with regard
to the equality of the sexes.

Among other thinkers, both male and female – so Barlas believes,
with allusion to the South African theologian Farid Esack and to Amina
Wadud – there is a tendency to say "No" to the text and to state that
one simply has to move away from the text and cultivate a new Muslim
identity. By contrast she herself explicitly says "Yes" to the text and yet,
she reads it in a way that is the exact opposite of the prevalent way of
reading it today. She believes that an anti-patriarchal interpretation with
reference to theology and methodology offers a firmer footing than the
prevailing patriarchal mode of interpretation. Hence, she wants, in her
own words, to interpret patriarchy out of the Qur'an:

> When I ask whether the Qur'an is a patriarchal or misogynistic text,
> I am asking whether it represents God as Father/male or teaches that
> God has a special relationship with males or that males embody
> divine attributes and that women are by nature weak, unclean,
> or sinful. Further, does it teach that rule by the father/husband is
> divinely ordained and an earthly continuation of God's Rule, as
> religious and traditional patriarchies claim?[17]

---

16 Barlas, *Believing Women in Islam*, 3.
17 Barlas, *Believing Women in Islam*, 1.

By patriarchy she means two things: on the one hand, the style and manner in which a patriarch reacts, which again is based on the representation of God as father (the traditional patriarchy) and, on the other, the politics of differentiation of the sexes that favours men and excludes women (the modern/worldly patriarchy).

Two factors brought Barlas to the realization that the Qur'an supports neither the traditional nor the modern form of patriarchy. First, the Qur'an does not present God as father but instead explicitly rejects this notion. The Islamic view of God is considerably different in this respect from the Christian for which the idea of God the Father is not alien. In contradistinction to Christianity, the Qur'an undermines patriarchy. It does not attribute rights to fathers and fatherhood in the traditional form; it does not elevate fathers and fatherhood to something sacrosanct. On the contrary, it expressly condemns following the way of the fathers, for this is a wrong way and leads away from God's path. Here Barlas spots a clear rejection of traditional patriarchy. Of course, the Qur'an recognizes throughout that patriarchies exist and that power lies in the hands of men. This is why it turns often towards men. Nevertheless, recognition of patriarchy or appeals to men are something different from advocacy of male domination.

Above all, however, God is not represented in the Qur'an as father/male; instead it prohibits every sort of image of God. According to the Qur'an God was not created but is uncreated, and accordingly, not depictable even if human language always provides God with a masculine pronoun. For Barlas, God stands above identification through gender.

To be sure, the weightiest argument against patriarchy proceeds from the very nature of the divine self-representation. A God who rejects being made a patriarch cannot be a model for patriarchy. Furthermore, the Qur'an stresses the ontological equality of man and woman by teaching that men and women were created from the same *nafs*, "self" or "soul", that they are morally fully responsible for themselves and that they are brought to judgment according to the same criteria. So it is written in verse 33:35:

For men and women who are devoted to God –
believing men and women,
obedient men and women,
truthful men and women,
steadfast men and women,
humble men and women,
charitable men and women,
fasting men and women,
chaste men and women,
men and women who remember God often –
God has prepared forgiveness and a rich reward.

Women are just as capable of moral behavior as men. They must act in the same way as men. So, for example, the Qur'an addresses both sexes alike in verse 2:177 when it explains what God expects of them:

Goodness does not consist in turning your face
towards East or West. The truly good are those
who believe in God and the Last Day, in the angels,
the Scripture, and the prophets; who give away
some of their wealth, however much they cherish it,
to their relatives, to orphans, the needy, travellers
and beggars, and to liberate those in bondage;
those who keep up the prayer and pay the prescribed alms;
who keep pledges whenever they make them;
who are steadfast in misfortune, adversity, and times of danger.
These are the ones who are true,
and it is they who are aware of God.

Moreover, women are just as much positioned for *taqwa*, awe of God, which is the central demand God makes of human beings. In verses 39:17–18 we read:

But let those rejoice who keep from idol-worship
and turn to God in repentance. Give good news

to My servants, who listen to My precepts
and follow what is best in them.
These are they whom God has guided.
These are they who are endowed with understanding.

For Barlas it is not logical that human beings who are morally equal
should not be equal in actuality. Moreover, in the Qur'an, biological
gender is not employed to furnish men with privileges and to exclude
women, as is the case in the modern and worldly forms of patriarchy.
The Qur'an does not link sex even once with gender. It recognizes the
biological (sexual) distinctions throughout but accords them no specific sexual symbolism. Not a single verse assigns particular spheres of
work to men and women or implies that the biological differences of
men and women make them dissimilar, incompatible, incomparable
or opposite to one another. Furthermore, sex is not stigmatized in the
Qur'an. It thus enhances the image of woman too that Islam is not
so hostile to sexual pleasure as Christianity is. Moreover, woman is
not responsible for the fact that Adam ate the apple. In the Qur'anic
description of the Fall, Adam and Eve were seduced together and both
are responsible. In Barlas' view patriarchal constructs of sexuality come
from Judaism and Christianity and were insinuated into Islam.

All her statements about the Qur'an show that her hermeneutics
rests on her theology. God's word has to be connected with God.
For this reason she considers His three essential characteristics. The
first principle is oneness, tawhid, which symbolizes God's indivisibility,
that is, the indivisibility of His sovereignty as well. God is the absolute sovereign; no one can share in His sovereignty. Therefore, there
cannot be any sovereignty of men over women; that would be heretical. The second principle is God's justice which permits no injustice
towards one of His creatures. God's incomparability, particularly in an
anthropomorphic sense, constitutes the third principle. God may not
be represented as man, as father. The ban on images, so important in
Islam, confirms this.

For Barlas it isn't only a hermeneutical failure that Muslims have
not engendered any contextually legitimate procedure for interpreting

the Qur'an; it is also a theological failure. They have developed no connection between their image of God and their understanding of the text. This is why a coherent image of God is quite important for women's emancipation. For obedience is due solely to God and not to anyone else.

The Appeal for Another Image of God

According to Barlas then, reform will take place less through a new interpretation of the so-called misogynistic verses which relate to the supposed superiority of the man (wife-beating, polygamy, legal testimony, inheritance, etc.). A critique of theology and of methods of exegesis is far more important. And assuming that another image of God can be introduced into theology, the problem of the misogynistic verses of the Qur'an may be solved.

By a closer scrutiny, for example, it becomes clear that in the Qur'an the word "level" (daraja), which many seemingly pious Muslims routinely gloss to mean that God created men at a higher level, is employed only in connection with the husband's privileges in a case of divorce. It isn't clear, however, what exactly his privilege may be. Some scholars believed, according to Barlas, that the privilege lies in his ability to initiate a divorce; others think that it lies in his prerogative to cancel a divorce. In no instance, however, does it have anything to do with his existence as a male or his biology. From the ontological viewpoint men cannot be superior in any way to women since it is written in the Qur'an that both of them have their origin in a single soul (nafs).

Likewise the word qawwamun can denote the financial role of husbands as family breadwinners but not any guardianship over women. Rather, the Qur'an has intended men and women to be awliya', "friends", or models for one another and has obligated both to prescribe the right and forbid the wrong. How, Barlas asks, could they do this if men had complete power over women?

Even the verse about "wife beating" can be resolved as long as one recognizes that the word translated as "beating" can have several meanings, one of which is "to separate". For Barlas, therefore, the question arises as to why Muslims have preferred one meaning – and indeed, one disadvantageous to women – over all the others. The Qur'an teaches, moreover, that love ought to be the foundation of a marriage and it prescribes compassion and generosity between spouses, even if they have just been divorced.

With regard to testimony in court, only in one case does it apply that the testimony of a man is worth exactly that of two women, namely, when the witness statements relate to liabilities arising from a contract. In the much more decisive instance of adultery, by contrast, the wife's testimony weighs more than that of her husband; specifically, if a husband accuses his wife of adultery on the basis of his own testimony, she can refute the charge by her own statement – thus, in a real sense she has the last word.

Barlas wants to show by all these examples that interpretation of the Qur'an is dependent on who interprets it, on how it is done and in what context. When it is interpreted only by men – as has always been the case historically, and indeed only in a fragmentary way, and always within a patriarchal context – the outcome is hardly surprising. In her view, the Qur'an *could* be read throughout as a patriarchal text but only if specific parts are singled out and the totality of the message is ignored. She shares this approach with Wadud and Rahman, both of whom emphasize repeatedly that it is a matter of understanding what the larger whole is, and not just minute individual directives. Contextualization is thus one of her magic words – who said what and when and why:

> In other words, a restrictive and oppressive exegesis results both
> from the failure to historicize the Qur'an's teachings and to read the
> text as "a whole, a totality."[18]

Asma Barlas takes the Qur'anic summons to heart to interpret it in its "best meaning". If Muslims don't manage to do this and read sexual inequality, oppression and even polygamy into the Qur'an, it is unfair to hold the Qur'an responsible for this. Texts cannot interpret

---

18 Barlas, *Believing Women in Islam*, 169.

themselves. Only Muslims can do this and as a result they have to bear
the burden of their own misinterpretations. The question also arises in
this connection as to whether the text itself is not responsible when it
is wrongly understood.

> My own view is that the Qur'an's auto-hermeneutics serves
> Qur'annot only as a guide to how we read it but also as an argument
> for the fact that it cannot be made responsible for how it was read or
> how not.[19]

The Qur'an anticipates the fact that it can be misunderstood. In
verse 41:40 it is written:

> Those who distort the meaning of Our message are not
> hidden from Us. Is he who is hurled into the Fire better,
> or he who comes through safely on the Day of Resurrection?
> Do whatever you want,
> God certainly sees everything you do.

The distortions of the interpreters, according to the Qur'an, demonstrate moral as well as hermeneutical failure. For this reason those who
obscure God's revelations for some personal advantage are condemned.
Just how people obscure revelation becomes clear when the Qur'an
refers to the law that was given to Moses. It is written, "You put it on
parchments, revealing them but concealing much" (6:91). Veiling thus
crops up if God's message is read in a fragmentary and selective manner:

> Moreover, the Qur'an urges us to read in the best possible way.
> And while it leaves it open as to what this may be, it states that not
> all readings that we can derive from it are apt. In sum, the Qur'an
> not only anticipates that we may misunderstand it but it also tries
> to prevent this by propagating some moral and textual strategies
> while warning about others. This is why I believe that responsibility

---

19 Barlas, *Believing Women in Islam*, 205.

for reading the Qur'an rightly lies with the reader; and I see nothing wrong with the argument that meaning resides in the Qur'an while the responsibility to discover it correctly lies with its readers.[20]

Nevertheless, Muslims are constrained to read it in the best way. Verse 39:18 says:

Who listen to the declaration and follow the best of it. Those are the ones whom God has guided.

Theological principles aside, the Qur'an itself states how it should not be read. In verse 15:91 those who "have broken" the Qur'an "into portions" are addressed, and they are threatened:

By your Lord! We shall question them all about all their doings.
(15:92–93)

Will the Best Interpretation Prevail?

Barlas denies that her ideas will lead to freedom for women and to democratization. One cannot simply read the Qur'an and acquire a functioning democracy in one stroke. But she does see a connection between democracy and Qur'anic interpretation. In her view, the prerequisite for democracy in Islamic countries lies in a fundamental change in the way in which believers confront their sacred scripture and interpret it. Even though she comes from a country in which Benazir Bhutto was sworn in as the first female head of state in the Islamic world, in 1988, Barlas is anything but optimistic that her female-friendly interpretation will succeed at any time soon. She is not even sure that she will live long enough to see Muslim thinking change substantially – even women themselves still defend the patriarchy. And yet, it is always women who have suffered the most from this conservative mentality. The battles over the cultural supremacy of interpretation

---

20 Barlas, *Believing Women in Islam*, 206.

are waged on their backs. Whether or not they wear a headscarf is only one of these battles. Notwithstanding all this, she means to fight for what she thinks is right. She feels an ethical responsibility towards her religion and herself.

Reception of her ideas has not been confined in the US to a purely academic readership; she receives invitations from Muslim organizations and associations and thereby reaches a wider public. Among these are, for example, are the Muslim Public Affairs Council (MPAC) and the Council on American Islamic Relations (CAIR), the largest Muslim organization in the US, which has taken up certain of her theses. Of course, the public often reacts in dismay; for example, to her argument that one should not automatically make God male. Nevertheless, Barlas holds that such pronouncements as this are in absolute conformity to the Qur'an; and so she fails to understand how they could be seen as controversial. True, it is a fact that in many Muslim communities today it is men who define religious knowledge. Hence, her claim that every Muslim must have the right to read and interpret the Qur'an for himself is upsetting to some simple believers. Many of them believe that this is the preserve of specialists who are versed in the various Islamic sciences. One of Asma Barlas' fundamental theses is, therefore, that the Qur'an is addressed even to uneducated Bedouins in the desert. And so it cannot be monopolized by legal experts and scholars. Finally, there is, at least in Sunni Islam, no clerical caste.

She believes that one reason for the attacks on her statements and ideas, which should be self-evident in any case, is that they threaten certain male structures of authority in Muslim communities. Furthermore, many view her as a kind of advance submarine in a Western cultural invasion. In the end, equality is considered a Western value and for this reason, it is perceived as difficult to fight for within an Islamic framework. For still others she is merely an apologist.

Conversely, however, she hears from young Muslims, and especially from Muslim women, who are extremely happy to have read such thoughts in her works, and for whom whole new horizons have been opened up. For a younger generation of Muslim daughters of immigrants, who no longer identify with the conservative Islam of their parents, Asma Barlas serves as a significant role model with the central question that she tackles: How can I believe in the religion of my fathers and mothers, in which I still have some share, but in which the conservative interpretation handed down to me stands in glaring contradiction to those values I have made my own?

She frequently hears the reproach that as a woman she possesses no authority to speak about the Qur'an, she is also criticised for being a non-Arabic speaker. But she replies that, as a believer, she too may speak about her belief. The Qur'an is not addressed solely to men nor to Arabs alone. It is addressed to all who wish to hear it. And quite by virtue of being a woman she has to express herself: "As a woman I have much at stake here."[21] That she has very little chance of being acknowledged an authority is quite obvious to her, all the more so since states that derive benefit from patriarchal interpretations are not about to relinquish this.

Her critics don't come only from the ranks of conservatives. For example, the reformer-theologian Farid Esack writes that the Qur'an cannot be read as a gender-equitable text nor as a human rights document. One must consciously free it from its literal meaning whenever it runs against equity between the sexes. If he himself were forced to decide whether he would do violence to people or to the text, he would sooner do violence to the text. All religious writings that do not serve the goals of justice between the sexes must be subjected to a series of hermeneutical principles that range from contextualization through reinterpretation up to abrogation in order to arrive at another interpretation.

Barlas cuts in here. Of course, when Esack urges contextualization and reinterpretation, she can hardly oppose him. But she sees a problem in his methodology; when she considers societies such as the Saudi Arabian or the Afghan under the Taliban, where indeed there is no consensus as to what gender justice may be, who then determines this? This is why she believes it to be a better strategy to read the text anew with a just and non-patriarchal God in mind, rather than to seize upon the brutal tool of abrogation for which Esack argues.

---

21 Barlas, *Believing Women in Islam*, 209.

Another well-known critic of Islamic feminism is the reforming thinker Ebrahim Moosa. He states that one must resign oneself to hearing the Qur'an in its patriarchal voice. Generations of scholars have confirmed that the Qur'an propagates patriarchal norms. Barlas parries both objections. Generations of scholars could hardly have represented such an opinion since Muslim women and feminists only began some 20 years ago to employ the notion of patriarchy in their interpretation of the Qur'an. Moreover, for her part she deems it textual fundamentalism to say that a patriarchal voice speaks in the Qur'an. Furthermore, she also rejects Moosa's criticism that Islamic feminists cling to a few verses that confirm their views in order then to assert that the Qur'an proclaims gender equity as a norm. What Moosa here describes as hermeneutical acrobatics is what he himself practices when he interprets certain verses in a certain way and then proclaims that the Qur'an propagates patriarchy as a norm. Readings by women are slanted while readings by men are objective and authentic? Barlas does not accept that in the least.

7

'Abdolkarim Soroush: More than Ideology and State

A Revolutionary in the Name of Islam

'Abdolkarim Soroush, born in Tehran in 1945, is today one of the most important Muslim intellectuals in the world. In 2005 *Time* magazine called him one of the most significant intellectuals worldwide. He comes from a traditional religious family as Farajollah Hajj Husayn Dabbaq, his full name, shows. He was born on *'Ashura*, the day of the Shi'ite Imam Husayn's death. He was named Husayn for that reason. His pseudonym is composed of the names of two of his sons; Karim is one of the 99 "beautiful names of God". The prefix *'abd* means "slave" or "servant"; taken together, the name 'Abdolkarim means "servant of the Beneficent". Soroush is the name of the angel responsible for poetic inspiration.

Soroush received his education at the Alaviye School, an institution that was founded in the 1950s by pious Bazaris as an alternative to both the secular education offered by the state and to the traditional theological academies. Here students were to be educated in modern as well as traditional disciplines. The school quickly became one of the most significant teaching institutions in Iran. Many revolutionary intellectuals passed through it. The cornerstone of Soroush's later scientific research was put into place in this school. His physics teacher alerted him to the questioning that enjoyed a wide popularity at this time.

Eminent Iranian scholars, among whom was Mehdi Bazargan (1907–1995), later the Iranian president and minister (January to November 1979) and Allame Tabataba'i (1903–1981), one of the most esteemed philosophers among the clergy, sought to reconcile modern science with religion by showing that scientific knowledge did not stand in contradiction to the Qur'an and the traditions of the Prophet.

Soroush was dissatisfied with their solution. At the age of 17, while still at school, he took up the study of Islamic philosophy and the classical disciplines of *fiqh*, *usul al-fiqh* and *tafsir* with a cleric. Soroush studied the Qur'an commentaries of earlier scholars, such as al-Razi (1149–1209), al-Tabarsi (d. 1153) and Fayz Kashani (d. 1680) along with those of such moderns as Sayyid Qutb, Mahmud Taleqani (1914–1979) and Allame Tabataba'i. The diversity of their interpretations of the Qur'anic revelation fascinated him and he began looking for the reason for this diversity.

After earning his diploma Soroush began to study pharmacy in Tehran. His military service followed. When this was over he moved to the Iranian city of Bushehr where he worked for 15 months as director of the laboratory of nutrition and sanitary materials. Finally, for a brief period he worked in Tehran at a laboratory of drug control. In 1973 Soroush went to England. He registered there for a master's programme in the Faculty of Analytical Chemistry at the University of London, while at the same time studying philosophy and epistemology at the Faculty of History and Philosophy at Chelsea College. Soroush stayed for five and a half years in England, completing his studies with a doctorate in chemistry.

At this time in Iran the confrontations between the shah and segments of the populace were intensifying. Iranian students living in America and Europe, who had been in any case long since strongly politicized and quite often engaged in the opposition, were drawn increasingly into the revolutionary upheavals at home. Soroush became a member of a Muslim community which he used from that time on as a political platform. In the months leading up to the victory of the Islamic Revolution, their meeting place became a centre for active opposition where Iranian opponents of the shah who were living in England gathered. Alongside Soroush, then relatively obscure, such well-known personalities as Ayatollah Morteza Motahhari (1920–1979), a confidente of Khomeini, and Ayatollah Mohammad Hosein Beheshti (1925–1981) gave lectures there over the political situation in Iran.

Soroush's speeches from this time were published during the revolution in pamphlet form. In these he dealt with left-wing ideas and Marxist tendencies, devoting himself to so-called dialectical antagonism. His objective was to check the growing influence of left-wing Iranian groups, in particular that of the *Mojahedin-e khalq*, the "people's *mojahedin*". Soroush criticized them for having wrongly interpreted Marxism. They blended their wrong interpretation with Islam, seeking to develop an ideology out of this melange that would establish their own claims to power. Soroush countered the People's Mojahedin with arguments taken from Karl Popper's *The Open Society and its Enemies* and thereby became one of their harshest critics.

From Court Theologian to Dissident

Soroush returned to Iran in 1979 after the revolution and taught at the faculty of education at the University of Tehran. In addition, he often appeared as a theoretician of the Islamic Republic on television. Here, once again, he deconstructed left-wing ideology. His book *Satanic Ideology (Idiuloji-ye sheitani)* came out of these addresses and interviews. In 1981 he moved to an institute for the study of Western philosophy (the "Society for Philosophy") that had been founded during the shah's time. He also became a member of the newly established "Islamic Cultural Revolutionary Staff" which in 1984 was renamed the "Supreme Council for Cultural Revolution" and is better known under this name. This body was supposed to Islamicize the universities (which had been deliberately shut down for this purpose) and to do so by drafting new teaching schedules and expelling any teaching staff and students who did not behave in conformity with the system. Soroush is criticized by those in the opposition for his long-term membership in this council. In his own defence he says that by so acting he wanted to get the universities reopened. By an "Islamicized" university he had envisaged an increase in the branches of knowledge as intended by the Prophet.

After 1984 Soroush accepted no further political posts but devoted himself entirely to research. He taught at Tehran University, served as a guest-professor at various non-governmental universities and even taught in the theological academies in Qom during the 1980s. Alongside mysticism, Soroush also taught the philosophy of religion, epistemology, comparative philosophy and the philosophy of the empirical sciences. From 1988 to 1994 he also gave talks for the faithful in mosques. His sermons in Tehran's Imam Sadeq Mosque were especially well known. His lectures on mysticism were broadcast on television and because of his eloquence as a speaker they brought him fame and a high level of public recognition. With the same obvious assurance and authority with which he addressed his auditors in mosques or on television, at scholarly conferences he ranged over al-Ghazali and the theosophical philosopher Sadreddin Mohammad Shirazi (1571–1640). He always speaks in a highly literary style, enriched with quotations from the Qur'an or the poetry of Jalaleddin Rumi (1207–1273).

In his work Soroush has continually dealt with Western scientific and intellectual developments. As he himself puts it, he tries to rise to the challenge of Western thought. For Soroush it is imperative to receive scientific theories and philosophy and confront them. Unfortunately, traditional religious scholars would not share this position; they would dismiss everything Western a priori as unreligious. By contrast Soroush employed Western methods in his own investigations for he began to explore from an epistemological perspective how the diversity of Qur'anic interpretation came about. He discovered an explanation for the plurality of interpretative variants in the Western philosophy of science. In his own work Soroush's basic attitude towards the West is plainly on view: He argues for fruitful exchange.

His stay in London provided him with still further intellectual promptings. Since the Renaissance the West has emphasized the life of this world, whereas in his own mystically steeped culture, renunciation of the world is propounded. In oriental thinking earthly happiness loses all meaning alongside salvation in the next world. Confrontation with the European viewpoint, so opposed to his own, provided Soroush with a new impulse and he set about occupying himself with the function of

religion from that time on. He began to ponder modern man's expectations of his religion. A study of modern Christianity finally confirmed
his supposition that the interpretation of religion alters over time; otherwise how could a person today call himself a believing Christian?
At this point his interest in the relationship between reason, and the
modern concept of reason, was stirred; and this is the scholarly theme
to which he has devoted himself in the years thereafter.

Right after the death of Khomeini – the founder of the state – in
1989, Soroush began to direct criticisms at the Iranian system. This may
have been due to the admiration he felt for the leader of the revolution. He respected Khomeini because of his struggle against the shah's
regime and, furthermore, because he gave religion, ordinarily mute, a
voice and transformed it into revolutionary activism. Because he criticized the ruling clerical class and its claim on a monopoly of religious
knowledge, however, Soroush fell into disfavour in 1996. The media
attacked him initially, but then he became a target for physical assaults
and even death threats. The occasion was the publication of his article
entitled "Freedom and Clergy" (*Horriyat va-Ruhaniyat*). In it Soroush
criticized Shi'ite clerics for having lost their freedom and degenerated
into a social class: they allowed themselves to be supported by believers who were obliged to pay the so-called *khums,* meaning "a fifth". As
a class, the clergy automatically took on all the negative characteristics
that are ingrained in rigidly defined social groups:

> These benefits turn a group of people into a guild and a unified
> community and allow them to distinguish themselves from others.
> It is the notion of status that drives a distinction between one's own
> people and others; produces "Us" and "the Other"; keeps watch
> to safeguard the secrets of the guild; nurtures certain traditions and
> ways of behavior over others; creates stages and levels; of one we
> say we will protect this from external threats, holding it to be holy
> and important, a bearer of knowledge and the law's mysteries,
> gradually becoming a dominant tradition and ideology; chooses
> a few great personalities as practical and intellectual holy guides;
> follows set intellectual models; equates religion with the truth; and

regards any offence against the basic precepts of accepted thinking as a crime against religion.[1]

His argument may be summarized as follows. Through being financed, the clergy have become a class. As a class concerned about its own prerogatives, it claims a monopoly. The ossification of religious thinking can be attributed in turn to this monopoly. He writes:

A guild that conceives of itself as the preserver of a single way of interpreting religion and bases its political power and its material advantages upon that must be rejected.[2]

This was strong stuff in a theocracy. Following repeated threats Soroush, remained sporadically abroad and officially accepted only guest professorships. For some ten years now he has been living permanently in exile. He has carried out research and taught at such celebrated institutions as the Wissenschaftskolleg in Berlin, the Institute for the Study of Islam in the Modern World in Leiden, as well as at Harvard, Princeton, Chicago and Yale. In Spring 2008 he was a visiting fellow at the Berkeley Center for Religion, Peace and World Affairs in Georgetown.

Soroush has thus held distinguished guest professorships and fellowships that come with great esteem and recognition. Even so, his life is one in exile. Soroush needs Iran, however, as a nurturing soil, a field of resonance. He has published little since leaving Iran. That may be connected with the fact that he is first and foremost an orator. His addresses were published in Iran both in book form and in the journal *Kiyan*. Soroush possesses the gift of spontaneity in confronting his public to speak about burning issues from which he then arrives at fundamental matters and develops his themes. His ideas emerge out of what he observes. This is why he needs an Iranian public, people

---

1 Abdolkarim Soroush, "Saqf-e ma'ishat bar sotun-e shari'at" (Basing Livelihood on Religion), *Kiyan* 5 (1995), 3.
2 Soroush, "Saqf-e ma'ishat bar sotun-e shari'at" (Basing Livelihood on Religion), 25.

who are fired up about the same things as he is, as well as a close proximity to Iranian problems. Only in this setting do his immense learning and his critical and innovative spirit come into play. This does not happen in exile. This doesn't mean that in exile he does not also deliver remarkable lectures. Nevertheless, they clearly have less of an impact in Iran; they suffer from his distance from events in Iran that not even the internet can bridge. This loss of impact also affects the open letters through which he intervenes in discourse inside Iran. Many of these do find their way to Iran; for example, a letter from the year 2010 addressed to Iran's religious leaders under the title "They have turned Iran into a dismal country". But the effect that he has via foreign media or his homepage is not nearly as great as when he himself is in Iran. On the other hand, even thinkers living in Iran find most ways of communicating with their readers blocked since they cannot appear publicly and hardly any newspaper will dare to print their contributions.

Soroush is married and has five children four of whom also live abroad. His son has followed in Soroush's footsteps as a philosopher and so had to leave Iran. His son-in-law Hamed has been so badgered that he too together with Soroush's youngest daughter Kimia has gone into exile. Hamed was tortured both mentally and physically because he refused to say on television that his wife was a slut and his father-in-law a good-for-nothing, a stooge of foreign powers, and an enemy of religion. What Soroush wrote in reaction to this is his most personal settling of accounts with the Islamic Republic. For when he said to his son-in-law after this episode that God would never forgive his torturers, the latter replied, "There is no God. I swear by God, there is no God."[3] His torturers had robbed him, an innocent creature, of his faith, Soroush writes in his distress and he appends a conversation with God, "O Almighty God, I have learned from al-Ghazali that I may not curse anyone, not even Yazid. But now I most humbly beg your

---

3 'Abdolkarim Soroush, "There is no God, I swear to God, there is no God..."
February 2011. http://drsoroush.com/English/By_DrSoroush/E-CMB-20110200-
TherelsNoGod.html.

permission to be permitted to curse this pack of infidels of the Islamic Republic."[4]

Today Hamed and Kimia live in London. Both sons are in Canada; another daughter is in Washington. Only Soroush's wife together with another daughter still lives in Iran. She comes to visit him from time to time. She cannot live abroad, she says. She realized that when she lived in London with him during his student years. That moving from one university to another, from one fellowship to the next, is not any sort of life for him becomes clear when one sees him with children. He misses his family, especially his grandchildren: "This is not the right sort of life but what can you do? The situation in Iran will change at some point. Then we'll all go back."[5]

The Variability of Religious Knowledge

Soroush's goal is primarily to change political and social conditions in Iran. This is why he concerns himself with religion. The knowledge that he has gained from that can, however, be transferred to other countries and other circumstances, for the change that he wants is to be attained through an altered understanding of religion. He doesn't concern himself therefore with the specific doctrines and provisions of religion but proceeds in epistemological mode. From Karl Popper he adopted a theory of knowledge that contains two elements essential for his approach. First of all, it presupposes the possibility of an infinite increase in knowledge and the merely approximate nature of knowledge. Second, it proceeds from an understanding of development that may possibly be qualified as "wrong" on occasion but never as historically "worthless".

Soroush subsumes his main epistemological theory under the general heading *Kalam-e jadid*. The series in which his work appears with Sarat Publishers has this name. The same name is used for his lecture series in Qom and at various universities in Tehran. He himself renders this "modern theology" in English. He isn't much bothered by the fact that

---

4 Ibid.
5 'Abdolkarim Soroush, Interview with the author, 9/9/2012.

the Christian concept of theology is not transferable to the Islamic concept of *kalam*. In both instances, however, it is discourse about God that is involved. The variability of religious knowledge is the substance of Soroush's principal thesis. Because human knowledge is intrinsically variable – it is dependent on the time and the condition of the sciences – man's knowledge of his religion changes as well. With the passage of time ever new interpretations of belief emerge, according to Soroush; they are suited to the circumstances in which the interpreters live.

Soroush is not concerned with the question of whether religion can be an object of knowledge in any sense; his epistemological approach allows him to affirm that the traditional understanding of Islam does not have to be devalued. In any case, religion's absolute claim still remains intact. Soroush's central tenet is:

If there is a religious law in this absoluteness, then it is only with the lawgiver, namely, God.[6]

Soroush's epistemological starting point is thus the possibility of an infinite increase in knowledge together with the merely approximative nature of knowledge. In his view, man can never really know what God expects of him. He can never understand what God's law really is or what its purpose is, since God's intentions are fathomless. Each and every alleged knowledge about this is only suppositional, as Soroush says with reference to Popper. Epistemology has taught him that what human beings understand of the Qur'anic text can never be equated with the text and its real intentions. Humans can only know God's ultimate goal and this goal of religion cannot stand in any way in contradiction to human conceptions. Like every other text the Qur'an is an open one that invites interpretation. Human understanding of the Qur'an – like every other form of human knowledge – is dependent on the epoch and the status of the sciences. As time passes, Soroush says,

---

6 'Abdolkarim Soroush, *Qabz va bast-e te'orik-e shariat. Nazariye-ye takamol-e ma'refat-e dini (The Theoretical Contraction and Expansion of the Sharia – the Theory of the Development of Religious Knowledge)* (Tehran: Sirat, 1994), 305.

ever new interpretations of faith will result that are appropriate to the conditions in which the interpreters are living.

Soroush doesn't try to present this as a new insight. On the contrary, he says rather that the rigid interpretation of belief is a modern phenomenon. Previously one always started from some change in religious knowledge. In evidence for this he cites *ijtihad* and the diversity of Qur'anic interpretations. The various interpretations that the interpreters of religion arrived at demonstrate, moreover, that a fundamental distinction obtains between religion in itself and the human understanding of religion. Soroush thus distinguishes between religion and religious knowledge. True, religious knowledge is based on religion and yet, it does not correspond to it. This opens up space for new interpretations. That a separation can be made between religion and religious knowledge proves unequivocally that there are differences between them. As one example of this difference, he notes that religion, at least in believers' minds, contains no contradictions or antitheses. By contrast, religious knowledge, that is, religious scholars' understanding of religious texts, points up many contradictions, and this is just as true whether knowledge of law or theology or exegesis is at stake.

Soroush introduces yet another argument, namely, that religion is complete but that religious understanding, by contrast, is not. By the first statement he means that God has revealed everything necessary for the right guidance of humans in His scripture. Nothing is lacking in the religion, but religious knowledge is not perfect, in Soroush's opinion; were it so, then the branch of the sciences devoted to Qur'anic exegesis would have been done away with centuries before.

By this differentiation between religion and religious knowledge Soroush believes that he has found a formula for the separation of the mutable components of religion from the immutable, and the profane from the sacred, He takes these at the same time as points of departure for the revivification of religious thinking. He dismisses all other attempts at interpreting religion in a contemporary sense. This applies especially to the so-called "scientific interpretation" (*tafsir 'ilmi*). In his view, this has engendered nothing but contradictions. *Tafsir 'ilmi* hasn't solved believers' problems; instead, it has made them doubt the truth

of religion. The exegetes who devoted themselves to scientific interpretation wanted to show that modern scientific findings, such as, for
example, the discovery of microbes, or modern ideas, do not stand in
contradiction to the Qur'an, but in fact, can even be derived from it.
They are of the opinion that only now, since the technical and natural
sciences of the 19th and 20th centuries have become known in the
Islamic world, can the Qur'an be correctly understood.

Ayatollah Mahmud Taleqani is the leading proponent of the scientific
interpretation of the Qur'an in the Iranian context. In his Qur'an commentary *A Ray of Light from the Qur'an* (*Partovi az Qor'an*), Taleqani
puts forth a modernistic interpretation that strongly influenced left-
wing groups in particular. Taleqani regarded the Qur'an as a living
document, as a book of great relevance to contemporary problems
and, in this way, he found present-day formulations, such as those
dealing with social justice, already articulated in the Qur'an.

Soroush notes positively that Taleqani perceived how claims might
be made for religion with respect to science and current problems. He
too wanted to reconcile religion and modernity. Nevertheless, Soroush
criticizes his conclusion and considers his approach wrong. For him,
it cannot be proved that the findings of modern science have already
been given in the Qur'an; the discovery of microbes cannot be logically
inferred from the Qur'an. But for Soroush, his method demonstrates
that Taleqani too introduced forms of knowledge into his interpretation
that he had acquired from outside the religious sciences. He had interpreted the Qur'an with the aid of knowledge drawn from politics and
social theory. Political theory taught him that social justice is a value.
Taleqani then made such knowledge the basis of his Qur'anic exegesis.
This marked feature of *tafsir 'ilmi* confirms for Soroush his theory of the
natural exchange of the sciences.

Soroush bases this view on the epistemological theory that proceeds from a continuous dialogue between different human fields of
knowledge. The understanding of a theologian, an exegete and a legal
scholar of both the Qur'an and the sunna changes inevitably when
his other, extra-religious knowledge changes. Because all understanding of religion is based on knowledge that lies outside of it, religious

understanding too is in flux. With this argument Soroush explains the diversity of Qur'anic interpretations by renowned scholars, a diversity that was once the leaping-off point for his own scholarly endeavors.

To be sure, Soroush's theory relativizes the knowledge of the ruling powers and that makes it dangerous to Iran's religious establishment. Because a human being cannot really comprehend the exact will of God, different views about religion must be tolerated and ideas that have not stood the test of time should be abandoned, regardless of who formulated them. Soroush undermines the authority of the *vali-ye faqih* (the highest legal scholar), the supreme religious and political authority in Iran and his demand for absolute obedience, when he argues that even his religious knowledge is only a human, and therefore fallible, interpretation of religion. He explicitly reproaches the *vali-ye faqih* Ali Khamenei (b. 1939) for claiming – contrary to law – to have a monopoly on religious interpretation.

For Soroush there can be no univocal religious knowledge, nor any monopoly on interpretation, because the Qur'an, like every text, is open and invites interpretation. For the same reason, it can also be interpreted, in his opinion, so as not to stand in contradiction to human rights and democracy. This position was bound to cause problems for him in Iran where discussion always had to be in conformity with the opinion of Khomeini, the founder of the state, according to whose image of man and God only one being – God – had rights. By contrast, man has no rights; he has nothing but obligations to God. In the end, God or His representative on earth, the *vali-ye faqih*, can accord rights to man, but because these are not intrinsic, God can take them away from him if He, or his representative on earth, so wishes. For Khomeini, moreover, each person must subordinate himself to the general good, the good of the *umma*, and so has no individual right to freedom vis-a-vis the state. These arguments correspond to Khamenei's own position. Against Western claims for the universality of human rights it is asserted that Muslims, because of historical and social developments within their own cultural sphere, have decided to observe God's rights rather than human rights.

Soroush has left the cultural relativism of the ruling clerics quite far behind, nor does the question of a possible agreement between Islam and human rights or the idea of the origin of human rights in Islam – as Muslim apologists formulate it – interest him either. Human rights are for him simply a dictate of human reason. Hence, they cannot stand in opposition to religion, given that God's will cannot be contrary to reason. The fact that human rights emerged within a framework outside of religion does not stop Soroush from regarding their realization in an Islamic system as possible and indeed, imperative. God's right would be safeguarded and the result would be a complete concord of human and religious values. Soroush thus assumes a position usually taken only by secularists; for he proceeds from the conviction that a human being also possesses rights beyond religion, and fundamentally so, simply by virtue of being human. In other respects, however, he bases his position on religious grounds.

A consequence of his argument is that an entire series of laws that the Islamic Republic recognizes must no longer be applied; for example, the *hadd* penalties, the so-called transgressive punishments, among which are stoning and the amputation of limbs. For Soroush it isn't requisite to follow all Islamic laws in detail. He justifies this by distinguishing between values of the first and second order. The second-order values relate solely to the minute prescriptions of law – e.g., prescriptions as to clothing – which differ from one religion to the next. But the different religions, not to mention human reason, are completely unanimous on the significance of first-order values, including, for example, justice and human dignity.

A Religious and Democratic Government

Proceeding from these premises Soroush attempts to develop a political system that would be both Islamic and democratic and thereby arrives at his second apposite notion, that of a religious and democratic government. Just because his faith means so much to him – and drawing on his own experiences with Islamism as it actually exists – he comes to the conclusion that religion and state must be separated. As he observes, more and more people are turning away from Islam because of abuse of power, censorship, lack of freedom, corruption and nepotism. It is for this reason that Soroush supports democracy. It protects religion, i.e., God's rights, from all types of regime; through democracy religion is protected from misuse by would-be men of God for their own purposes, but which run counter to the Creator's will. If human rights are respected, religion cannot be misused. In this respect, Soroush's ideal government is not only democratic but religious as well. Accordingly, he no longer dwells on interpretation of individual Qur'anic passages but instead turns his attention to the Creator's ultimate will. In this respect, in particular, he stands apart from those thinkers who set out to show how tolerantly Islam has behaved in its history towards other religions. According to their approach, attacks on apostates are glossed over and presented as rare or politically motivated. These interpretations are irrelevant to Soroush's argument since he tries to accommodate his understanding of religion with the modern concept of human rights, and not vice-versa. In this regard he is far ahead of Islamist thinkers who want to confer an Islamic significance, based on quotations from Qur'an and sunna, on universally valid human rights, and so can be considered a post-Islamist thinker. For Soroush, human rights are not religious but they are acceptable to every religious person, and necessarily so.

He wants an Islam with a human face and considers the *velayat-e faqih* (the rule of the supreme legal expert), the Iranian system of government, as having failed. As a "government by Islamic law" (*hokumat-e feqhi*), it has been incapable of solving society's problems. That religion first and foremost is meant for the life to come, "for ordering this life and otherworldly bliss", certainly doesn't mean that "faith here and now in this life is of no use", but nor does it mean that "religion from the very beginning was sent down for this world and for life in this world."[7] Because of his conviction that the answers to all questions cannot be found in religion Soroush stands far removed from the universalism of fundamentalist groups whose political strategy comes down to "Islam is the solution" (*al-islam huwa al-hall*).

---

7 'Abdolkarim Soroush, "Khadamat va-hasanat-e din" (Function and Benefits of Religion), *Kiyan* 5, (1995), 27, 12.

The failure of the *velayat-e faqih*, in Soroush's opinion, clinches the argument for democracy as an alternative. As a form of government that goes hand in hand with a liberal economic system it could even, over the long term, be the best way to bring society to piety since "a hungry belly knows no religion."[8] In Soroush's ideal state satisfying people's material needs also belongs among the religious duties of government. At that point, the religious-democratic government will deserve its name: "religious" because it gives believers the possibility of a devout life, as well as "democratic" in its manner of exercising power.

It is Soroush's view that a "religious-democratic government" (*hokumat-e din*) is more religious than a "government of Islamic law" (*hokumat-e feqhi*). The *hokumat-e fiqhi* merely enacts the prescriptions of the sharia within society. He doubts that a society that resorts to the sharia is truly religious according to the Creator's intention. No "religious society" is constructed by recourse to the sharia but only a society "that lives by Islamic law". From mere outward appearances it isn't possible to infer any actual rootedness of the community in faith. Christians too might end up introducing Islamic law; they might take a fancy to veiling, could prohibit alcohol and come to believe that cutting off hands is a reasonable expedient against stealing. Hence, what is more important for Soroush than the application of Islamic law is that a pious motive underlie religious activity. But this piety cannot be compelled:

> Hypocrisy and dissimulation are the greater sins, not drinking alcohol and gambling. But the perspective of the legal scholars (*binesh-e feqhi*) places more importance on outward activity than on the promptings of the heart. The difference between the two approaches is evident when the two types of government begin their work. When the scholarly-juristic perspective begins to operate, the government's first endeavor is to give the society a countenance that conforms to the religious law. It will start to employ the *hadd-* punishments, to collect blood-money, to insist on veiling, etc.

---

8 Soroush, "Khadamat va-hasanat-e din" (Function and Benefits of Religion), 12.

But the perspective that relies on faith (*binesh-e imani*) does not
start from this point but saves these matters [that is, introduction
of Islamic law (author's note)] for later and makes people devout
through wisdom, sermons and discussions.[9]

For Soroush, therefore, the religious soul of the government is more
important and it proves itself insofar as it realizes God's will. A society
is not religious just because it employs religious law but because the
people within it freely acknowledge their belief. Accordingly, his ideal
is a religious state in which a spirit of faith prevails, not as a legislative
or political tribunal but rather as the spirit and conscience of society.
It follows logically from this that a religious government will also
have no specific, fixed form but will take on different configurations in
every age. Soroush thus maintains that the form of government is not
specifically granted by God and that every government that realizes
the goals of religion is itself religious. As a result there is no formal difference between his religious-democratic government and any current
democratic government.

In fact it shouldn't be expected that a religious government will
be distinct in nature from a non-religious one. And it just isn't the
case that in this world rational people walk on their two legs while
religious people do so on their heads. What is so terrible about the
fact that people in other societies have accepted the same methods
in dealing with the question of government as we have hit upon in
our definition of a religious government?[10]

Even so, despite this almost complete accord there is a small but
decisive difference. Soroush's democratic state is not indifferent with
respect to religion but rather, has a divine purpose. To this extent the

---

9 'Abdolkarim Soroush, "Tahlil-e mafhum-e hokumat-e dini" (Analysis of the Term
"religious rule"), *Kiyan* 6 (1996), 32, 3.
10 Soroush, "Tahlil-e mafhum-e hokumat-e dini" (Analysis of the Term "religious
rule"), 11.

religious-democratic state envisages quite a different goal than the merely democratic one; it is still incumbent on it to bring about a perfect society. To be sure, this should occur within a free and democratic order, even if not within a liberal democracy that "with its dubious support for immoral social behavior is not in tune with Muslim sensibilities", as Soroush, who was chosen in 2004 by the Washington Center for the Study of Islam and Democracy as the "Muslim Democrat of the Year", formulates it.[11]

Nevertheless, freedom is a necessary prerequisite in his utopian Islamic state, and one that is pleasing to God, thereby providing an argument for the superiority of a democratic order. Genuine religiosity can exist only in a democratic society since faith is founded on freedom of the will; a coerced religiosity runs counter to the Creator's intention. The prophets too understood their mission in this way:

> The prophets came to win over people's hearts with the spell of
> their words and not to rule over their bodies.[12]

Soroush takes freedom as a value in itself. For this reason it should not be sacrificed for the sake of the diffusion and protection of Qur'anic truth.

> Humanity has made more mistakes and suffered more harm in an
> order that it wanted to cram violently with the truth than in an order
> in which it might even make mistakes.[13]

Freedom is in any case more important than compliance with Islamic regulations:

---

11 Abdolkarim Soroush, (Religion and Democracy: Iranian Experience, Mashhad and Tehran, 1–2 December 2004). http://csidonline.org/images/stories/ pdfiles/56900_eng_iran%5B1%5D.pdf.

12 'Abdolkarim Soroush, (Lecture, London, November 17, 1996).

13 'Abdolkarim Soroush, "'Aql va-azadi" (Reason and Freedom), *Kiyan* 1 (1992), 5, 15.

Free societies, whether they are religious or not, are godly (*elahi*) [i.e., in accord with God's will] and human (*ensani*); in totalitarian societies, by contrast, neither humanity nor divinity remains.[14]

Against the Ideologization of Religion

Another milestone occurred at the beginning of the 1990s when he broke with the so-called ideologization of religion for which 'Ali Shariati, the most important ideologue of the 1978–79 revolution, was particularly responsible in Iran. Soroush does not deny that at the time this was utterly necessary. He stresses Shariati's significance, even considering himself to stand in his tradition and repeatedly pays tribute to his achievements in strengthening religious thought. Shariati helped Islam discover a new zest for action and rejuvenated it, and this was imperative for the revolution.

But Soroush, who has suffered under this conceptual worldview, today states quite openly that he would like to "de-ideologize" the religion. His main argument for this is that religion is not "ideologizable" because of its diverse characteristics. Religion is more, is fuller, is more capacious than an ideology and when it is subjected to ideology, it is inevitably diminished and fixed within a single interpretation. Soroush lists the following as the evils of ideology:

1. An ideology is used as a weapon, true to Lenin's words: revolutionary action demands a revolutionary theory.
2. An ideology must be succinctly, vividly and precisely formulated.
3. From these two points it follows that a choice of rules must be made so that the ideology can be more easily demarcated from other ways of thinking and its representatives more easily distinguished from others.
4. Ideology is forged with regard to an enemy. For this reason ideologies are always time-bound and in need of an image of the enemy.

---

14 Soroush, "'Aql va-azadi" (Reason and Freedom), 24.

5. For an ideology the launch of a movement is paramount, not the discovery of truth.

6. Ideology possesses no theory applicable for a constructive phase, but only for the revolutionary phase and its battles.

7. Ideology requires ideologues, i.e., a leader or a designated class since somebody has to formulate the ideology.

8. Ideologues speak of ideology as if speaking of their beloved, i.e., in the loftiest tones, and as a result are blind to every defect.[15]

One of the arguments that Soroush adduces to show that Islam is not "ideologizable" runs as follows: the Qur'an is a profound book; it has many meanings. An ideology is the exact opposite of that; it is simple. "This is why religion was not sent down as ideology."[16] Moreover, he understands religion as a mystery, as a phenomenon that arouses amazement in a positive sense. And so it stands in opposition to the precision that an ideology requires. All the mysterious paths of interpretation are reduced to one if Islam is turned into ideology: "It is as though a poem were to be translated into prose."[17] In addition, ideology is the garb of a particular society, a remedy for a specific sick person, and because of this its validity is automatically delimited in time. But for religions these characteristics do not apply: religions are eternal.

Soroush further criticizes ideological societies for their readiness to use force. Holding that the end justifies the means, they regard the furtherance of their goals by means of violence as legitimate. Moreover, everything is interpreted from their perspective and placed at the service of their own ideology. Such a society is built on hatred. So much love is lavished on the ideology that those who think otherwise must be hated unremittingly. A variety of opinions isn't possible; to every

---

15 'Abdolkarim Soroush, "Farbehtar az Idiuloji" (Richer than Ideology), *Kiyan* 3 (1993), 14, 4–7.

16 Soroush, "Farbehtar az Idiuloji" (Richer than Ideology), 10.

17 Ibid.

question there is a firm fixed answer based on a claim to exclusivity that brooks no opposition and no one alongside it – and especially not reason. "To open the door to ideology is to lock the door on thought."[18] The findings of science, among other things, cannot be trusted in an ideological society since even these must be put into the service of ideology and serve as propaganda. As a logical conclusion of this process it turns out that it is not the law but rather human beings – grossly elevated and credited with superhuman capabilities – who are in charge.

According to Soroush ideological societies permit no questions about their meaning and goals. Ideologies proceed on the assumption that human beings are there for its sake whereas religions are there for the sake of human beings.

> Is it right then that ideology take precedence over humans and
> that they cannot overtake it? Or that people be trampled under its
> feet and end up poor, humiliated, helpless and enslaved? Can any
> ideology be so sacrosanct that no analysis and no investigation ever
> reaches it?[19]

A religion turns into an ideology, in Soroush's view, when a single interpretation is declared to be the official one and is represented by a particular class as the only true way of reading. At that moment religion automatically takes on all the weaknesses of an ideology. The religion that has been made ideological then usurps the place of religion but then, on the other hand, becomes human through being made ideological. Soroush criticizes Shariati explicitly as being responsible for this. Thanks to his efforts to make Islam an ideology, a class of official interpreters of ideology came into being. Inevitably they had all the failings that Shariati had wanted to avoid. Through his book *Islamic Community and Imamate* (*Ummat va-Emanat*) Shariati smoothed the path for the clergy; he had to have been aware of the danger that the clergy would immediately claim the role of ideologues for themselves.

---

18 Soroush, "Farbehtar az Idiuloji" (Richer than Ideology), 14.
19 Soroush, "Farbehtar az Idiuloji" (Richer than Ideology), 16.

The religious society that Soroush promulgates is, in his opinion, the complete opposite of that.

But the ideal religious society, in which religion is the judge, in no way resembles such an ideological society. In the ideological society the government ideologizes society while in a religious society the government makes society religious. In an ideological society an official interpretation of the ideology prevails but in a religious society there are various interpretations and no official interpretation of religion. In an ideological society the ideology is given over to the ideologues. In a religious society, by contrast, religion's significance (*amr-e din*) is too great to be transferred solely to the official interpreters. In a religious society there is no single person and no single legal opinion that cannot be questioned, and no understanding of religion will be taken as the last and the best. Religion takes on the coloration of different societies but one fixed coloration of religion does not result therefrom.[20]

In the belief that only a specific part of religion, namely, the sharia, can be turned into ideology, he attempts by way of mysticism to rescue religion from an ossified ideology that benefits only those in power. For Islam is not made up only of sharia but also of *haqiqat*, "truths", and *tariqat*, "ways of mysticism, gnosis, theosophy". Both of these, moreover, are impervious to ideology. Since, in his view, an ideological religion displays only the negative face of religion, mystical Islam becomes for Soroush, the post-Islamist, the counterpoint to juristic Islam.

Whose Qur'an?

In 2007 Soroush was accused of having abandoned his faith. This came about because of an interview that he granted a Dutch journal in which the English translation of one of his books that had appeared in Iran in 1999 under the title *The Expansion of the Prophetic Experience* (*Bast-e*

---

20 Soroush, "Farbehtar az Idiuloji" (Richer than Ideology), 20.

Tajrobe-ye Nabavi) was announced. In Iran there were harsh reactions, which must have been prompted by the title that headed the interview: "The Word of Muhammad". Soroush had said in the suspect interview:

> But the Prophet is also in another way the creator of revelation. What he receives from God is the content of revelation. But this content cannot just be offered to people for it surpasses their understanding and even goes beyond words. It is amorphous. The Prophet's task consists in giving form to the formless in order to make it accessible. Like a poet the Prophet transfers inspiration into the language that he knows, into the style that he has mastered and into the images and knowledge that he possesses.[21]

In particular, Soroush clearly formulates the consequences that this important role which the Prophet played had in the formation of the text:

> A human perspective on the Qur'an makes it possible to distinguish between the essential and the accidental aspects of the religion. Certain parts of the religion are historical and culturally determined and are no longer relevant today. That is the case, for example, with the corporal punishments prescribed in the Qur'an. If the Prophet had lived in another milieu, these punishments presumably would not have formed part of his message.[22]

The book, which had appeared in Persian in 1999, hadn't led to any comparable uproar. The reason for this – apart from the title of the interview – must have been that in 2007–8, social and political conditions in Iran had become far more restrictive. It must have lain as well in the fact that Soroush's position in the interview, widely disseminated through the Iranian-registered homepage *Aftab*-News (http://aftabnews.ir/), found a broad readership – including, among others,

---

21 'Abdolkarim Soroush, "The Word of Muhammad," Interview with Michel Hoebink, *Zem-Zem* (2007). URL: http://www.zemzem.org/zemzem/?q=node/21
22 Ibid.

the Ayatollah Ja'far Sobhani of Qom who learned of the interview on *Aftab*-News on 3/2/2008 and was very disturbed. Furthermore, Soroush expressed his opinion in the interview far more clearly than he had in the corresponding article. This applies especially with respect to the aforementioned consequences of his statements. In the essay he expresses himself in a more oblique and coded manner.

In *The Expansion of the Prophetic Experience* Soroush – quite like Rahman and Shabestari – rejects the traditional Islamic conception according to which the Prophet Muhammad is viewed as a messenger who received revelation from God and proclaimed it with the same content and in the same words. For Soroush this view degrades the Prophet's personality, turning him into an involuntary instrument of God. He holds the view, by contrast, that Muhammad accepted the revelation, assimilated it and then proclaimed it in his own words. This is why he was specifically chosen and summoned by God. According to Soroush, who goes into far more detail in his explanations than Rahman, we are indebted to Ibn Khaldun, the celebrated fourteenth century Arab historian, for some of the most interesting observations about the nature of revelation and the prophetic experience. The latter writes that the Prophet grew gradually better and better able to endure the revelation; this is why the Meccan suras are short while the Medinan ones are longer.

Quite in the spirit of Ibn Khaldun, Soroush goes on to argue that the message of revelation changes in relation to its context. In Mecca the Prophet wanted to shake people up, to alarm them and rouse them. Hence he used vivid sermons that affected them strongly and he was forced to set out clear positions. In Medina, however, it was a matter of advancing the mission and consolidating its teachings. Legislation was now needed, as well as extensive explanation and dialogue with the populace. Since the Prophet was now better able to sustain the revelations and had gained prophetic experience, the form and the content of the message changed as well.

The longer an experience lasts, Soroush argues, the more complete it becomes. A poet becomes an ever better poet the more he composes poetry. An orator becomes an ever better orator the more he speaks. This holds true for every experience although the essence of what is experienced does not change, the truth of the experience remains always the same, and its validity is not called into question. The Prophet's innermost experience progressed through this sort of expansion and development. With every day he grew more and more accustomed to his position, his mission and his goals. He became firmer and more direct in fulfilling his duties, better prepared to realize his goals, more successful in his work and more self-confident about his success.

According to Soroush, the Prophet's personality was his capital; it was at once the receptive vessel as well as the generator, both the subject and the object, of his religious experience of the revelation. The more his personality developed, the more his experience did also, so that revelation followed him and no longer he the revelation. In the language of the mystics, as a result of his closeness to God, the Prophet attained a level that brought God to dwell within his sight. It follows from this for Soroush that the Prophet's reactions and responses would have become even more comprehensive had he lived longer. In his view the Qur'an could have become even more capacious; and he tries to clarify this with several questions. If Aisha had not been accused of adultery, would we have had the sura al-Nur? If there had been no war between tribes, would the sura al-Ahzab have come into being? If Abu Lahab had not existed or if his wife had not been hostile towards the Prophet, would there be a sura al-Masad? These were all historical events, of greater or lesser importance, traces of which remain in the Qur'an.

Soroush compares this with the ways in which students influence their teacher. They pose a question here, they ask for an explanation there. All of these questions and explanations get written into the religion. This is precisely what Soroush means when he says that religion is human, historical and in progress. The upshot is that Islam was born within the context of these interactions and involvements. The Prophet did not have a book that was sealed which he then offered to people. He didn't say to them, "Look what you can make of this and act accordingly." The Qur'an, Soroush argues, was revealed progressively. While the spirit of the message was still intact, it took shape in reaction to events. The relationship of the Prophet to his people has to be envisaged as a dialogue. He said something and he heard something. Then he told them what he heard. In other words, everyday events played a role in the genesis of the religion; had something else occurred, Islam would have had a different genesis – so Soroush, much like Rahman, believes.

As further proof of his thesis that its milieu formed the Qur'an's contents, Soroush notes that the Qur'an treats only of matters that occurred in Mecca and Arabia during the Prophet's time. For example, the Iranian prophet Zoroaster goes unmentioned because he was unknown, and yet, the ethnic group that went by the name of the Magi, who lived in Iran at this time and had contact with the Arabs, is mentioned once or twice. All the prophets mentioned in the Qur'an were Israelite prophets of whom the Arabs had heard and with whose names they were more or less familiar. Soroush explains that just as the Arabic language – the language spoken in the Prophet's milieu – finds expression in the Qur'an, so too do the beliefs and viewpoints of his immediate surroundings find expression there as well.

He proceeds quite critically with regard to the historical Muhammad. Despite his chosen status, the Prophet was still a man and so subject to all the limitations that the time in which he lived and the place in which he acted imposed upon him. What made Muhammad an annunciator was that he was to convey a revelation to human beings that lay beyond the human ability to comprehend. He had to make the ungraspable graspable, the infinite and inconceivable conceivable, to humans. He had to be able to accomplish this mission necessarily in his own language and through his own understanding which were, however, both historically conditioned and hampered by shortcomings.

This state-of-affairs also explains the errors and contradictions that occur in the Qur'an, according to Soroush. The educational level of the Prophet as well as the extent of his knowledge can also be deduced from the Qur'an. While errors can also occur here, the Qur'an itself contains pronouncements which must be free of error since they relate to the fundamentals of the faith and are meant for eternity. Here Soroush includes the pronouncements on God's attributes, on life after death or on the rules for prayer. These portions of the Qur'an are identical with God's word. Nevertheless, errors and contradictions are on display in the statements, directives and prescriptions that concern historical events, other religions or especially, human society and day-to-day earthly life. Passages of this type are expressive of the cultural and mental stage of development at the time. Since they have been shown to be wrong and outmoded, they should be supplanted by modern knowledge.

While many see in this epistemological turn a possibility for the introduction of an *aggiornamento* within Islam, Soroush's critics accuse him of having abandoned his religion at last. This is how Ayatollah Ja'far Sobhani, who has grappled most intensively with Soroush's theses and composed several responses to it, sees the matter. Even the reforming cleric Mohsen Kadivar who, unlike Sobhani, is not under suspicion of parroting the opinions of Iran's clerical establishment, regards Soroush's effort critically. Kadivar, who largely shares Sorough's opinion in his political criticism, fears that Soroush's approach to the Qur'an will lead to the "dissolution of religious new-thinking" (*enhelal-e nouandishi-ye dini*), and that not much will remain of religion if Soroush's approach is thought through to its conclusion. The moderate Grand Ayatollah Hosein 'Ali Montazeri (1922–2009) has also raised questions on this score.

On the other hand, Soroush's proposals about what God's word actually is and about how revelation is to be conceived, has led to renewed questioning in Iran's religious discourse where it has been taken up and discussed. Through Soroush's initiative too, there has been for the first time in Iranian discourse some search for an answer to this complex and as yet unanswered question. So, Ayatollah Ja'far Sobhani, for one example, reacts to Soroush in earnest and quite unpolemically. Sobhani believes that Soroush entangles himself in contradictions. On the one hand, he claims that Muhammad was in a position directly to transmit the revelation insofar as it dealt with life after death, or God's attributes, and to express it as God communicated it. On the other hand, however, he states that because of the historically conditioned state of his knowledge Muhammad fell into error and contradiction in those parts that deal with earthly life. How is it that he could accomplish the one but not the other? This is a counter-argument that is at least worthy of consideration. In addition, Sobhani points out numerous Qur'anic passages that explicitly stress that the Qur'an is God's word and that Muhammad is the bearer of revelation. Sobhani thus argues on the basis of the Qur'an's own content. In fact in numerous passages of the Qur'an it is stated that it is God's word. The only question is whether Soroush has ever disputed that.

As the argument heated up, Soroush gave an interview in the Iranian periodical *Kargozaran* in February 2008 in which he was asked directly about all this:

Question: Several newspapers and websites say that Soroush has officially denied that the Qur'an was revealed by God and has said that it is the earthly word of Muhammad. Is that true?

Reply: Maybe you're joking or have political motives, God forbid! I hope your intentions are good and that you have simply misunderstood the matter. In the end no one who is familiar with God's universal lordship and with the closeness of the Messenger of God to HIM – and who knows of his experience of union with HIM – would speak in such an heretical way. God's emissaries are so close to God and they lose themselves so utterly in God that their word is the same as God's word, and their commandments and prohibitions and their preferences and aversions are God's commandments and prohibitions as well as His preferences and aversions. The beloved Prophet of Islam was a human being and he conceded that he was a human being and was aware of that. And yet, this human essence had assumed such a divine coloration and quality at the same time...that everything that he said was simultaneously worldly and godly; these two things were not separable one from the other.[23]

---

23 'Abdolkarim Soroush, *Expansion of Prophetic Experience: Essays on Historicity, Contingency and Plurality in Religion* (Leiden: Brill, 2009), 289.

The Qur'an is thus both divine and human at once for Soroush, and indeed, in a classification that can be termed mystical. Here in the West Soroush has become known as a political philosopher, but in Iran he also counts as one of the most important literary critics, and as a specialist in Persian mysticism. Furthermore, he is himself recognized as a poet. This is the background from which he argues when he compares the Prophet Muhammad's inspiration with that of a poet and elaborates his mystical approach to revelation. Certainly this is no easy approach. But Soroush has always argued that he stands in a more complicated relationship with religion than is easily understood by a conventional believer.

8

Mohammad Mojtahed Shabestari: The Prophet Reads the World

Tradition and the Break with it

Of the notion that a reform of Islamic thinking is, by and large, not a matter for clerics, Mohammad Mojtahed Shabestari may stand as a living counter-proof. In addition, Shabestari proves that to think about Islam in a new way doesn't invariably lead to exile. Shabestari is a Shi'ite cleric who holds the rank of *hojjat al-Islam* "authority on Islam". Thus, he stands in the clerical hierarchy just one step below an Aya-tollah. Shabestari was born in 1936 in comfortable circumstances in the vicinity of Tabriz, that is, in the Iranian part of Azerbaijan. His father and grandfather were also clerics. He is proud of his designation "Shabestari", someone who comes from Shabestar, since many associate his native town with the popular poet Mirza 'Ali Mo'ez Shabestari (1873–1934) who fought against religious fanaticism.

At the age of five he went to Tabriz where he attended the state primary school and the state gymnasium in an environment that was quite open. The inhabitants of the city had the reputation, which they still enjoy, of being liberal nationalists; moreover, Tabriz was at the centre of the constitutional movement from 1905 until 1911. There, a strong middle class composed of traders, clerics and intellectuals had developed which nurtured contacts with Istanbul, Baku and Europe.

At the age of 14 Shabestari began a study of the Islamic sciences in

Qom that would last for 18 years. His most important teacher was the philosopher and Qur'anic scholar Mohammad Hosein Tabataba'i. As the author of the most significant twentieth-century Shi'ite Qur'an commentary, the *Scales of Qur'anic Exegesis (Tafsir al-Mizan)*, Tabataba'i was one of the greatest Shi'ite authorities of the age. His method consisted in interpreting the Qur'an through the Qur'an itself. For him, moreover, any Qur'anic interpretation had to be completely reconcilable with modern reason.

Still, Shabestari did not study only with Iran's greatest exegete and philosopher of those years. At the beginning of the 1960s he was also roused by the incendiary political speeches of the Ayatollah Khomeini. The man who would later become the founder of the state struck him, like many clerics of his generation, as a bearer of hope and the embodiment of a revolutionary Islam. In this he was the complete opposite of the man who was Shabestari's third important teacher, Kazem Shariatmadari (1905–1986). Shariatmadari later became one of Khomeini's most telling adversaries; his public humiliation by Khomeini was one of the catalysts for Shabestari's estrangement from the regime of the Islamic Republic. As a teacher, Shariatmadari stood out especially because of his interest in foreign languages and Western culture in general. In this, Shariatmadari differed markedly from most of the scholars of Qom who were completely against any new form of knowledge; for everything that didn't belong within the narrow circle of their competence they had nothing but scorn. Shariatmadari by contrast read Jean de La Fontaine (1621–1695) in Persian translation as well as the *History of Western Philosophy* by Mohammad 'Ali Foroughi (1877–1943). This influence marked Shabestari. Inspired by Shariatmadari, Shabestari also gave himself over to topics in his student years that did not belong within the traditional curriculum, such as comparative religion. He also learned English.

In 1959 he married Robab with whom he lives till today in what he calls a mixture of a "traditional and a modern marriage". He won't explain in further detail what that means exactly. "That's enough as a statement", he declares.[1] He got to know his wife's family in Qom. She

---

1 Mohammad Shabestari, Interview with the author, 2/11/2009.

hails from Arak in central Iran; his wife is thus not an Azerbaijani. For this reason, Persian is spoken at home. The children too do not speak Azeri. "Today I have few family connections with Azerbaijan. And yes, I have been Persianified", he says, alluding to his wife.

Shabestari had four children; one daughter died at the age of 18 in an automobile accident. Faride, the other daughter, is a dermatologist, his son Mohammad Kazem a pediatrician. The fourth child of this marriage, Mohammad Reza, is an engineer. *Doktor ya mohandes*, "doctor or engineer". That these two professions –which according to an old Iranian cliché, still current today, count as the two professions most worth striving for – are represented so exclusively even in the family of a cleric is not without a certain irony; nevertheless, it is one of intellectual status that is customarily passed on from one generation to the next. That he hasn't pressed his sons to become clerics is not the only tradition with which Shabestari has broken.

As a Cleric in Hamburg

In 1968 Shabestari accepted an offer to direct the Islamic Centre in Hamburg. With the support of Iranian businessmen, who from 1953 on had financed the building of a mosque in the Außenalster, the Imam Ali Mosque, the fourth-oldest German mosque, came into being. Since then, a cleric sent from the city of Qom, the centre of Iranian spirituality, had always administered it. Shabestari came after Mohammad Beheshti, who would later play an important role in the Islamic Revolution, and before Mohammad Khatami (b. 1943), later president of the State and the third cleric who administered this mosque.

Like many of his contemporaries Shabestari too wanted to undertake missionary activity and move Islam out of the narrow circle of the theological academies, so when the opportunity came at the right time for him he went with his family to Hamburg and stayed there for nine years. But it wasn't easy, as he tells it, to live as a Muslim in the 1960s in the Hanseatic city. His wife and his daughter, who wore the headscarf, were stared at on the street and had abusive words hurled after them: "Compared to those days the city of Hamburg has changed greatly for the better. Today it is much more open."[2] Despite his negative experiences, Shabestari today says that, in retrospect, the years in Hamburg were the best of his life. Now he enjoys coming to Germany for two or three weeks a year; he stocks up on new literature and meets old friends in Hamburg. To be sure, he can't extend his stay longer because he gets depressed; he becomes homesick for Iran, he says, even though he feels that Germany is his second homeland.

> At the beginning of my stay I did find the country and its achievements quite interesting but since I didn't yet know the language I couldn't form any connection with the world around me and this pained me very much. Two or three years later, after I had learned the language and could form relations with the people and the world around me, I was very impressed by the order and discipline that I observed. And I was glad that finally I could study Christian and Western culture and literature.[3]

Of course, by "literature", belles-lettres is not meant. Neither then nor now does Shabestari concern himself with that, but he does like classical music: Mozart, Beethoven, Bach. In addition, Shabestari particularly liked the forests in Germany; he enjoyed strolling and, as a fan of German coffee, he especially loved the "coffee-and-cake break" in the afternoon. His recollection is also marked by romanticism when he enthuses over German scholarly virtues. That Germans could manage to promote the notion, down to the smallest detail, that they are so exact, so rational and systematic, corresponds charmingly to the standard cliché that many Iranians entertain in their regard. But it becomes credible when he speaks of it. Moreover, these scholarly virtues correspond thoroughly to Shabestari's own. His friends describe him as a very critical and meticulous thinker, as someone who reflects a long time before he says something.

---

2 Mohammad Shabestari, Interview with the author, 18/6/2012.
3 Shabestari, Interview, 2/11/2009.

The teaching that he did at that time took the Qur'an in particular as its subject. In this, he was especially concerned with the question as to whether Islam was compatible with modern science, but less so with politics, even though the atmosphere all around him among Iranians in Germany was politically quite charged. Still, Shabestari held back from the activities of the Confederation of Iranian Students, the Iranian opposition abroad.

In 1977 he returned to Iran. Such contemporaries as the cleric Hasan Yusufi Eshkevari, who has collaborated frequently with Shabestari over the past 30 years, came to value him as someone who possessed a deep knowledge of Western culture and its thought and who "had returned to Iran with a valuable capital."[4] When Shabestari came back to Iran, the country was already in its pre-revolutionary phase. He joined the revolution with great enthusiasm. For a brief time he published the well-regarded periodical *Andishe-ye eslami* or *"Islamic Thought"* which, however, had to be shut down after 15 issues for financial reasons. Although the contributors to the journal felt indebted to the revolution they often engaged in open political criticism. With the revolutionary fervor and its many excesses in mind, Shabestari warned of the danger that people could come to think they were God or like Him.

In 1980 Shabestari was elected a delegate to parliament from his home town of Shabestar. This led to some personal meetings with Khomeini during which their differences became apparent. Shabestari took issue with the leader of the revolution over freedom of speech and demanded the right to be able to identify political grievances. Because his criticism went unheard he did not run again for parliament. He accepted an offer to become a professor of comparative religion at Tehran University and from then on devoted himself intensively to his research. Now he found the time to read the authors who had sparked his interest during his years in Hamburg: Protestant theologians such as Paul Tillich (1886–1965) and Karl Barth (1886–1968) as well as the hermeneutical philosopher Hans-Georg Gadamer (1900–2002). During his stay in Hamburg, Shabestari had heard a lot about these thinkers,

---

4 Hasan Yusefi Eshkevari, Interview with the author, 3/12/2009.

but now, for the first time, he began to delve thoroughly into their works. To the question as to why it was especially Protestant theologians that he took on he replied:

It wasn't completely accidental that I concerned myself more with Protestantism. The Protestant way of thinking is closer to my own. It is a rather critical way of thinking. This led me to study Protestantism more. In addition, I found the existentialist interpretation of Christianity that Protestantism practises quite interesting.[5]

In his teaching and research, Shabestari was particularly preoccupied with the question of reconciliation between Islam and democracy, Islam and human rights, that is, with the question of how Islamic concepts could be reconciled with the accomplishments of modernity. To establish this reconciliation he enlisted the aid of modern hermeneutics and Christian theology, his application of which was a direct result of the knowledge that Shabestari had been introduced to in Germany. In order to familiarize the Iranian public with his modernizing ideas Shabestari wrote regularly from the mid-1980s for the journal *Keyhan-e farhangi* "The World of Culture" which at that time served as a medium for Islamic reformist thought. Thus, from 1987 to 1990 there appeared a series of articles in *Keyhan-e farhangi* on the relation between reason and religion. Later Shabestari wrote for the periodical *Kiyan* "Firmament" which was a forum for so-called religious intellectuals (*roushanfekran-e dini*) up until it was banned in the year 2001. Most of the protagonists of Iranian reform discourse wrote for *Kiyan*. Because of this, parallels were drawn with the French *Encyclopédistes* and there was talk of a "school" of the periodical *Kiyan* or of an intellectual "salon" of post-Islamist thinking.

Shabestari had withdrawn from political activity but he saw himself as part of a project in support of religious modernism, reform and new interpretation, in short, Islamic new-thinking. Thus, among his publications in *Kiyan* there appeared a critique of traditional thinking

---

5 Shabestari, Interview, 2/11/2009.

in Islamic theology, an article about revelation and the freedom of the human intellect, as well as articles on religious pluralism. His objective was comprehensive social change and he wanted to contribute to this through his publications.

His status made it possible for him to participate in a debate from which others were *a priori* excluded. At least since the 1978–79 revolution, in Iranian usage in public discourse, as well as in politics, there has been a distinction between "religious intellectuals" (*roushanfekran-e dini*) and secular "non-religious intellectuals" (*roushanfekran-e gheir-e dini*). The latter were persecuted, shut out from universities and considered by the ideology of the regime as "not our own" (*gheir-e khodi*); the former, however, were considered as "our own" (*khodi*). Their basic loyalty to the regime was not in question. As a result they could articulate dissent and argue for reform. The demands for reform of both groups do not display so many differences in any case, nor were the intellectuals who offered secular arguments in any sense so non-religious as the term *roushanfekran-e gheir-e dini* might lead one to believe. Even so, they were presumed not to possess *ta'ahhod*, that is, to have no connection with Islam. Because of this they weren't allowed to have a say. Those, however, who did belong, might formulate ideas about Islam or Islamic thought that were advanced and novel and indeed, even unheard of in comparison to what was being written in other Islamic countries – until, that is, they stepped across a line that was never precisely defined but which mostly affected the manipulations of the conservatives and the immense power and pretensions to a monopoly of the *vali-ye faqih*. Then they too became *gheir-e khodi*. Shabestari, like Soroush, underwent this. But because he expresses himself rather more cautiously than Soroush, he has at least been spared the experience of exile.

Truth and Method in Iran

In 1996 Shabestari's *Hermeneutics, the Book and the Tradition* (*Hermeneutik, Ketab va-Sunnat*) appeared, the first book published in Iran that explicitly proposed modern Western hermeneutics and even left the term untranslated in its title. The author thus made his programmatic starting-point clear and stressed a specific perspective. The Egyptian Nasr Hamid Abu Zaid, who greatly influenced Shabestari, and with whom the latter kept up a lively exchange, emphasizes throughout his writings that with his hermeneutical approach to the Koran he is employing an old approach firmly anchored in Islamic tradition. This is why Abu Zaid quite consciously always used the term *ta'wil* – a term that stems from Islamic tradition – for hermeneutics. Abu Zaid calls an interpretation that gives precedence to reason *ta'wil*, and so, employs a term that in the early period of Islamic theology served as a technical term for exegesis. Over the course of the history of theology the term took on increasingly negative connotations and came more and more to designate a purely arbitrary textual interpretation. Eventually it was almost totally supplanted by *tafsir*, which was considered more objective. By using this term, Abu Zaid also wanted to show that *ta'wil* is a procedure that is in no sense foreign to classical Islamic exegesis. At the same time he was concerned to emphasize that he was not using a modern Western method, nor did he want to introduce it into Islamic scholarship. According to him *ta'wil* is the term that the Qur'an itself recommends for its interpretation. For this reason, the Egyptian designates the understanding of the Qur'an by this term in his book *The Concept of the Text* which revolves around the notion of *ta'wil*.

Unlike Abu Zaid, however, Shabestari does not make his own tradition his starting point but instead speaks explicitly of hermeneutics in the Western sense. He not only introduced the term into everyday speech, he also made it presentable. In the meantime *hermeneutik* is used even by clerics as a matter of course. Shabestari is thus a pioneer in the field of hermeneutics in Iran, at least in its modern sense. His colleague 'Abdolkarim Soroush, for example, doesn't derive his theses from hermeneutics but rather from epistemology.

Shabestari's ideas revolve around one idea: the text cannot basically be read in an objective way. When he reads a text, every reader will be guided in great measure by knowledge that he already possesses before he reads. Shabestari draws a conclusion from this that has wide-ranging consequences: no way of reading the Qur'an can claim to be the only right one. In this way he orients himself essentially towards German hermeneutics. Solely by virtue of his assimilation of the sources in their original languages Shabestari occupies a commanding position on the Iranian academic scene; by contrast, even supposed specialists on Kant or Hegel possess only rudimentary knowledge of German.

Regarding hermeneutics, he adopts Immanuel Kant's argument: in a philosophy of understanding it is the case that limits have been set to the human capacity for knowledge. Accordingly, hermeneutics highlights the problem that human thinking and understand are historically-conditioned. Shabestari wants to apply this Kantian idea to the Qur'an as well. He writes:

> Whatever has been formulated within a specific historical horizon needs, in order to be understood within another historical horizon, a kind of translation of its contents and a new formulation.[6]

Modern hermeneutics has picked up the problem that Kant defined and teaches that the meaning of every text is a hidden truth which is revealed first through interpretation. The text is first brought into spoken expression through interpretation. Without interpretation, no text, no speech, can be understood.

At this point Hans-Georg Gadamer comes into the picture. Shabestari adopts his approach, which turns the limitation defined by Kant into something positive, and declares that understanding must involve a conversation that is basically inconclusive about the interpretation of significant reports in the historical and cultural tradition. He seizes upon Gadamer's notion that there can be no interpretation free from all preconceptions "however much our will to know must be directed towards escaping the spell of our preconceptions."[7] Even though there can be no understanding that is free from preconceptions, the preconceptions have to be put constantly to the test in the process of

---

6 Mohammad Shabestari, *Hermeneutik, ketab va-sonnat [Hermeneutics, the Book and Tradition]* (Tehran: Tahr-e now, 1996), 14.
7 Hans-Georg Gadamer, *Wahrheit und Methode*, vol. 1, (Tübingen: J.C.B. Mohr, 1990), 494.

understanding. A text can be understood only when the question to which the text supplies an answer is recognized, Gadamer concluded, and Shabestari adopts this fundamental hermeneutical principle.

He never says "Qur'an" and yet it is clear that he means the Qur'an when he declares, with regard to the fifth hermeneutical principle, that the interpretation of a text is particularly difficult when several centuries intervene between the text's composition and its interpretation. When the interpreter lives in a period in which his experiences are utterly different from those of the author, he has to translate the words in the text into his own horizon of experience. Shabestari puts this in a general way but what he means is clear: the Qur'an must be contextualized.

Even when he states that one has to discover the original starting point of the author – by which is meant, however, the centre of the text's meaning, "around whose axis all the text's content is ordered" – Shabestari is speaking in general of religious texts and yet, for him, it is always about the Qur'an.[8] Of course, he can hardly state this openly since in a religious discourse the method by which the Bible has been historically and critically analyzed has connotations that are too negative to permit their application to the Qur'an. Shabestari wants to pose "questions to history" – something virtually tantamount to heresy in the Iranian context.

He is intent on investigating the concrete situation in which the text was composed, what its author wanted his public to know, what linguistic endowments and possibilities he had at his disposal and how the historical conditions looked in which those whom he addressed were living. These questions, by which he positions himself directly in relation to Gadamer who understands "speech as a medium of hermeneutical experience"[9], can be answered only by means of an exact historical analysis, Shabestari writes. Only in this way can one come as close as possible to the true meaning of the text. Otherwise the

8 Shabestari, *Hermeneutik, ketab va-sonnat [Hermeneutics, the Book and Tradition]*, 28.
9 Gadamer, *Wahrheit und Methode*, 387.

interpreter only imposes his own ideas on the text and slips his own opinions into it. Shabestari clarifies his thesis that objective reading isn't possible but that every reader and interpreter has a preconception and a prior knowledge that is not disinterested by means of an example taken from the history of Islamic theology. This concerns the opposing positions of the Ash'arites and the Mu'tazilites towards the Qur'an.

Abu al-Hasan 'Ali ibn Isma'il al-Ash'ari (873–935) is deemed to have had an anthropomorphic understanding of the Qur'an. Shabestari refers to al-Ash'ari's statement that God is seated on His throne. According to Shabestari, al-Ash'ari held the opinion, based on his own personal bias or preconception, that when the Qur'an says that God is seated on His throne or that God has a hand, precisely this is what is actually meant. What the statement "God is seated on His throne" or "God has a hand" might mean beyond a first glance is something that al-Ash'ari didn't try to understand. He was content with a literal explanation.

Conversely, the Mu'tazilites, a rationalistically oriented school, disagreed that by "God's hand" an actual hand of God was meant. In Shabestari's view these theologians, just because they were rationalists and so possessed a preconception stamped accordingly, took this in a further, metaphorical sense. The Mu'tazilite position was also grounded in the ideas of 'Abd al-Jabbar ibn Ahmad al-Asadabadi (936–1025) who provided the true meaning of the expression by means of linguistic expertise and who interpreted obscure Qur'anic passages against the background of the Qur'an as a whole.

Shabestari arrives at the conclusion that there is no *zehn-e khali*, a term that he presumably is familiar with in the context of Zen Buddhism and which he translates into Persian. Zen Buddhism has the term *mu shin* that in Japanese usage literally means "innocence" but which in interpretation denotes the mind's lack of intentionality (freedom from "I-willing"), that is, a condition of complete naturalness and independence from dualistic thinking, a mental attitude without any kind of fixation, open to intuitive perception, and that is capable of regarding a situation unclouded by one's own ideas.

And yet, according to Shabestari, a human being is not a *tabula rasa*, or "blank slate". In his view there exists a presupposition, an interested knowledge and so, correspondingly, a multiplicity of possible interpretations because of which the reading of Islam prevailing today in Iran, the Islam of jurisprudence (*eslam-e feqahati*), can only be one of many, even if it does claim to be the only right one. It is not to be set up as absolute and cannot claim that it is one with God's will. Hence, the ruling clerics ought not pull the wool over people's eyes by claiming that their own human knowledge of religion is religion itself. Shabestari rejects this juristic Islam, as it is called today in Iran, in contrast to spiritual Islam (*eslam-e ma'navi*) or to traditional, quietist Islam (*eslam-e sonnati*). It is incompatible with human rights and democracy; it has pledged itself to carrying out the Qur'anic punishments, for example, or to a supposedly Qur'anic notion of human rights and has caused the crisis in which Iran finds itself in political and social terms.

Shabestari is convinced that not Islamic law but rather *iman*, "faith", is the important component of Islamic religion. Here too he is reacting against conditions in Iran. At the founding of the Islamic Republic legal expertise moved into the forefront since according to the constitution, a jurist-scholar is the supreme political and religious authority in the country. The latter decides authoritatively which interpretation of Islam the populace has to follow. For Shabestari, however, it is genuine faith, not the observance of juristical prescriptions that is authoritative. Faith cannot be strengthened by forcing people to observe the juristical prescriptions. His thesis is that the basis of all belief is freedom of thought and human free will.

According to Shabestari, Ash'arites and Mu'tazilites, along with the philosophers, say that faith is something "that must be *acquired*".[10] Thus, a human being doesn't get faith as a matter of course. Man must bear witness actively, otherwise he cannot be considered a believer. Nevertheless – and this is the crucial argument here – only free human beings can bear credible witness. From this it follows, in Shabestari's view, that the very logic of belief is that people be free. They should be able to act and decide in accordance with their own free will.

---

10 Mohammad Shabestari, *Iman va-azadi [Belief and Freedom]* (Tehran: Tahr-e now, 1997), 21. (His emphasis)

Shabestari brings his second argument to this conclusion too. The relation between God and man in religious texts is one between me and Him, between Him and you. Revelation is a dialogue. And the whole philosophy of this relationship, as of revelation itself, is that God recognizes human freedom.

> If God did not view man as free, He would not speak with man but compel him.[11]

The third argument for the rightness of his thesis is the fact that in accord with the Islamic conception, the intellect ('aql) was the first created thing. God confronts man as a free being when He wants to lead human beings to belief. For the same reason, Shabestari disallows any taqlid, any slavish imitation, in belief. No one can imitate anyone else in belief; rather, every person stands before God. In contemporary Iranian culture, however, in which belief means something that can be imitated, in which God is viewed as someone violent, and in which there can be no relationship between God and a human being – what might be described as "Thou and I" – belief cannot flourish, according to Shabestari. Belief is not a commodity that can be recommended to people; belief is not a law to which people are obligated, nor is it an ideology to which people can be compelled, or a body of knowledge that can be appropriated. Belief is the freest decision that a person can take and the very one that most determines his destiny. In the relationship of God and man that Shabestari most favours, God respects human freedom. He does not want slavish obedience but freely chosen devotion. Shabestari's espousal of democracy is clarified by this as well. For his weightiest argument is that only a faith arrived at freely is an authentic belief that is pleasing to God.

---

11 Shabestari, Iman va-azadi [Belief and Freedom], 28.

The Reception of Protestant Theology

Shabestari wants to answer the following question by means of theology: How can I bring God close to people in this modern world? The strengthening and consolidation of belief should be assigned to theology and not to Islamic law, the conception of which on the part of the scholar-jurists is responsible for the present crisis in faith. He writes:

According to the definition of theology it is a science that determines the following:

1. What are the principles of Islamic belief and convictions?
2. How can they be proved; how can they be made accessible to reason and a rational explanation found for them?
3. How can doubts that are articulated be addressed?[12]

For this, Shabestari refers to the works of Paul Tillich (1886–1965) and Karl Barth (1886–1968). He frequently cites Tillich's *Systematic Theology*, which is devoted to the thematic realms of "Reason and Revelation" and "Being and God", with manifest admiration.

Broad-based attempts such as this (the *Systematic Theology*) help in speaking about God. In this sense we might say that speaking about God has become easier.[13]

Tillich's quasi-mystical approach to revelation is of special significance for him. Revelation represents for Tillich the manifestation of something hidden to which no access can be found in the usual way. Here Shabestari recognizes clear similarities with Islamic spiritual history, and especially with the Arab mystic Ibn 'Arabi (1165–1240).

A further aspect of Tillich's theology that Shabestari seizes upon is his critique of theism. By this, Tillich understands that God has been turned into an existent object. This God, as object, stands over against the subject; this God has died under the weight of modern doubt.

---

12 Shabestari, *Iman va-azadi [Belief and Freedom]*, 92.
13 Shabestari, *Iman va-azadi [Belief and Freedom]*, 115.

Shabestari takes up this critique, characterizing the relationship of God to man as a primordial I-Thou connection which has, however, gone missing in the Islamic Republic of Iran. Through institutions that portray themselves as custodians of the truth between God and man the infinite God has been made finite, turned into an object. In this way he comes very close to Tillich who thinks that the "God above God" is not something existent but rather Being-itself, and accordingly, not an object. Since all thought persists in a subject-object structure, God can be grasped only in a direct, preconscious state of "being stirred to the depths by what matters to us unconditionally" that encompasses and surpasses both belief and doubt.

Tillich was also known for his thesis intended to establish a modern image of God, namely, that God is that which "concerns us unconditionally", since He is the unconditioned truth, as opposed to that which merely "concerns us", such as money or success. For Tillich, belief was something that comes over man, that deeply stirs him, seizes and holds him, so that nothing and no one can keep man away from Him. He identifies belief with the phenomenon that Rudolf Otto (1869–1937) called "the Holy" in his pioneering work of that title.

This absolute form of "being stirred to the depths by what matters to us unconditionally" is decisive for Tillich and for Ibn 'Arabi in equal measure. For Ibn 'Arabi God's word has such an indescribable effect on him, to whom it is addressed, that it suspends his ability to reflect. In this, Shabestari finds the content of a new experience of belief which replaces observance of juristic norms. In an Islamic context this "being stirred to the depths" is especially situated within mysticism. The mystics see God in everything, they see only God and, in particular, they listen to God. Shabestari positions himself here too when he advances an I-Thou concept in connection with the new notion of revelation that it requires. Belief as a religious experience that occurs between God and man must stand at the centre of the new theology which the Islamic world has to find in the modern age. The relationship between God and man, in his view, must be laid out in this way.

Karl Barth interests Shabestari too for this reason. In his theology Barth processed the crisis of the modern world and instead of turning away from God because of war and destruction, he elaborated the idea of God as "the wholly Other". Through this notion he could turn to God. Barth also effected a shift in emphasis from the judging God to the gracious God and thereby arrived at a new image of God. Pursued further, this notion leads almost automatically to Persian mysticism which positions God as the beloved at the centre of its religious experience. Islamic mysticism has always stood as the opposite pole to juristic Islam; mystics have always reproached legal scholars for reinforcing the outer aspects of the religion, being themselves incapable of recognizing the inner aspects. Perhaps, through his openness to Protestant theology, Shabestari has arrived back at his own tradition within Islamic history.

Political Movements in Religious Garb

This kind of reform, which he calls true reform, is for theologians something different from the reform movements that have existed for the last 150 years in the Islamic world. These have not been religious movements for reform but merely political movements in religious garb. When political changes occur in a society and take on a religious coloration, he states, no religious reform in any shape or form has come about. For example, Jamal al-Din al-Afghani – always called Astarabadi in Persian – merely used religion. It is actually disputed whether he was religious at all. But Shabestari does not consider even Muhammad 'Abduh as a religious reformer. True, 'Abduh wanted to change people's approach to education and so he argued that Islam stood for progress and development; however, this was no religious reform.

> In my opinion these two were little more than social and political reformers. One of them was active in political movements and the other wanted to change Muslims' worldview. But if we compare the effect of these two reformers with Luther's effect within Christendom, we see that Luther's effect lay more within the realm of the religious experience of Christianity whereas the effect of these

two personalities [i.e., 'Abduh and Afghani] lay in the realm of social and political reality.[14]

Shabestari is alluding here to the "Tower Experience" as the quintessence of a meaningful religious experience of faith that had far-reaching consequences: *sola gratia* "by faith alone". In his lonely meditation on *Romans* 1:17 Luther suddenly discovered what he had been looking for in vain for a decade. The verse led to Luther's new understanding of the Bible that God's eternal righteousness is a gift of grace, given to humans only through belief in Jesus Christ. No one could compel this gift on his own.

For Shabestari such a new thought betokened true religious reform since the core of belief lay in religious experiences of this sort, not in "a heap of political movements". Here Shabestari is alluding unmistakably to the Islamic Revolution of 1978–79. Just because clerics lead a movement doesn't make it religious. Their movement had not been a religious one even if religion had cried out for a struggle against oppression:

> If someone with a lofty purpose struggles against oppression and
> dispossession and if this struggle is accompanied by a spiritual and
> religious experience, then this act is certainly a religious one. But
> here it's a matter of something else, namely, that the social reality
> which certain reformers in Islamic societies want to change, cannot
> be achieved through a change in religious views. They wanted
> to realize an industrial economy, a democratic society, universal
> health-care, up-to-date knowledge, a changed culture and the like.
> But in the religious texts we have no instructions to tell us how these
> things are to be realized.[15]

For religious reform, Shabestari argues, the individual's religious experience, the truly important part of religion, is requisite; and he

---

14 Shabestari, *Iman va-azadi [Belief and Freedom]*, 123.
15 Shabestari, *Iman va-azadi [Belief and Freedom]*, 133.

explains that there are three levels of religion. In Islam the first level consists in saying the prayers, keeping the fast, giving alms and participating in political and social life on the basis of religious motivations. The second level involves ideas and convictions such as, for example, knowledge of prophethood, knowledge about God, the resurrection and the human being. At this more inward level convictions are at stake, not outer actions. But there is a still farther level. To describe this, Shabestari uses the comparative form of "inner" which is difficult to translate. This *deeper, more inward* level refers to religious experience, what is lived through religiously. Precisely here something new must occur.

> In our society, unfortunately, rumour has it that being religious
> consists in accepting a few principles of belief; that when somebody
> says, "I believe in God's oneness, justice, prophethood, the imamate
> and the resurrection", that person is religious. But in fact that isn't so.
> In the Qur'an someone is religious who is a believer and a believer
> is someone who has had an experience of belief.[16]

Because religious reform should occur within the realm of religious life and experience, Shabestari considers Muhammad Iqbal (1873–1938) to have been the only true Islamic reformer. He is full of praise for him, believing that he hearkens back within the sphere of Islam to Luther and the modern Protestant theologians because, like them, Iqbal elaborated a new approach to his religion. Iqbal, and particularly his book *The Reconstruction of Religious Thought in Islam*, have been known in Iran for decades. Thus, there are numerous references and allusions to the Pakistani poet; for example, in Soroush's work as well. Here Shabestari is following paths that have long been trodden before. Like Iqbal, his model, he openly promotes a spiritual democracy as an alternative to European democracies and Iranian theocracy. Such a spiritual and secular democracy would have an Islamic character insofar as the most important principles of the religion, such as righteousness, would be implanted.

---

16 Shabestari, *Iman va-azadi [Belief and Freedom]*, 119.

Iqbal is also a model for Shabestari because he did not lose God in modernity but found Him again in a mystical encounter. He found God again in a prayerful attitude. Like Iqbal, Shabestari elaborates a mystical approach to God. This is not prayer; rather, wonderment in the redeeming experience of God's speech is for him the new experience of belief through which God can still come close to modern men and women:

> God's speech is what God directs to human beings – and indeed, in such a way that man discovers himself as a being addressed by God.[17]

In this Shabestari is a bit reminiscent of the Egyptian Amin al-Khuli who located the miraculous nature of the Qur'an (a key concept of the classical exegetes by which the inimitability of its linguistic expression – in Arabic *i'jaz al-qur'an* – was meant) in the auditor's soul. For al-Khuli, the distinctive achievement of the Qur'an was to have stirred the hearer emotionally and so made him receptive to God's message. Shabestari has taken al-Khuli on board; he even cites him and refers to him in one of his few footnotes. And like al-Khuli, Shabestari does not mean by the miraculous nature of the Qur'an its linguistic inimitability, as is generally understood in Islamic theology. He focuses on the widening of horizons and the bewilderment (*hayra*) that is triggered in people in apprehending God's word. The proclamation that induces *hayra* in the hearer is the beginning of knowledge of God, just as in Islamic mysticism *hayra* is the final stage before self-annihilation, that is, the last stage before union with God. When man hears God's word, it so sweeps him away that, as Ibn 'Arabi puts it, his ability to think is unmoored or he swoons in a faint.

Shabestari follows him in this. God manifests Himself not as an avenger and judge who insists on observance of His rules and threatens with punishments for any infractions but rather as a lover who brings the beloved into a state of confusion with His words, who astonishes

---

17 Mohammad Shabestari, *Qera'at-e rasmi az din [An Official Reading of Religion]* (Tehran: Tahr-e now, 2000), 323.

and rescues. For him any speech that doesn't achieve this is not God's speech.

> Until a person is illumined inwardly God's word is not present and no word of God's speech can be heard.[18]

This is Shabestari's religious experience. He sees mystical Islam as a counterforce to juristic Islam. He is in search of a new theology, a new discourse about God, and he wishes to place a genuinely old experience of faith back at the centre-point. In his view, the experience of faith, the perception of the revealed word (*sokhan-e vahyani*) as something that in a positive sense paralyzes man with wonderment and leaves him stockstill and moved to his depths, which mystical poets and thinkers exalted, has now, however, been shunted aside to the margins. And yet, how must a system be constituted in which a Muslim can live his belief or come to belief and have such a religious experience? For the modern theology that Shabestari wants stands as a matter of course in close connection with the monistic image of Islam that prevails in Iran today and in which he sees a false relation between faith and power.

For him the only consequence arises from his Qur'anic hermeneutics: the Qur'an hardly addresses the question of rulership. Only in a general sense is it written that rulership must be just and nothing further. Details about the question as to how this is to be organized in practice are simply not there. As evidence for this assertion Shabestari notes the fact that when Imam 'Ali ibn abi Talib, the first imam of the Shi'a and the fourth caliph, gave his governor in Egypt instructions for ruling, he enjoined him only to rule justly and to respect the traditions of the people that were prevalent in the conquered country.

The theologian is here referring to the so-called "letter on rule from Imam 'Ali to Malik al-Ashtar" and is playing on a well-known register since this letter on rule is viewed by most Shi'ites as normative for Shi'a leadership. In point of fact its contents confirm Shabestari's assertion that government must be in the first instance just. Further instructions

---

18 Shabestari, *Qera'at-e rasmi az din [An Official Reading of Religion]*, 329.

relative to governmental institutions or the need for the application of the Islamic punishments, as claimed by Khomeini, do not appear in this document in any way. This is telling for Shabestari's argument inasmuch as Imam 'Ali is considered by Shi'ites to have been the pre-eminent interpreter of the Qur'an.

In any case a state that applies the Islamic punishments is not necessarily Islamic, Shabestari observes in passing but with unmistakable reference to the Islamic Republic of Iran. The question is fundamental as to which form of government can best bring faith to fruition:

> It follows from the logic of belief that believers must demand the
> establishment of a political and social order...in which they can
> more knowledgeably and freely practice their faith... Such a society
> will certainly not be an oppressive and totalitarian society.[19]

But since the Qur'an has not prescribed any concrete system, people must decide for themselves, in Shabestari's view, as to what kind of order they wish to live in as well as where their faith can best be realized. He proposes a democratic system that accords every freedom to its citizens "for faith is no ideology."[20]

At this point he distances himself considerably from Khomeini's claim that the ruler must be a religious authority and the populace rightly guided, even by force. In this he is unequivocally recognizable as the post-Islamist thinker that he would come to be ever more strongly in the late 1990s. He turned away from the notion of political Islam as ideology that had informed him in the 1960s and 1970s, and strove to oppose it with his own Qur'anic hermeneutics.

A Prophetic Reading of the World

In 2006 Shabestari fell victim to the purges of the Ahmadinejad regime. After he was forced into retirement Shabestari published what he

19 Shabestari, *Iman va-azadi [Belief and Freedom]*, 79.
20 Shabestari, *Iman va-azadi [Belief and Freedom]*, 80.

himself terms the pinnacle of his intellectual activity. His reflections, entitled *A Prophetic Reading of the World (Qera'at-e Nabavi az Jahan)*, first appeared in the form of an interview in the June/July 2007 issue of the periodical *Madrese* which afterwards had to suspend publication. It shouldn't be assumed that Shabestari was able to publish his ideas in Iran in book form. Nevertheless, those ideas were widely disseminated in Iran through a blog that one of his students mounted.

Shabestari reads the Qur'an as an historical and evidentiary document and in so doing departs markedly from the notions formulated by Islamic theology over its history. For him the Qur'an is indeed still a text with a divine origin as seen from Muhammad's perspective or at the least as ultimately referring back to God. But he believes that at the same time Muhammad understood it as his own words. The Prophet, so Shabestari argues, said about himself that he was a speaker because God had willed it so. Nevertheless, it wasn't only the form that the Prophet himself determined, but the contents as well. The theologian here takes an unmistakably new direction. He thus calls it *wahy*, often translated as "revelation" and understood as a "transcendent linguistic aid". In his view *wahy* is only an aptitude given the Prophet by God. It is this aptitude that enables Muhammad to carry out God's work, that is, to summon to faith.

Today Shabestari considers the Qur'an to be a prophetic way of reading the world. By this he means not only that the religious exegetes have formulated their own understanding of revelation but that Muhammad himself did so too. The Qur'an is the "result of *wahy*" (*mahsul-e wahy*), "not *wahy* itself" (*na khod-e wahy*); it is "a monotheistic reading of the world in the light of *wahy*."[21] By establishing this thesis as a theologian, and with reference to a theological tradition, Shabestari has come to be the leading exponent, among Iran's clerics, of a secular interpretation of Islam. He is one of the first Iranian clerics to apprehend secularization not as hostile to religion but as something necessary for rescuing faith. This is why he campaigns on behalf of secular and democratic politics nowadays. At the same time, however,

---

21 Mohammad Shabestari, "Qera'at-e nabavi az jahan" [A Prophetic Reading of the World], *Fazlnamah-yi Madrasa* 6, 2008.

it is religion that supplies people with values in their quest for meaning and morality in this secular life.

Two theses lie at the basis of Shabestari's idea. First, in light of the results of linguistic philosophy of the last two centuries, the Qur'an, an Arabic-speaking text understandable by all believers as well as unbelievers, has to be ascribed to a human being. Were it instead to be ascribed directly and immediately to God, this would stand not only factually but essentially in contradiction to its distinctive nature, that of being comprehensible to all. This first point has to be understood against the background of contemporary philosophical hermeneutics. The second thesis is of a literary-critical kind and runs: the dominant literary genre of the Qur'anic verse, which summons to belief, is that of narrative. The Qur'an is thus a narrative about the world in Muhammad's time. Hence it is the historical situation in which a text emerges that must be understood, in a manner indicated by the notion of a language game in Ludwig Wittgenstein's (1889–1951) sense and which Shabestari here takes as his starting point.

Wittgenstein's central notion is that every linguistic expression is lodged in a human praxis. Only within this praxis do the many and various language games have meaning. A word, a concept or a sentence has meaning only if it possesses a specific usage and function within a life-form. And so every language game has specific rules. These rules for the correct use of language are conventions or customs that are conceivable only in a specific social context. According to Wittgenstein a man in isolation would not be capable of creating language games. In carrying Wittgenstein's reflections over onto the Qur'an, Shabestari comes to the conclusion that the speaker in the Qur'an can only have been a human being. Only a human being would have been in a position to participate in the language game that the Qur'an presents; only he is at home in the human praxis of language. For this reason the theologian believes that the Prophet Muhammad cannot not have been *ummi*, that is, illiterate in both reading and writing, as most Muslims understand the term.

What the term *ummi* means in the Qur'an is disputed. Among Western scholars of Islam, however, the view prevails that the Prophet cannot have been *ummi* in the sense of "illiterate", and Shabestari shares that view. He does not conceive of the Prophet as a mere conveyor of sound but as a someone responsible:

> Our own experience tells us this: it is always a human who is speaking. It is always a human who says particular words. It is always a human who is the subject of the act of speaking. And in that he is intellectually in a position to speak he also takes personal responsibility for what he says.[22]

For Shabestari a human speaker is absolutely necessary for a word to be comprehensible to him whom is spoken to. This sort of comprehension is universally available; it is equally open to a believer and an unbeliever. Hence he writes:

> If it be assumed that the Qur'an is complete, i.e., that its entire wording, all its sentences and its content, are the direct and unmediated word of God that He transmitted to the Prophet and which he in turn passed on, like a recording device, then the consequence of this would be that the text, as a transcribed utterance, would be incomprehensible.[23]

A possible counter-argument to Shabestari might be that only believers understand the Qur'an and that those who don't believe don't understand it. The classical Islamic "science of the Qur'an" argues thus, since the Qur'an itself says so. But he rejects this counter-argument. Something that is not essentially open to everyone's understanding is not understandable. For Shabestari, understanding is the rational knowledge that is spoken of in modern philosophical hermeneutics.

---

22 Shabestari, "Qera'at-e nabavi az jahan" [A Prophetic Reading of the World], 2008.
23 Shabestari, "Qera'at-e nabavi az jahan" [A Prophetic Reading of the World], 2008.

It is a knowledge the origin of which can be explained. It is
possible to show by argument where and why something has
been understood or not understood. Understanding and not
understanding can thus be distinguished. Wherever that is not
possible we cannot speak of understanding. And so a person who
believes cannot speak with others who do not believe on any
rational basis about his understanding of a text: he cannot make
understandable to the other what and why he understands.[24]

What he means by this is that it is unmistakably clear from the
Qur'an that conversations and discussions took place between the
Prophet and those whom he addressed, among whom there were, in
particular, unbelievers and believers of other faiths. These latter too
must have understood the Qur'anic verses, otherwise they could not
have discussed them. Had Muhammad conveyed the Qur'an merely
as a pure transmitter he would have demanded that people follow him
out of sheer devotion as slaves. But if that were the case, the many
discussions and debates over social conditions, to which the Qur'an
attests, would have had no meaning. In Shabestari's view, the Qur'an
wants to persuade, it addresses people's intelligence, it doesn't want
slaves. This is why the Qur'an says of itself that it is insight, proof and
a clear sign.

Could a text lay claim to such characteristics if it were not
universally understandable? Were then all the manifold efforts that
were made after the Prophet's death on the part of Islamic scholars
to interpret the Qur'an correctly not senseless? They prove, however,
that people took the Qur'an for a text that could be understood, that
could be studied and analyzed. Today we still devote ourselves to
the Qur'an to learn better to understand it and more accurately to
interpret it. Is that all pointless in the end?[25]

---

24 Ibid.
25 Shabestari, "Qera'at-e nabavi az jahan" [A Prophetic Reading of the World],
2008.

Furthermore, Muhammad is respected as someone "who summons to God" as a result of the Qur'anic witness. He summons to God "based on a clear proof" (12:108). The Prophet sends servants "of great might" (17:5). Muhammad calls people "to a straight path" (23:73). He comes as someone who "teaches them the Scripture and the Wisdom" (62:2). According to Shabestari, no one who is a mere medium for sounds could have these functions and tasks. All the roles that the Qur'an names as Muhammad's are meaningful only if the Qur'an is the Prophet's own reading. He has introduced people to the meaning of the Qur'an. His calling was also a mission and went far beyond what falls to a mere medium. Nor, in Shabestari's view, did the Prophet ever claim that the verses of the Qur'an were sent down literally by God. The wording as well as the content of the speech that he conveys stem from him. Of course, Muhammad experienced God as the ultimate Mover, in the Aristotelean sense, of this recitation. And because he experienced Him as Mover, Muhammad called whatever befell him and whatever he expressed as *wahy* which is defined by Shabestari in turn as a "transcendent linguistic aid."[26]

Shabestari does not let the argument stand that Muhammad only passed God's word on in the way that a commander passes a command in its exact wording on to his army. The example is inadmissible because it implies anthropomorphism. Language cannot at one and the same time remain comprehensible to humans when God is the speaker unless God be made human. If one lets God really be God there is no plane on which what God communicates to the Prophet and what the Prophet transmits to human beings, coincides. The Prophet must function as a sort of translator of what is non-human into human language. And yet, human language can exist only in the human world, Shabestari argues, and even recourse to God's omnipotence is here of no help.

Even the Qur'an's inimitability (*i'jaz al-qur'an*) serves Shabestari for an argument for the human character of the Qur'anic discourse. This is astonishing in that the very inimitability of the Qur'an in Islamic

---

26 Ibid.

theology in general serves as a proof of the Qur'an's divine nature. Accordingly, the Qur'an is seen not only as God's word but also as a miracle that confirms Muhammad's mission. The miracle is seen in a linguistic form that is so unsurpassable that no human being is capable of creating anything comparable. On this Shabestari says only that had the Prophet been nothing more than a channel for carrying sentences whose wording and content were intended only for the devotion of believers and were in particular valid only for them, there would have been no sense in claiming that other people could not produce something comparable to these verses.

Shabestari deals quite briefly with the inimitability of the Qur'an, which he never once refers to by its technical term, even though it has played a major role in the history of Islamic theology and is one of the most significant arguments for the divine nature of Qur'anic speech. Does he consider the arguments that assert the miraculous nature of the Qur'an not watertight enough to concern himself further with them? Or does he perhaps not elaborate on the *i'jaz al-qur'an* just because it is one of the most important arguments in Islamic theology for the divinity of Qur'anic speech?

In the course of his reflections Shabestari draws the conclusion that Muhammad did not claim that the Qur'an was not his word; instead, he as much as presented it as his own utterance. Even so, the claim that he made and that he had to push through against his enemies was that he himself was an exceptional person who had been summoned by God and empowered by Him to speak these words. This empowerment to speak is the true significance of the Qur'anic *wahy*:

> From the Qur'an's standpoint *wahy* consists of God's speaking with the Prophet of Islam. This leads to his call and consequently to his speaking, i.e., to his delivery of the Qur'anic verses. Hence, the Qur'anic verses are the product of *wahy* (*mahsul-e wahy*) but not *wahy* itself.[27]

---

27 Shabestari, "Qera'at-e nabavi az jahan" [A Prophetic Reading of the World], 2008.

Abu Zaid, who likewise argues that the Qur'an must be understood as a product of its culture and so can be treated as a quite normal historical text, has noted that the need for elucidation arises when the claim is made that God speaks to human beings, that indeed two parties, different in essence, are engaging in communication. This cannot be explained by sound human reason. Shabestari too sees this very same difficulty and concludes that God did not speak at all. For Abu Zaid there has to have been some intermediary between God and the Prophet who transmitted the revelation to the Prophet, in other words, the angel Gabriel. The Egyptian distinguishes among the various levels of communication and explains that there have been diverse opinions throughout the history of Islamic theology on the question of just how the sending down of revelation actually happened. Many scholars insist that the formulation of the text was undertaken by Gabriel and that the wording of the divine message was thus revealed to Muhammad. This view implies that the angels had a verbal system – the Arabic language – at their disposal.

Abu Zaid does not subscribe to this view. Another theological tradition separated the levels of revelation and believed that the sending down of the text was a sending down of its meaning, independent of any verbal code. The Prophet experienced an inspiration and then expressed the divine message in Arabic. Hence, Gabriel drew close to Muhammad to inspire him with the revelation. Unfortunately Shabestari does not discuss this possibility. A few months before his death Abu Zaid said that he found Shabestari's thesis extremely interesting but not fully thought-through on this point. Shabestari had not sufficiently reflected on the fact that the Qur'an says about itself in various passages that it is God's word. The discussion that was planned between the two theologians could not take place, however, because of Abu Zaid's sudden death.

The Qur'an as Narrative

For Shabestari the Qur'anic text is, by and large, a religious story which explains and comments upon natural events, the history of peoples, social relations and the individual destinies of human beings. In his view the Qur'an is primarily about giving people living in the world religious meaning, based to be sure on the Prophet's experience. The text doesn't supply information about how the world actually is but gives instead Muhammad's way of seeing. He "reads" the world, Shabestari says. This "reading" is based on the Prophet's hermeneutical experience. Here Shabestari draws on speech-act theory according to which facts are not only described in verbal articulation but are themselves carried out as actions. Accordingly, every statement about reality is also an intervention in reality.

Shabestari concludes that a human being who experiences all existing things as a manifestation of God does not interpret what he understands; rather, his understanding is itself an interpretation. Considered thus, understanding, commentary and the seeing of the manifestation are one and the same. Just as the Prophet sees the world so too does he form and control the text. Furthermore, the prescriptions of sharia are traceable back to an interpretative understanding through the Prophet of the social conditions prevailing in the Hijaz. As a logical conclusion Shabestari arrives at the momentous consequence that he infers from his explanation:

> The decrees were not promulgated in any sense for all societies and for all times.[28]

Shabestari's reflections can be understood as the introduction of a rational ('aqlani) method of Qur'an interpretation. This rational way of reading in turn proclaims the religious message of the text which can be designated comprehensively under the rubric of tawhid. Tawhid betokens the devout consideration of the world with the existence of the one God as its background and the organization of life on the basis of this belief. Thus, the Qur'an is the expression of Muhammad's acknowledgement of monotheism. From this it follows logically that

---

28 Shabestari, "Qera'at-e nabavi az jahan" [A Prophetic Reading of the World], 2008.

the Qur'an is created, as the Mu'tazilites understood it in their time. For uncreatedness, the atemporal existence of the Qur'an, would contradict strict *tawhid*, the divine oneness. But if one proceeds from the Qur'an's createdness, it becomes easier to assume that it was conditioned in its form and content by the Prophet's personality.

The Mu'tazilites called themselves *ahl al-tawhid wa-1 -'aql* (the party of divine oneness and reason, in order to designate the main content and objective of their theological system, and this could apply just as well to Shabestari's theological system. For him too, a belief in the absolute oneness and the absolute justice of God serves as the foundation for an entire system of principles and articles of faith. It thus becomes possible for him to renew faith by appealing to God's justice as the most important commandment, and to dispense with those aspects of Islamic law that stand in opposition to justice as we understand it today. That relates to the law of punishments and to much else that is incompatible with human rights.

In Shabestari's view, if Islam were still to be for believers "what concerns them quite unconditionally", it could become – notwithstanding the Islamism currently so prevalent – that unique "dimension of mightiness" that Paul Tillich, his mentor described. Shabestari does want a religion that has been made private but he also wants to be stirred to the depths by religion. If it were freed from the clutches of the conservatives, it could indeed be a private matter while also bringing morality into secular life. Religion would become the bearer of sacred values and it could then enable these values to prevail in Iran.

> It is obvious that the realization of human justice and human rights
> is a religious concern for believing people. Believers believe that
> the realization of justice and human rights also guarantees human
> rights as healthy interpersonal relations and is a response to God's
> summons to justice. And in practice, by observing human rights they
> abide not only by the commandment to respect human rights but
> also by the commandment to respect God's rights.[29]

---

29 Shabestari, "Qera'at-e nabavi az jahan" [A Prophetic Reading of the World],

The Islamic Revolution brought the Islamists to power; the Islamic Republic has made post-Islamists out of many of them. One of the most important of these is Mohammad Shabestari who has tried through his thought and his work to resolve the contradictions that Islamic discourse in the 1960s, 1970s and 1980s produced. His idea that the Qur'an is a prophetic way of reading the world is his argument, new for him, against the notion that sharia must be applied and that the Qur'an offers a program for governing. It is not that. For Shabestari, moreover, there still remain the ethics, ritual and spirituality which Islam has founded and which can be summed up in the core notion of *tawhid* – *tawhid* as a human being's personal experience of God. *Say! God is one.*

2008.

The Future of Islam

The thinkers presented here have confronted a central problem of modern Islamic theology, namely, how to deal with specific Qur'anic statements. For us Muslims today this is an existential question since many Qur'anic statements do not agree with what we accept as values – at least when these statements remain uninterpreted. This complex of problems taken in itself can be discussed and a new way of interpretation devised and developed, for example, one that is favorable to women. But it can also be placed within the context of a more far-reaching question and an answer can be attempted as to what the nature of God's word is, and therefore, how the essence of God's word is constituted. Out of the answer to this second question, countless answers to the first arise. Those presented here have given their answers and they have also raised new questions. But it is less a matter of being able to come up with ready answers as of becoming aware of the necessity of discussing these important questions; this should be initiated now. Our six thinkers exemplify this: they are aware of a problem and they confront it. I regard their efforts as innovative, interesting and worthy of consideration. Whether they will be supportable for Muslims over the long term cannot be determined here. What is important, however, is that they be considered and reconsidered.

The objection could be raised that these thinkers are fighting a losing battle because they live in exile or are isolated as free thinkers at home. But as to the first point, they are not cut off from their public in this very globalized world. This is true of Abu Zaid, for example, who over the years has found acceptance in the Islamic world. As to the second, they have already accomplished much: the democracy movement in Iran, which in Germany is often said to be dead but is not, would be inconceivable without the ideas of Soroush and Shabestari. That Mohammad Khatami, a reform-minded president, was elected in 1997 by 70 percent of the population, is in great part due to them because they smoothed the way with their modernizing ideas towards an openness to democracy and human rights. The election of Mahmoud Ahmadinejad, a hardliner, in 2005 doesn't invalidate this thesis since every social movement that promotes change will provoke a counter-movement.

Four of the six thinkers here had to leave their homelands for political reasons. In the cases of Abu Zaid and Soroush it was their criticism of the monopolization of textual interpretation and its misuse for political motives that caused them to be driven into exile. In Rahman's case it was his statements about the nature of revelation that brought the pot to a boil for his opponents; in his case too, the fact that he criticized the power of the religious scholars and challenged them with his new interpretation of Islam stood very much in the foreground. Finally, power and primacy of interpretation are also at issue here; in other words, the question of who is authorized to speak for Muslims. Muslims themselves, and not any sort of pre-emptive structures, should decide this. It is relatively certain that they will decide on an interpretation that corresponds to their needs; in the modern world this cannot be backward-looking one. Over the long term, in a country such as Iran, for example, in which 65 percent of all students are women, the religiously based principle that the testimony of a woman counts for half that of a man in court cannot be maintained. That holds to an even stronger degree for Europe and the US where hundreds of thousands of Muslim women have now grown up in a much less patriarchal milieu than in the Islamic world.

And so two things come together here: a societal necessity and a religion that historically has shown that it has a potential for plurality and adaptability and that it can admit and incorporate ambiguities. Islam is as pure as rainwater and as it has taken shape over history in various places, it has assumed the different colours, tastes and fragrances of the traditions on which it has fallen. That will happen again, even now, with Islam in the 21st century, with Islam in Germany, with Islam in Europe. It is for us Muslims to make the best of our religion. We must prepare the ground for it here. In the words of the poet Sa'di:

> The blessed rain brings forth
> tulips in the garden,
> but in the salty steppe
> it brings forth nothing but weeds.

Acknowledgments

I thank Ulrich Nolte for his notes and corrections as well as for his constant friendship. And I thank Stela Muminovic for preparing the index. I thank those who are depicted here for instructing me in the abundance of our Islamic tradition. I hope that I have done justice by them. I thank my husband Navid Kermani and my parents Sibylle and Manutschehr Amirpur for always being there.

Bibliography

(Translations of citations are by the author, except as noted.)

Introduction

Abu Zaid, Nasr. *Ein Leben mit dem Islam*. Freiburg im Breisgau: Herder Verlag, 1999.

Bauer, Thomas. *Die Kultur der Ambiguität: eine andere Geschichte des Islams*.

Berlin: Verlag der Weltreligionen, 2011.

Engineer, Asghar Ali. "The Compatibility of Islam, Secularism and Modernity." In *New Voices of Islam*, edited by Farish Noor, 29–34. Leiden: ISIM, 2002.

Qur'an:

The Qur'an: a New Translation by M.A.S. Abdel Haleem. Oxford: Oxford University Press, 2004.

The Qur'an with Parallel Arabic Text. Translated with notes by N.J. Dawood. London: Penguin, 1993.

The Qur'an. Translated into English by Alan Jones. s.1. [London]: Gibb Memorial Trust, 2007.

Safi, Omid, ed. "Introduction: The Times They Are A-Changing – A Muslim Quest for Justice, Gender Equality, and Pluralism", in *Progressive Muslims: On Justice, Gender, and Pluralism*. Oxford: Oneworld, 2003, 1–29.

Zentralrat der Muslime e.V.. Grundsatzpapier des Zentralrates der Muslime in Deutschland (ZMD) zur Kopftuchdebatte, 23.10.2003, http://textfabrik.islam.de/2652_print.php

1 On the Way to Modernity

Meier, Andreas. *Der politische Auftrag des Islam: Programme und Kritik zwischen Fundamentalismus und Reformen: Originalstimmen aus der islamischen Welt.* Wuppertal: Peter Hammer, 1994.

2 Islamic Reformers Today

'Ali ibn abi Talib. *Nahj al-balagha*, edited and interpreted by 'Ali Naqi Feiz ol-Eslam. Tehran, 1972.

Dernbach, Andrea. "Elastischer Islam." *Tagesspiegel,* 2/10/2007.

Esack, Farid. "Den Islam neu denken." *Der Wille Gottes in unserer Zeit – ein Gespräch über Aids, Widerstand und einen modernen Islam mit dem südafrikanischen Theologen Farid Esack. Zenith, Zeitschrift für den Orient,* 1/2002.

Kadivar, Mohsen. "Freedom of Religion and Belief in Islam." In *The New Voices of Islam: Rethinking Politics and Modernity,* edited by Mehran Kamrava, 119–142. Berkeley: University of California Press, 2006.

——. "Vom historischen Islam zum spirituellen Islam." In *Unterwegs zu einem anderen Islam: Texte iranischer Denker,* edited by Katajun Amirpur. Translated from the Persian by Katajun Amirpur, 80–105. Freiburg: Herder Verlag, 2009.

Mir-Hosseini, Ziba. "Muslim Women's Quest for Equality: between Islamic Law and Feminism." *Critical Inquiry* 32 (2006): 629–645.

——. *Islam and Gender: the Religious Debate in Contemporary Iran.* Princeton: Princeton University Press, 1999.

Moosa, Ebrahim. "The Debts and Burdens of Critical Islam." In *Progressive Muslims: on Justice, Gender and Pluralism,* edited by Omid Safi. Oxford: Oneworld, 2003, 111–127.

Mudhoon, Loay. "Mohammed Arkoun. Kritiker der islamischen Vernunft". http://www.eurasischesmagazin.de/artikel/?artikelID=20110215.

Ramadan, Tariq. *Muslimsein in Europa*. Marburg: MSV, 2001.

——. *Peut-on vivre avec l'islam?* Entretien avec Jacques Neirynck, 2d. rev. ed., Lausanne: Favre 2004.

Saadawi, Nawal. *Fundamentalismus gegen Frauen*. Munich: Diederichs, 2002.

——. Interview with the author, April 1999.

Shahrour, Mohammad. "The Divine Text and Pluralism in Muslim Societies." Muslim Politics Report of the Council on Foreign Relations 14 (July-August 1997): 8. http//www.quran.org/library/articles/shahroor.htm.

3 Nasr Hamid Abu Zaid

Abu Zaid, Nasr Hamid. *Naqd al-khitab al-dini*. Cairo: Dar Sina, 1992.

——. *Islam und Politik: Kritik des religiösen Diskurses*. Frankfurt: Dipa-Verlag, 1996.

——. Interview with the author, 1999.

——. *Ein Leben mit dem Islam*. Freiburg im Breisgau: Herder Verlag, 1999.

——. *Mohammed und die Zeichen Gottes*. Freiburg im Breisgau: Herder Verlag, 2008.

——. *Gottes Menschenwort: Für ein humanistisches Verständnis des Qur'an*, selected, translated and with an introduction by Thomas Hildebrandt. Freiburg im Breisgau: Herder Verlag, 2009.

Andrae, Tor. *Muhammad: Sein Leben und sein Glaube*. Göttingen: Vandenhoeck & Ruprecht, 1932.

Kermani, Navid. "From revelation to interpretation: Nasr Hamid Abu Zayd and the literary study of the Qur'an." In *Modern Muslim Intellectuals and the Qur'an*, edited by Suha Taji-Farouki, 169–192. Oxford: Oxford University Press, 2006.

——. *Offenbarung als Kommunikation: Das Konzept* wahy *in Nasr Hamid Abu Zayds* Mafhum an-nass. Frankfurt am Main: Peter Lang, 1996.

——. "Die Affäre Abu Zayd. Eine Kritik am religiösen Diskurs und ihre Folgen." *Orient* 35 (1994): 25–49.

Libforall: http//www.libforall.org/background-islamic-mysticism-and-tolerance.html.

Negus, Steve. "Professor charged with apostasy." *Middle East Times* 6, 12/7/1993.

Nöldeke, Theodor. *Geschichte des Qorans.* Vols. 1 and 2 revised by Friedrich Schwally, Leipzig 1909, 1919.; vol. 2 by G. Bergsträsser & O. Pretzl, Leipzig 1938. One-volume reprint, Hildesheim 1961.

——. *The History of the Qur'an.* Leiden: Brill, 2013.

Orth, Stefan. "Historische Kontext stärker berücksichtigen: ein Gespräch mit dem Islamwissenschaftler Nasr Hamid Abu Zaid." *Herder Korrespondenz* 7/2008, 340–344.

Tabataba'i, Seyyid Mohammad Hosein. *Qor'an dar eslam* [The Qur'an in Islam], s.l. 1983.

Thielmann, Jörn. *Nasr Hamid Abu Zaid und die wiedererfundene hisba: sharia und qanun im heutigen Ägypten.* Würzburg: Ergon, 2003.

Twardella, Johannes. *Religiös-philosophische Profile: Positionsbestimmungen jüdischer und islamischer Intellektueller im Säkularisierungsprozess.* Hildesheim: Olms, 2006.

Wild, Stefan. "Die andere Seite des Textes: Nasr Hamid Abu Zaid und der Qur'an." *Die Welt des Islams* 33 (1993): 256–61.

4 Fazlur Rahman

Esack, Farid. *Qur'an, Liberation and Pluralism.* Oxford: Oneworld, 2002.

Koshul, Basit. "Fazlur Rahman's *Islam and Modernity* Revisited." *Islamic Studies* 33/4 (1994): 403–406.

Moosa, Ebrahim. "Introduction." In *Revival and Reform in Islam,*
by Fazlur Rahman, edited and with an introduction by Ebrahim
Moosa, 1–29. Oxford: Oneworld, 2000.

Rahman, Fazlur. *Islamic Methodology in History.* Karachi: Central
Institute of Islamic Research, 1965.

———. "The Concept of Hadd in Islamic Law." *Islamic Studies* 4/3
(1965): 237–251.

———. "The Impact of Modernity on Islam." *Islamic Studies* 5/2 (1966):
113–128.

———. *Islam.* Chicago: University of Chicago Press, 1966.

———. *Major Themes of the Qur'an.* Chicago: University of Chicago
Press, 1980.

———. *Islam and Modernity: Transformation of an Intellectual
Tradition.* Chicago: University of Chicago Press, 1982.

———. "Islamic Modernism: its Scope, Method and Alternatives."
International Journal of Middle East Studies 1 (1970): 317–333.

———. "Islam: Challenges and Opportunities." In *Islam: Past Influence
and Present Challenge,* edited by A.T. Welch *et al.,* 315–330.
Edinburgh: Edinburgh University Press, 1979.

———. "Islamic Studies and the Future of Islam." In *Islamic Studies:
Tradition and its Problems,* edited by Malcolm Kerr, 125–133.
Malibu: Undena Publications, 1980.

———. "Islam's Attitude toward Judaism." *Muslim World* 72/1 (1982):
1–13.

———. "Some Key Ethical Concepts of the Qur'an." *Journal of Religious
Ethics* 2/2 (1983): 170–185.

———. "My Belief in Action." In *The Courage of Conviction,* edited by
Phillip Berman, 153–159. New York: Dodd, Mead & Company,
1985.

———. "Approaches to Islam in Religious Studies: Review Essay." In
Approaches to Islam in Religious Studies, edited by Richard Martin,
189–202. Oxford: Oneworld, 1985.

Sonn, Tamara. "Fazlur Rahman's Islamic Methodology." *Muslim
World* 81/3–4, (1991): 212–230.

Waugh, Earle. "The Legacies of Fazlur Rahman for Islam in America." *American Journal of Islamic Social Sciences* 16/3 (1999): 27–44.

5 Amina Wadud

Abu Zaid, Nasr. *Reformation of Islamic Thought: a Critical Historical Analysis.* Amsterdam: Amsterdam University Press, 2006.

Abugideiri, Hibba. "The renewed women of American Islam: Shifting lenses toward Gender Jihad?" *The Muslim World* (2001): 1–8.

Ali, Kecia, Juliane Hammer & Laury Silvers, eds.) *A Jihad for Justice: Honoring the Work and Life of Amina Wadud.* Austin: University of Texas Press, 2012. http://www.bu.edu/religion/files/2010/03/A-Jihad-for-Justice-for-Amina-Wadud-2012-1.pdf

Anwar, Zainah & Rose Ismail. "Amina Wadud and Sisters in Islam – A Journey towards Empowerment." In *A Jihad for Justice: Honoring the Work and Life of Amina Wadud,* edited by Kecia Ali, Juliane Hammer & Laury Silvers, 63–72. . Austin: University of Texas Press, 2012. http://www.bu.edu/religion/files/2010/03/A-Jihad-for-Justice-for-Amina-Wadud-2012-1.pdf.

Barlas, Asma. "Amina Wadud's hermeneutics of the Qur'an: women rereading sacred texts." In *Modern Muslim Intellectuals and the Qur'an,* edited by Suha Taji-Farouki, 97–124.0xford: Oxford University Press, 2004.

Fatah, Tarek. "I am a nigger, and you will just have to put up with my blackness". Professor Amina Wadud confronts her hecklers in Toronto. 11/02/2005. http://najat-fares-kessler.blogspot.de/

Hammer, Juliane. "Reading Gender in the Quran. Text, Context and Identity in the Work of Amina Wadud." In *Zwischen Orient und Okzident: Studien zu Mobilität von Wissen, Konzepten und Praktiken. Festschrift für Peter Heine,* edited by Anke Bentzin, Henner Fürtig, Thomas Krüppner & Riem Spielhaus, 129–146. Freiburg im Breisgau: Herder Verlag, 2010.

Safi, Omid. "Walking with Amina." In *A Jihad for Justice: Honoring the Work and Life of Amina Wadud,* edited by Kecia Ali, Juliane Hammer & Laury Silvers, 225–231. Austin: University of Texas

Press, 2012. http://www.bu.edu/religion/files/2010/03/A-Jihad-for-Justice-for-Amina-Wadud-2012-1.pdf.

Sisters in Islam: http://www.sistersinislam.org.my/page.php?35.

Wadud, Amina. "On Belonging as a Muslim." In *My Soul is a Witness: African-American Women's Spirituality*, edited by Gloria J. Wade-Gayles, 253–265. Boston: Beacon Press, 1995.

——. *Qur'an and Woman: Rereading the Sacred Text from a Woman's Perspective*. Oxford: Oxford University Press, 1999.

——. *Inside the Gender Jihad: Women's Reform in Islam*. Oxford: Oneworld, 2007.

——. 2008: http://www.dradio.de/dkultur/sendungen/religionen/858172/

——. 2011: http://www.taz.de/1/archiv/digitaz/artikel/?ressort=ku&dig=2011%2F08%2F17%2Fa0115&cHash=fdea1cb346/

——. Interview with the author, 25/9/2012.

6 Asma Barlas

Barlas, Asma. DW=http://www.dw.de/dw/article/0,,1919362,00.html

——. *Believing Women in Islam: Unreading Patriarchal Interpretations of the Qur'an*. Austin: University of Texas, 2002.

——. "Der Koran neu geselen," *Islam und Gesellschaft* 6, Friedrich-Ebert-Siftung Politische Akademie, Berlin (May 2008): 5–10. http://library.fes.de/pdf-files/akademie/berlin/05440.pdf

——. "Morality: for women and girls only." *The Daily Times*, Pakistan, January 14, 2003.

——. "Muslims in the US (I)." *The Daily Times*, Pakistan, June 17, 2003.

——. "Muslims in the US (II)." *The Daily Times*, Pakistan, July 1, 2003.

——. "Un-reading Patriarchal Interpretations of the Qur'an: Beyond the Binaries of Tradition and Modernity". Presentation to the Association of Muslim Social Scientists, *Conference on Islam: Tradition and Modernity*, Toronto, November 4, 2006.

——. "Re-understanding Islam: a Double Critique". *Spinoza Lectures*. Amsterdam: Van Gorcum, 2008.

———. Interview with the author, 28/8/2012.
Moghissi, Haideh. "Women, Modernity and Political Islam." *Iran Bulletin*, no. 19–20 (Autumn/Winter 1998): 42–44.

7 'Abdolkarim Soroush

Amirpur, Katajun. "Ein iranischer Luther? 'Abdolkarim Soroushs Kritik an der schiitischen Geistlichkeit." *Orient* 37 (1996): 465–481.
———. "The Expansion of the Prophetic Experience: Abdolkarim Soroush's New Approach to the Qur'anic Revelation." *Die Welt des Islams* 51 (2012): 409–437.
———. *Die Entpolitisierung des Islam, 'Abdolkarim Soroushs Denken und Wirkung in der Islamischen Republik Iran*. Würzburg: Ergon, 2002.
Boroujerdi, Mehrzad. *Iranian Intellectuals and the West: the Tormented Triumph of Nativism*. Syracuse: Syracuse University Press, 1996.
Cooper, John. "The Limits of the Sacred: the Epistemology of 'Abd al-Karim Soroush." In *Islam and Modernity: Muslim Intellectuals Respond*, edited by John Cooper, Ronald Nettler & Mohammed Mahmoud, 38–56. London: I.B. Tauris, 1998.
Dabashi, Hamid. "Blindness and Insight: the Predicament of a Muslim Intellectual." In *Iran: Between Tradition and Modernity*, by Ramin Jahanbegloo, 95–116. Oxford: Lexington Books, 2004; reprinted in Hamid Dabashi, *Islamic Liberation Theology: Resisting the Empire*, 99–142. London: Routledge, 2008.
Dahlén, Ashk. *Islamic Law, Epistemology and Modernity: Legal Philosophy in Contemporary Iran*. London: Routledge, 2003.
Ghamari-Tabrizi, Behrooz. *Islam & Dissent in Postrevolutionary Iran: Abdolkarim Soroush, Religious Politics and Democratic Reform*. London: I.B. Tauris, 2008.
Matin-Asghari, Afshin. "Abdolkarim Soroush and the Secularization of Islamic Thought in Iran." *Iranian Studies* 30 (1997): 1–2, 95–115.
Soroush, 'Abdolkarim. "'Aql va-azadi" (Reason and Freedom), *Kiyan* 1 (1992): 5, 13–25.

———. "Eine religiöse demokratische Regierung?" *Spektrum Iran* 5 (1992): 4, 79–85.

———. "Farbehtar az Idiuloji" (Richer than Ideology), *Kiyan* 3 (1993): 14, 2–20.

———. *Qabz va bast-e te'orik-e shariat. Nazariye-ye takamol-e ma'refat-e dini* (The Theoretical Contraction and Expansion of the Sharia – the Theory of the Development of Religious Knowledge). Tehran: Sirat, 1994.

———. "Saqf-e ma'ishat bar sotun-e shari'at" (Basing Livelihood on Religion), *Kiyan* 5 (1995=1995a): 26, 25–31.

———. "Khadamat va-hasanat-e din" (Function and Benefits of Religion), *Kiyan* 5, (1995=1995b): 27, 2–17.

———. "Tahlil-e mafhum-e hokumat-e dini" (Analysis of the Term "religious rule"), *Kiyan* 6 (1996=1996a): 32, 2–13.

———. Lecture, London, November 17, 1996.

———. "The Evolution and Devolution of Religious Knowledge." In *Liberal Islam: A Sourcebook*, edited by Charles Kurzman, 244–251. Oxford: Oxford University Press, 1998.

———. *Reason, Freedom and Democracy in Islam: Essential Writings of Abdolkarim Soroush*, translated, edited and with a critical introduction by Mahmoud Sadri and Ahmad Sadri. Oxford: Oxford University Press, 2000.

———. "The Word of Muhammad." Interview with Michel Hoebink, *Zem-Zem* (2007). URL: http://www.zemzem.org/zemzem/?q=node/21

———. *Expansion of Prophetic Experience: Essays on Historicity, Contingency and Plurality in Religion.* Leiden: Brill, 2009.

———. "There is no God, I swear to God, there is no God..." February 2011. http://drsoroush.com/English/By_DrSoroush/E-CMB-20110200-ThereIsNoGod.html.

———. http://csidonline.org/images/stories/pdfiles/56900_eng_iran%5B1%5D. Pdf last queried on 5/8/2012.

———. Conversation with the author on 9/9/2012.

Vakili, Valla: "Abdolkarim Soroush and Critical Discourse in Iran." In *Makers of Contemporary Islam*, by John L. Esposito & John O. Voll, 150–176. Oxford: Oxford University Press, 2001.

——. *Debating Religion and Politics in Iran: the Political Thought of Abdolkarim Soroush.* Washington: Council on Foreign Relations, 1996.

Wright, Robin. "Islam and Liberal Democracy: Two Visions of Reformation." *Journal of Democracy* 2 (1996): 64–75.

8 Mohammad Mojtahed Shabestari

Dahlén, Ashk. *Islamic Law, Epistemology and Modernity: Legal Philosophy in Contemporary Iran*, 163–186. London: Routledge, 2003.

Eshkevari, Hasan Yusefi. Interview with the author, 3/12/2009.

Gadamer, Hans-Georg. *Wahrheit und Methode*, vol. 1. Tübingen: J.C.B. Mohr, 1990.

——. *Truth and Method.* London: Bloomsbury, 2013.

Hajatpour, Reza. *Iranische Geistlichkeit zwischen Utopie und Realismus: Zum Diskurs über Herrschafts-und Staatsdenken im 20. Jahrhundert*, 305–319. Wiesbaden: Dr Ludwig Reichert, 2002.

Sadri, Mahmoud. "Sacral Defense of Secularism, Dissident Political Theology in Iran." In *Intellectuals and the State in Iran: Politics, Discourse and the Dilemma of Authenticity*, by Negin Nabavi. Florida: University Press of Florida, 2003.

Shabestari, Mohammad. *Hermeneutik, ketab va-sonnat* [Hermeneutics, the Book and Tradition]. Tehran: Tahr-e now, 1996.

——. *Iman va-azadi* [Belief and Freedom]. Tehran: Tahr-e now, 1997.

——. "Qera'at-e rasmi az din" [An Official Reading of Religion]. *Rah-e nou* 19, 29/8/1998: 18–24.

——. "Qera'at-e rasmi az din" [An Official Reading of Religion]. Tehran: Tahr-e now, 2000.

——. *Islam und Demokratie.* Erfurt: Sutton-Verlag, 2003.

——. "Göttliches Recht?" *Die politische Meinung* 48 (2003): 5–12.

——. "Qera'at-e nabavi az jahan" [A Prophetic Reading of the World]. *Fazlnamah-yi Madrasa* 6, 2008.

——. "Demokratie und Religiösität." In *Unterwegs zu einem anderen Islam: Texte iranischer Denker*, edited by Katajun Amirpur. Translated from the Persian by Katajun Amirpur, 25–36. Freiburg: Herder Verlag, 2009.

——. "Die Menschenrechte und das Verständnis der Religionen." In *Ibid.*, 37–44.

——. Interview with the author, 2/11/2009.

——. Interview with the author, 18/6/2012.

Vahdat, Farzin. "Post-revolutionary Islamic modernity in Iran: the inter-subjective hermeneutics of Mohammad Mojtahed Shabestari." In *Modern Muslim Intellectuals and the Qur'an*, edited by Suha Taji-Farouki, 193–224. Oxford: Oxford University Press, 2006.

The Future of Islam

Saadi. *Rosengarten, in der Übersetzung von Karl Heinrich Graf, neu bearbeitet und herausgegeben von Dieter Bellmann*, 33. Leipzig & Weimar: Gustav Kiepenheuer Verlag, 1982.

——. *The Gulistan (Rose Garden) of Sa'di*. Bilingual English & Persian edition with vocabulary; new English translation by Wheeler M. Thackston, 17. Bethesda: Ibex Publishers, 2008.

Glossary

'Aql: The intellect, used to denote the use of reason as a source of *sharia*.

Ahl al-kitab: Literally "People of the Book"; the Islamic designation for Jews and Christians.

Asbab al-nuzul: The occasions or context of revelation, a description of when, in what circumstances, and why divine revelation took place.

Fiqh: Islamic jurisprudence, the human understanding of *sharia* as developed by Islamic scholars.

Hadd pl. *hudud*: Crimes which have set penalties enumerated in the Qur'an and hadith, such as the amputation of the hand, for example, in certain cases of theft.

Hadith qudsi: Literally, "sacred hadith", designating certain hadith that some regard as being "spoken" directly by God and relayed by Muhammad as such.

Hisba: The concept that Muslims, and especially Muslim rulers, have the responsibility to intervene in order to "command what is good and forbid what is wrong", as enjoined by the Qur'an.

Hashiye: Farsi word for the concentric, circular structure of Qur'anic exegesis.

Hayra: A state of bewilderment, such as that induced by the apprehension of God's word.

Ijtihad: Pertaining to Islamic law. The formulation of a judgment in relation to a legal or theological question based upon the principles of Islamic jurisprudence.

Ilahiyat: Theology.

Ilham: Divine inspiration, see also *wahy*.

Iman: Faith or belief.

Kafir pl. *kuffar*: Disbeliever (in Islam).

Kalam: Discourse or dialectic. The use of reason and theological debate to defend the tenets of Islam.

Khalifa: "Caliph" in English. God's representative on Earth and, therefore, the political leader of the Muslims.

Kitab: Literally, "book", often in reference to the Qur'an.

'Ibada: Worship through the following of Islamic practices and beliefs, obedience to God.

Mu'amalat: Social matters and rules governing humans' worldly conduct, according to Islam.

Niya: "Intention", especially with regard to the actions of a believing Muslim.

Shahada: The Muslim declaration of faith, whereby one affirms the oneness of God and that the Prophet Muhammad is His messenger.

Sharia: the Islamic law.

Shura: Literally, "consultation" or "counsel".

Sunna: The body of Islamic custom and practice as derived from the words and actions of Muhammad as reported in the hadith.

Sura: A chapter of the Qur'an, which is composed of *ayat*, or "verses".

Ta'wil: Qur'anic 'interpretation', used to mean hermeneutics or esoteric exegesis. *Tafsir* is now the dominant form of exegesis.

Tafsir: Exegesis, interpretation of the Qur'an.

Taqlid: Following Islamic legal tradition, that is, adopting prior rulings of other Islamic scholars. This contrasts with *ijtihad* which involves independent interpretation of legal sources.

Taqwah: Literally, "fear of God", from which is derived the signification of "piety", or "devoutness".

Tariqa: Literally, 'way' or 'path', a mystical or esoteric method for seeking the ultimate truth (*haqiqa*) of Islam. The term is especially associated with Sufism.

Tawhid: Monotheism and the belief in the "oneness" of God, Islam's most fundamental concept.

Umma: Literally, 'nation' or 'community', but primarily referring to the community of Islam; i.e., all Muslims worldwide.

Ummi: Meaning "illiterate" or "unlettered", as the Prophet Muhammad was reputed to be.

Usul: "Principles", often in the context of *usul al-fiqh* (the sources of Islamic jurisprudence).

Wahy: "Revelation" or "inspiration", the word of God as transmitted to Muhammad.

Zulm: "Injustice" or "oppression".

Index of Persons